D1532990

Further Than Yesterday:

That's All That Counts

Medric "Cous" Cousineau, SC, CD
Captain Ret'd RCAF

To Karen Bryon.
You are "Pawsome"
3 FLY!
Cous

THAI

Copyright © 2015

Medric "Cous" Cousineau SC, CD

All rights reserved, including the right to reproduce this book or portions thereof, its' photos or any associated audio or performance videos in any form whatsoever, without the express written permission of the authour.

Published by: Invictus Maneo Publishing, Halifax, NS

ISBN-13: 978-1514661963

ISBN-10: 1514661969

Advance Praise for Further than Yesterday

"Medric and his family have been to hell and back. What they have done not only with this book, but with their lives inspires Hope for many other veterans and their families."

Peter Stoffer, MP, Sackville Eastern Shore

"This story is true and needs to be read. Thai, a PTSD Service Dog (trained in a prison in Kansas) has helped restore sanity to Medric Cousineau, whose act of heroism in the North Atlantic brought on his version of PTSD. Now, both partners reach out to help others who need a second chance."

MGen (Retd) Frank Norman

"Cousineau writes as he once played football...with passion and fire and heart! Thank God for his unconquerable soul!"

Valerie Mitchell-Veinotte, Executive Director,

Nova Scotia/Nunavut Command, The Royal Canadian Legion

"Captain (Ret'd) Cousineau's book offers a personal, play-by-play account of events that continue to shape his life. Military members and veterans will relate to the demands and pride earned from his military training and the tragic events of 1986 that took him down a very dark path. The book is also a story about his relationship with Thai, his dog, and his rediscovery of safety, trust, and renewed purpose - valuable lessons for those veterans living with PTSD. Medric's story offers an important message, namely that hope does not come from talk alone, recovery often requires the courage to take some action."

John J. Whelan, PhD (Clinical psychologist and veteran)

"When optimism, idealism and dedication meet injury, pain and loss, the result is isolation, betrayal and desperation UNTIL one talented service dog for PTSD makes possible enough recovery to create a new life with meaning, purpose and hope.

Even more remarkable is the author's dedication and generosity of spirit in his current partial recovery, as he advocates for the provision of service dogs to others suffering from PTSD. Thank you, Cous!"

Dr Beth Reade, Psychiatrist, Homewood Health Centre

Stigma surrounding mental illness in all walks of life is high, however in a world where you're trained to be tough emotionally and mentally, stigma is deadly. Medric Cousineau is shining a light on something that has been kept in the shadows for far too long. "Further Than Yesterday" is an intense look into the mind of a hero. A far too common story that needs to be shared more often in order to create change. An incredible story of one man being given his second chance in life, thanks to one incredible dog. It gives me chills to think about the work Thai does and how she is able to do it. And yet it boils my blood to think of the difference we could be making in the lives of so many people if we could just get them the services, or the service dogs, they need. Think of second chances we could be giving. Think of the lives we could be saving.

Sara Goguen - Inspiring Lives Award Winner 2014 for her work _Saratonin_

"Medric takes you to the dark awful place where PTSD controls your life to a future of hope with Thai, his service dog that changes everything and gives him back his life. It's inspirational the work that Medric & Thai are now doing to help other veterans battling PTSD."

Joyce Treen, MLA, Cole Harbour – Eastern Passage

"Further Than Yesterday: That's All That Counts" refused to sit among the mountain of reading materials that I had on the go and forced me to cast aside all the others so that I could immerse myself completely in its compelling journey and it's many powerful messages. This is one of those books I did not want to put down because the quick tempo and raw emotion got to me; maybe because I too fight to Put The Stigma Down and because I have had to accept my own "New Normal." Many of us lived in ignorance and/or denial prior to our diagnoses and all of us who have been diagnosed commit daily to "keep the Beast in our rear view mirror." "Further Than Yesterday" reminds us of the impact mental wellness can have on family and friends and of the incredible work and hope that talented animals can bring into the world of those who have suffered moral injury. It educates and informs those who have not lived with PTSD. Importantly Cous and Thai demonstrate that practice based evidence can be invaluable and may be required even as we seek to develop evidence based practice where none presently exists. Equally important is that Cous reminds us that moral injury affects many Canadians from many walks of life and, although every journey is unique, the consequences of moral injury are often where we find common ground. Finally the book challenges all of us to respect the life changing work of Service Dogs.

Russ Mann Col Ret'd, OMM, MSM, MBA, CD

This is one of the most powerful moving, and readable books I have ever read. It is disturbing, but educational – I felt like I was there with Cous throughout all his turmoil. This book should be put in the hands of everyone who has, is suspected to have, or is likely to get in the future (ie: all military and all first responders), PTSD, and should be required reading for the CDS, the CMP, and the Ministers of National Defence and Veterans Affairs Canada!!!

Michael J Brown CD LCdr (Ret'd) RCN (Class of '83)

"I have only had the pleasure of knowing Medric for a couple of years, but what was apparent from the outset is the man is a force of nature! After reading *Further Than Yesterday* I can see that his great spirit, dedication and passion is inherent and unwavering. He has consistently put it all on the line and in doing so has dramatically impacted the lives of others; past, present and future. Thank you for all you do. Stay Calm my friend and keep on walking that dog!"

Danielle Forbes, Executive Director, National Service Dogs

"Today I will do
what others won't,
So tomorrow I can accomplish
what others can't."

-Jerry Rice,
Pro Football Hall of Fame

;

Table of Contents

Dedication

"No one knows where I have been, down that long and dusty road to hell and back again. Everyone has been somewhere, but no one knows where I have been."

Each of us has a story and a journey. In this case, you are about to read about my messed up journey. If you find yourself saying "Why the hell would anyone put up with that crap?" you will be asking the same question that I asked countless times after I got Thai. Before Thai, I was in no shape to even contemplate such a question.

To my two daughters, Lindsey and Jennifer, I could not be prouder of the strong women you have become. Jennifer, your career as an Emergency Room Nurse will carry on the family tradition of caring. Lindsey, your life may have been cut short, but you have left an indelible mark on this world. Butterflies and Lady Bugs will serve as constant reminders for all of us till we meet in Heaven. Love you both so much.

For Jocelyn, love of my life, sweetie and best buddy… Thank you for never bailing out, even though I gave you reason to on more than several occasions. Thank you for walking the Long Walk to Sanity and being the voice of reason in Paws Fur Thought.

Perhaps the most fitting dedication is two of your favourite quotes:

1.   "Everything happens for a reason."

2.   "It is what it is."

Acknowledgments

It is impossible to have undertaken and survived a journey like the one outlined in Further Than Yesterday without the help and guidance of so many people who have no idea the impact that they have had on my life, on the life of my family, and now the lives of countless others who are battling PTSD and other Mental Health Challenges.

To friends and family, who have been there through it all, the good, the bad and the ugly, thank you one and all.

To HMCS Nipigon and her Helairdet, members of 443 squadron: Only those who were out there during that 48 hour period will ever truly know. To Hans Kleeman, Bill Ropp, Brad Renner, and Doc Hagey (now deceased) your professionalism was without equal. To Ken Whitehead and Al Smith (now deceased) I live because you two were the very best that ever were when the stakes were human lives, namely mine.

To Lefty, Michael G, Gerry C, Stu L and mostly Tony H, we made it when everyone was betting against us and for good reason. Yet!

To my technical staff including my Editor, Cover Photographer Sophie Pyne of 4memories2last4ever and Photo fixer Karin of Karin's Photography thank you for making us look and read well.

To a group of veterans and serving military who did not give up on me, when in fact I had given up on myself, I have no way to tell the stories and their impact without a whole pile of pollen clouds and none of us want that. To my adopted little Sister Kate MacEachern, you go girl. To Paul "Trapper" Cane, Chris "Red" Hatton and Dennis "Corporal Justice" Manuge, thank you for being there. To WO Renay Groves of the Poppy Memorial Team, thank you for a legacy that will not fade for the families of our fallen.

To the Silver Cross Mothers and Fathers, especially Darlene Cushman and Angela Reid, thank you for the greatest of gifts to this country and for helping ensure my moral compass stays fixed on True North Strong and Free. They will never be forgotten.

To Vaughn Cosman, Hugh Ellis, Jeff Paige, Harold Wright, Lise Charron, Francine Harding, Terry O'Hearn, Becky Kent, Garry Pond, Wilma Bush and Dee Brasseur, you made the Long Walk to Sanity a reality. Without you, there would be no Kevin and Donna McLean, Maggie Van Tassell, Sheila Clayton, Bob and Christine Philipson Steadman, Lisa Partridge, and Angie Arra-Robar on the Paws Team. Vaughn, without your voice of "Build bridges, don't burn them", I would have scorched the earth. To the countless others who made the Long Walk to Sanity the success it was, I cannot thank you enough for supporting our vision.

To Sarah Holbert and Megan Llewellyn, and the rest of the CARES family, you have helped our veterans get their lives back with their Service Dogs. I am forever indebted.

To Brenda Anderson, the "Blind Chick" who taught me to see, and more importantly enhanced my handler skills, know that Noble and you will always be a special part of my journey.

To the NS Nunavut Command of the Royal Canadian Legion, Valerie Mitchell-Veinotte, Ron Trowsdale, Steve Wessel and countless other legion members, you are helping veterans regain their lives and re-unite with their families.

To LGen David Millar, thank you for your guidance. To Vice Admiral Retd Duncan Miller, thanks for reminding me to keep it "Paws-itive"

To Doctor Dee, the calm in the voices of the chaos of my brain, Hugs.

To Scott Henneberry and Chelsea Bainbridge, thanks for tending the Home fires. Could not have done it without you two.

To Bryan "Beetle" Bailey, thank you for the Forward. Gratitude.

But of all those who have been there since before the journey started, right through to present is "Uncle Frank" and "Aunt Anne". MGen Ret'd Norman was the commandant in my fourth year at RMC. In 2012, when I desperately needed a confidant, and a consigliore, Uncle Frank became my go to. I have no idea how many emails, and discussions we have had, but rest assured, he saw me at my worst, and now I hope that he can say that he has been a part of the Best, Paws Fur Thought.

Harsh Language & Trigger Warnings

To you my readers, I am going to take the liberty of apologizing for some very harsh language that appears in this work. Things are what they are and in certain circumstances described herein, emotions ran high and the vocabulary is not the finest of the Queen's English. Please consider the vocabulary into the context of the moments in which it appears.

There are also some sections which may act as triggers for those who suffer from PTSD. Self-care is paramount, so forewarned is also forearmed.

Foreword

I was pleasantly surprised, humbled, and honoured when Medric, whom I will hereafter refer to as "Cous", as do most of his college and military friends, floated the idea that I pen an introduction to his captivating book, *Further Than Yesterday*. I could only surmise that he chose me because I knew him during his formative years at the College, which he describes in his book as "The Before Time" period of his life, and one who witnessed his incredible recent accomplishments. While I cannot claim to have PTSD expertise, I am all too cognizant of its real and ravaging impact on soldiers. In particular I have seen its effects during and in the aftermath of the Medak Pocket operation in 1993. I have also come to be absolutely convinced of the efficacy of PTSD trained service dogs through my exposure to Cous and his incredible service dog Thai. As you will very quickly discover in his book, Cous would simply not be where he is today without Thai. Having witnessed the interaction between the two, I now know how important service dogs are in enabling those afflicted with PTSD to regain their ability to function and cope with the stresses of life.

Although Cous and I graduated together from RMC in 1983, I knew him primarily by reputation as I spent my first two years at Royal Roads in Victoria. In fact, we only got to know each other better when we found ourselves thrown together as members of the Cadet Wing Headquarters at the start of our fourth year. While at RMC, most of those who knew Cous could testify to his larger than life persona and his boundless energy and zeal. Those who did not know him well may have made the mistake of regarding him primarily as a proud member of the Frigate or as a somewhat bitter and boisterous football player who lamented the fact that their varsity team had been sacrificed by the College. Those who knew him better understood that he was an exceptionally dedicated, articulate, and deceptively well-read professional blessed with a great sense of humour. It was also during this time that he unexpectedly found himself thrust into very high profile duties which included acting as one of the Personal Assistants to the newly arrived College Commandant. This twist of fate proved to be the start of an intensely personal relationship between Cous and Major-General (Retd) Frank Norman to whom Cous later reached out to during his drive to extricate himself from the depths of his depression, anxiety and mental health injuries. In many ways, Frank Norman proved to be his rock and mentor and supported Cous incredibly in more ways than one.

In May of 2013, a month or two into my new job as the Executive Director of the RMC Club, I received a call from Cous completely out of the blue. Remarkably, we were able to instantly reconnect as if we were still cadets despite the fact that we had not communicated with each other for 30 years. While I had heard tell of his infamous exploits as an Air Navigator, which merited a very rare Star of Courage, we had very much lost contact with each other. It was wonderful to hear his distinctively deep voice again and it was obvious that he was brimming with enthusiasm as he was preparing to embark on his Long Walk to Sanity which would bring him back to Kingston, his alma mater, and later to enjoy our 30th year Class reunion.

During his Long Walk to Sanity, I had the good fortune to listen to Cous give two of his many presentations during his campaign. The first was to local Kingston Legion members and the second was an incredible presentation to the RMC graduating class of 2014 to which he makes reference in his book. Cous, a gifted orator and natural story teller par excellence, spoke straight from the heart with a combination of remarkable eloquence and bluntness which was liberally sprinkled with humour and, at times, raw emotion.

To describe the reaction of the audience as spellbound would be a huge understatement. The entire fourth year class, and everyone else present, literally hung on his every word. He had no doubt mulled his messages and anecdotes over in his mind on innumerable occasions while completing his 50 days of half marathon length walks. He very vividly recalled the highlights of the search and rescue operation which was conducted in the direst of circumstances. He then went on to describe his personal battle with the "Beast" which ultimately led to his release from the Forces at a time when the military medical understanding of PTSD was embryonic at best. He freely and frankly shared the impact of his battle with PTSD as well as the toll it took on his health and his family. Lastly he recounted how Thai had transformed his life and how PTSD service dogs perform their duties. In fact, whenever Cous became emotional or a response was triggered, Thai was immediately there clearly demonstrating how a properly trained service dogs can bring their handlers back to a functional footing. Cous' presentation will be one that will remain ingrained to everyone present. Those cadets in the room were given a much better understanding of the reality of mental health injuries which is critical to their preparation as the leaders of tomorrow as they very well may need to assist subordinates or perhaps help themselves in the future. In some ways, this single presentation is a microcosm of this book.

Cous' book is about much more than his personal courage and dogged determination on the day that he undertook to rescue two critically injured fishermen from an American fishing boat, although that story alone is worth the read. In my opinion, it is his protracted battle with stress related injuries that is the most engaging and illuminating aspect. The fact that he is able to share his experiences is the direct result of his personal tenacity, loving and supportive family and friends, and his intimate relationship with the incredibly devoted, disciplined and talented Thai. Cous shares all of this in a manner which is very much Cous. Honest and sincere, his prose is authentic and filled with emotion betraying his personal experiences and pain.

Seldom do we learn the details of harrowing operations nor do readers have the ability to literally get into the head of an individual who continues to overcome debilitating mental health injuries. His transformational change after the introduction of Thai is truly astounding in a ground-breaking area of mental health treatment. Cous' passion and personal campaign to raise funds to pair injured veterans with PTSD service dogs is noble in the extreme. Equally important is his contribution as a catalyst for change in public policy. He continues to fight the good fight in an effort to obtain public recognition and support for PTSD trained service dogs.

Throughout his book, Cous delivers his messages in the vernacular of those who have served. While some may think it is at times on the salty side, it reflects the reality of his environment and era. To read his words is akin to having an intimate conversation with someone who is able to reveal their inner thoughts and mindset. Cous has experienced more danger and the ill effects of stress than anyone should; while he was decorated for heroism resulting from that rescue operation, his true heroism is his battle against the "Beast" and his quest to break down barriers, bureaucracies, stigma, and to advocate change through the introduction of service dogs. While all of this has exacted a heavy toll, Cous, to his credit, is one who never backs away from a challenge and one who does not have "quit" in his DNA.

Without reservation, I commend his book to a broad audience for a variety of reasons. Firstly, it is rare that anyone will share the account of a dangerous rescue in such rich detail including their private thoughts and fears. Secondly, everyone can benefit from Cous' life time of non-medical expertise in PTSD injuries which he unfortunately acquired as a decades-long patient. Everyone who has experience as a first responder will certainly relate to what Cous has experienced and endured. Thirdly, everyone who attended a Canadian military college or served in uniform cannot help but enjoy his recounting of his College days, including, the introduction of Lady Cadets, and his early career as a Naval Aviator. Lastly, readers will appreciate the importance of his recent contributions; particularly his passion for championing public support for PTSD trained service dogs. Cous certainly deserves a big Bravo Zulu as an ex-cadet who is a credit to RMC and who continues to exemplify the ideals of TDV!

Lieutenant-Colonel (Ret'd) Bryan Bailey
Executive Director, Royal Military Colleges Club of Canada

Prologue:

The Nightmare Begins

The Nightmare Begins
October 6th, 1986

The blackness was like nothing I had ever experienced. The gale that howled outside whipped the ocean into a crazed frenzy. The hungry ocean heaved the sixty eight foot long liner out of Massachusetts like a cork. Hanging out the back door of the ten ton Sea King search and rescue helicopter gave me a bird's-eye view of the impossible task the crew was attempting: threading a swaying guideline down through a tangle of shrieking wires, rigging and chaos onto a six by six foot heaving deck space already awash in the blood of the injured crewmen.

Having been near and out the back door before, I was used to the smell of burnt JP5 jet fuel, but today it was different. It was another straw pressing on my back, threatening to break it, and send me into the abyss. Coppery bile pushed up into the back of my throat as the Sea King was tossed by the gale. None of the hundreds of training sessions for this evolution touched this reality where the environmentals pushed well outside any envelope anyone had ever conceived. Failure was not an option. The stakes were human lives. They always were in Search and Rescue. Tonight though the Life and Death may very well be my own.

Finally, after countless attempts, the guideline hit the deck and the crewman somehow managed to hang on. In an instant, I swung out the door in the double lift harness attached to the rescue hoist and prepared to descend from the maelstrom above into the chaos below. Ken Whitehead caught my eye, and our glance confirmed what we both knew, that my life was in his hands, the skilled and steady hands of the hoist operator and Commander of HMCS Nipigon's Helicopter Air Detachment. But mostly my life was in the hands of a greater power, God if you will. Powerless as I descended towards the deck, I had no idea how long the fall would be, on that night, in that moment, and in the black dog shrieking horror that would ensue when I would be genuinely powerless for moments, weeks and decades, driving hard into the inner circles of hell that would follow.

Leaving the helicopter, heading out to help the men on the long liner fight for their lives against the Atlantic, the seeds of the torment that I would fight for the next three decades had just been planted. In that instant, I began a completely different fight for my own life, one that I almost lost on several occasions. This is my story...

Still Trembling
May 2012

Still trembling like a leaf, thoughts swirl through my head and I find it difficult to focus. The news that I may be getting my service dog as soon as early August still overwhelms me, and I find it hard to imagine after all these years that help is so close yet so very far away. The reactions of those I've told are mixed since some have no idea about the struggles and the battles one faces when they wrestle and confront the issues surrounding post-traumatic stress disorder.

The challenge of describing what it is like to live with post-traumatic stress is in of itself a daunting one. I often find myself wondering "what would life have been like if on that night so many years ago my actions had been different?" Perhaps, the more pertinent question would be "what would have been the outcome if my diagnosis and treatment had been more timely and effective?"

I've had the chance to reflect many times and realize that I would've done what I did that night because it was my duty. Yes, ultimately I volunteered, but when I did it was because we had a job to do and in many ways I was the most logical choice to leave the helicopter and try to get on to the deck of the fishing vessel. Although I felt physically prepared and well trained, I had no idea of how deeply the emotional trauma of what I would experience combined with how the threats to my physical well-being would affect the rest of my life.

Years ago, while still a cadet at the Royal Military College of Canada, the cadet wing was briefed by the officer commanding the British forces at the Battle of Mount Tumbledown in the Falkland Islands. During his presentation, he wished he could change one thing. If he had the power, he would ensure that all of his leaders and all of his troops would be exposed to dealing with physical injury and trauma. Even though the conflict in the Falkland Islands was short by modern standards, the fighting at Mount Tumbledown was intense and brutal. Little was I to realize at this point that he foreshadowed what would become the initial triggering event in my battle with post-traumatic stress disorder.

Within a few nights of the rescue itself I found myself unable to sleep, and what little sleep I did get was shattered by intense vivid nightmares. Later in the story I will try and expand upon what happened that night, and my role in it. The entire crew of both sorties on the helicopter were placed in great physical danger, the margin of error was a razor's edge that narrowly missed fatally cutting us. During this evolution, there were points where I stood on that razor's edge and looked deep into the abyss. The difference between life and death in certain circumstances is blurred and definitely, upon reflection, only then does one come to appreciate how close one has come shaking hands with the Grim Reaper himself.

The macabre dance on the precipice while cheating the devil his due comes with the nature of the beast. The military and its members are often asked to do things that go beyond the scope of human experience and to do so at grave emotional and physical costs. The picture that I am about to paint for you is a reflection of the canvas of my life. Many parts of the story are blurred or lost in a sea of prescription pharmaceuticals. I wish the story was different but alas, it is what it is. For so many years I have plunged into the depths of despair and anguish, countless times planning out the sequence of events that would conclude the story.

There are those among the readers who have never dealt first hand with someone who has battled post-traumatic stress. There will be points where my descriptions of events and thoughts will be shocking and disturbing. I apologize in advance. Additionally, my experiences and my thoughts are not to be confused with the fact that my story does not completely or adequately address the circumstances of all who battle the "Beast".

In the end, if I raise the bar of consciousness for those who know not the impact of this horrible injury, then my work will not have been for naught. If I can shed some light for family and friends who care for someone who struggles, I will count myself lucky. In the end, the true measure of success will be whether any of the afflicted reach out for help and regain part of their lives, a degree of sanity and a sense of peace that eludes them.

DND 417

DND 417 (Oct 73) 7530-21-870-4620. Pretty damn official sounding. One. Blue. Hardbound. Department of National Defence Flying Log book for Aircrew other than pilot. Namely, if it wasn't for the facts and documents and images in my flying log book, so much of the story would be too obscured in the fog of time and medications, too much of both, to recall with any accuracy.

My flight log book was tucked out of sight in a corner of the barely organized chaos of my office. I wanted it to be everything the military office was not. I had a "Shit pit". I wanted no reminders of my past. Considering every one of my immediate family proudly served Canada in its military, it might have been odd to realize that not one picture, painting, portrait, or other memorabilia depicting anything military was displayed in my home. The closest we come is a Dusan Kadlec print of old war ships in Halifax harbour circa 1890. A glorious time of wooden ships and men of steel. A time before naval aviation.

My log book is a veritable march through time of my aviation career, with some interesting addenda. One of my instructors at Nav School had pointed out that a log book could be so much more than a historical list of aviation facts. A few notes here and there, and what would be nothing more than a chronology could become something that puts concrete to the memories of a career, however short that may or may not be. By adding brief notations, a few photos and a couple of newspaper articles, that instructor paved the way for a large part of the journey that you are undertaking. When I say that parts of the story are so clear, that clarity only comes from those facts and notations and the times that were the "before time". The before time was a happy place, and maybe that's why I'll talk about it first.

The log book, its tape yellowing with the passage of time, was tucked away. One would not trip across it by accident. My log book was not proudly displayed or even reserved for some place of honour.

Thankfully it remains. My log book was not destroyed in the passage of time. When something seems just a bit of a stretch, just a little too hard to believe, the recorded facts are what they are. Or as my bride loves to say, "It is what it is. No more, no less."

I wish that it were that simple. I long for simpler days and simpler times. Names, dates, places that would have been lost are at my fingertips. Actually it is a good thing. For if it needed to appear from the fog of my mind, it would be lost. A navigator, lost? We may be temporarily unsure of our position, we are never lost! In my case, I have no idea how you even begin to describe it.

What follows in the next section will be things that are published as a matter of record, or in fact available in some dusty old archive somewhere. Truly keep in mind, this is from my view point with my perception of reality, which may or may not be how others saw certain events. I am sure that from their view point things were much different. I honour that. I respect that. In the journey we are about to undertake, please don't judge anyone else in the story. In my case, know that whatever you come to think and feel is on me. Mea Culpa. Or for the younger at heart, "My bad". If it is negative, I have probably been wherever you think and then some.

At this point, dear reader I am also going to have to get you to indulge me. We are going to take a very long and convoluted journey. The reason it's this way is that at some point we will make a transition. A transition from historical events to a very different place. This place will give you insights into things you may have suspected. The journey will arrive at a destination. I know. I have been on this journey a long time.

Part One:

The Before Time

Things are going great
Summer, 1983

"Things are going great, and they're only getting better

I'm doing all right, getting good grades

The future's so bright I gotta wear shades"

-Timbuk3, The future is so bright.

The summer of 1983 was probably one of the greatest times of my life. Even though I have a French name I was no more bilingual than I could fly to the moon. Still was not, even though Richard "Cayou" Cayouette and I had survived Rook camp together in the fall of 1979. They had paired us up two-by-two in sequential alphabetical order and there you were, you had your rook term roommate. That was all the science there was to it at the time. The military was not going to over think something as simple as "you two grab your gear and get in there and square yourselves off." Cayou's English was better than my French and between the two of us we fumbled along, at that point neither of us linguistic superstars. We also figured out that the fourth years honestly could give a tinker's damn if we were having problems communicating. That was our problem, not theirs. The limit as X rapidly approached zero. "Yes I can close the lights". Not only did Cayou and I have that bond of being Rook term roommates, Cayou was in my section in my second term of 4th year. As Cadet Section Commander (CSC), Cayou was in my section, which was a mix of cadets from every year. The rooks had been let loose on the rest of the Wing and it was undoubtedly an interesting time. Rooks where trying to survive long enough to see us March off the square and to see a new crop become First years at the Royal Military College of Canada. Our marching off would officially mark the end of First year. Second Years were enjoying that glorious period of knowing enough to work through the system but honestly not being more than rank and file. Ranking ahead of the rooks and behind the Third Years. In a few short months, the Third Years would assume the mantle of the cadet command structure. The Fourth Years were counting down the Days to Grad. Fourth years were trying to finish theses, others trying to finish essays and papers to complete the course work. Some fourth years who had struggled academically in a course were pretty much left alone so that they could complete their studies, not "Supp out" and have to finish their fourth year a second time, and not graduate with our class. The time had arrived to turn the page on this chapter of our lives. Four years is a long time to be in the pressure cooker. We were done, and in some ways I am sure the college was glad to be done with us.

Our class was certainly going to be unique. We took immense pride in the fact that we were "LCWB." We were the last all male class of "gentlemen cadets" of the Royal Military College of Canada. We prided ourselves on it, and every attempt to quell the thing that unified us actually resulted in a renewed effort on our part to remain united and defiant. You cannot change the facts once established in history. In our second year, the world had changed dramatically and the college would never be the same. The First 32 took their place in infamy. The First 32 refers to a play on the Old 18. Every rook since time immortal had been drilled to know the names of the original 18 cadets who were enrolled into the Royal Military College of Canada. Ask any ex-cadet today and they will spurt out Wurtele, Freer, Wise... In the fall of 1980, the first 32 Lady Cadets entered through the arch to assume their place among the cadets of first year. Being wedged in between those that had never known Lady Cadets and the first class with them was us. The view of how well the experiment was going would certainly be different depending on who you talked to.

There is a not a grad alive who has not got his "When I was a rook stories." Every rook has had his or her share of horse shit to endure, but at least ours was not attached to a real horse. The point I am driving at is that there have been certain things that have not changed since the inception of the college. Other items have been shaped and molded through an evolutionary process to advance the college to the point it needed to be to produce officers who were to become instrumental in shaping Canada's role on the international global geo-political stage and Canada's military roles and policies along with it. Not every officer who becomes known as a great leader is a product of the Military College System. But I can guarantee you that there are a very large number who are. Did the Military College experience give them everything they needed to become the officers they were? No, it would be impossible. But just like every structure built to the top and meant to last, if there is an inadequate foundation the structure will not last. The college experience gave the graduates a foundation to shape their destinies.

The Lady Cadets Arrive
Fall of 1980

The class of 1983 was a bit of an administrative handful filled with a cast of characters and a host of challenges that had not faced previous staff and students. In some cases solutions would be simple and straight forward, in others, things followed a natural evolutionary path. This may give you an insight into how one simple thing changed a lot of cadet's lives. I do not mean to add levity to the situation but the arrival of Lady Cadets heralded changes in buildings as old as the Stone Frigate. Since the storied structure had been modified to become cadet quarters I think very little had been done to the building other than the addition of electricity and indoor plumbing. The College grounds are full of interesting and historical buildings steeped with rich history, but the Frigate is an icon. When the College went to multiple squadrons in 1948, Hudson Squadron was ensconced in the Frigate to remain there as I write. The building was originally built to house ship and naval stores on the shores of Navy Bay under the watchful eyes of "Old Fort Henry". Construction was completed between 1819 and 1821, and the "Stone Boat" maintains much of its character, unimpeded by time and technology.

Sometimes the mundane concerns of life become obscured in the details and so it is when you have approximately eighty guys sharing three washers and dryers, one per floor. For those of you unfamiliar with the life at Military College, one thing that cadets tend to do a lot of is laundry. Even though there were dry cleaning services available across the parade square, there was a never ending supply of athletic gear and daily wear uniforms to be washed in the Frigate. The few machines available would be humming morning, noon and night. If you had laundry in the inevitable queue and you walked by, you just moved the things along from bag to washer to dryer through the cycle. The routine became one of those daily rituals that became a part of life. In the Frigate, that took a serious turn for the better when the women arrived. There were three female washrooms added, one per floor, with accompanying washers and dryers. But their laundry facilities were outside the washrooms and were accessible for one and all. Originally, the machines sat idle, reserved for the use of the Lady Cadets. Then very quickly the machines became fair game, but with a catch. The laundry bags were readily identifiable, and since we were talking 4 ladies and 3 machines, well you get the idea. Some of the men would not move the ladies' laundry. But if they were open, it is funny how many bags of gear that looked distinctly male got set out in the hallway after the cycle was done, a solution that evolved with the times.

Other parts of the system did not fare as well and to say that all levels of commands faced challenges would be an understatement. The addition of Lady Cadets was here, like it or not. Many did not. My second year gave me a front row seat to watch what it was like to be them. First year is a trying event for everyone, but for the ladies, it was more so. Not because they were incapable. No, more so that they were the first and nobody knew exactly what to do. Later in this story, much will be added to this theme. Just know that being at the leading edge of anything, especially if it involves change at an institution steeped with the culture and history of a place as grand as RMC, change was not going to come easy.

Under those conditions that then Brigadier General Frank Norman assumed command of the College in 1982. For me personally there was soon to be an issue that made the Lady Cadets seem like the onset of inevitability and a time that was going to come. With our graduation, Lady cadets would assume the Cadet leadership roles in the Cadet Wing and would graduate a year later and be commissioned and join the Officer Corps of the Canadian Military. For those who told all within the college system that women were there to stay, they would soon be facing challenges of their own. Just as the last all male year of "Redcoats" was about to leave, whispers of women in combat roles were beginning to surface. If you thought that the fourth year class at RMC was having issues being the last all male class and all that it entailed, the rest of the pointy end of the military was about to have issues of their own, big issues at that. Perhaps there is one thing that history may come to know in the fullness of time. Other than their own classmates, the rogues, scoundrels and other scallywags that composed the motley crew of the "Last Class with Balls" (LCWB) had more chance to see the Lady Cadets rise to the task and become leaders than any other group. So what may be seen as "our class' great shortcoming," will in reflection become a source of great pride. We were the last all male class, and a sign of the evolutionary forces at work. The Class of '83 was soon to be the line officers when women broached the ramparts of the operational theatres and MOC's in the Canadian Military. Perhaps it was time? We had our celebration that we were the last and those that came behind us, with their mixed genders, replaced us. Maybe we were the last to know that the times have actually changed. I know that for me personally, that time had long since come and gone.

Combat Arms Battle Schools
Summer, 1981

The summer of 1981, at the end of my second year, was spent at CFB Gagetown. One of the largest land bases in Canada, it was home to the various "battle schools" that would take young officers and mold them into what would become the junior officers of the combat arms. Lest anyone doubt one very simple fact, though every military occupation comes with challenges and expertise unique to their own needs and requirements, the combat arms are absolutely different. There are countless books and articles written by lifers who can describe that situation in much better words and with much more insight than I ever will.

The first part of the summer was genuinely a nightmare. Keep in mind that we had survived BOTC, we had survived two years at RMC and now we were in Gage-nam (CFB Gagetown: A Military training base in New Brunswick renowned for its swamps) and it was different. Lest we had any thoughts that anything we had accomplished up to this point amounted to a hill of beans, we were instantly and totally removed from the frying pan and thrust into the fire. If memory serves as guide, we had ten "Military College" pukes and thirty-two "RESO-s", Reserve officers who came from units spread across Canada. What we had in fitness, drive and motivation, most of them had in experience. We were about to be exposed to pieces of kit in the military arsenal that they had been using for, in some cases, years. We had two officers and ten senior NCO s who would guide us through infantry battle school and then our exposure to the big guns, 105 mm howitzers.

I was certainly in a crossroads of crisis. I wanted to be an aviator. To do so, one needed out of the combat arms, and that was a trick that was easier said than done. The sharp pointy end does not like to give up its troops or resources easily. But it was my right to ask for a reclassification to Air Ops. In fact the second last thing I did before heading to Gagetown was to do my Air Force selection boards and initial aero medical screening at CFB Downsview. The last thing was a trip to my "Squad Bomb's" office. Squad bomb was the nickname we had given to Squadron commanders, who in many cases, were not much more than super cadets who had one tour, mostly from operational trades, under their belt. In keeping with its fine naval tradition, our squad bomb was a Naval Lieutenant who very clearly and succinctly summed it up as follows : "Lest you think you are going to Gagetown, screwing the dog, selling the pups and walking back in here to force our hand for your reclassification, you young man have another thought coming. Anything less than the effort that I know you are capable of, and you will never, ever get what you want. Am I perfectly clear on that point? I will make the remainder of your time in the military as uncomfortable as I can possibly make it."

Sure he huffed and puffed but I had no doubt he had the power to do exactly what he said and blow my house down. So it came to pass that I arrived at CFB Gagetown to spend the summer doing some of the most exciting stuff that I had ever done. Not that it was all wine and roses. Anything but. I started with them turning us out in our PT gear and combat boots and starting us running. And run we would, everywhere, at all times. Defensive linemen have a certain build that doesn't exactly suit itself to running. If you were a phase 2 Artillery officer you would double time or better. No exceptions, no excuses. This day was different. They took us on a long run out the back gate of Gagetown, and then returned us to the track at the gym, where we continued to run laps. Confession time: I hate running. Loathe it. Despise it. Even though I am nearly five foot eleven inches, I have just a 30 inch inseam, no neck and a really long body. Great build for a defensive tackle in football, but honestly not a gazelle. I did not say I was bone idle, it is that I absolutely do not like running. But then again, what I liked was of little consequence and with this particular group it actually would have been a bad idea to show any weakness. Unlike the previous exposure to the military, I certainly do not think we, as gentlemen cadets, were quite ready for what was coming. We had seen the flying beds at basic. We had been screamed at and verbally assaulted by our fourth years during rook term, and now we were exposed to a whole new cadre. These guys were all that we had seen before with one huge difference. These guys had been trained to kill people, and it showed.

The first guy fell out of formation a few laps later and was gasping for wind at the side of the cinder track. One of the DS (Directing Staff) stopped beside him. In a parade square voice that carried for miles the next thing we heard above our laboured breathing sounded some like this:

"What are you looking for some sympathy? You want to find sympathy? Check the dictionary. You will find it right between shit and syphilis. Now you slimy little piece of shit better get your unmotivated ass up there with the rest or you will pay. You'll all pay."

The diatribe continued and we ran. We knew what we could look forward to if we chose to stop running. The time came when I had to puke. I know I was going woof so I broke ranks, walked to the side of the track and let her rip. Three massive heaves later, hands on my knees, I was bagged. I also knew one other thing. My summer and my life was not going to turn out very well if I showed any weakness. So before my own CF personal motivational speaker had a chance to let fly with a vengeance, I came, I saw, I ran, I puked, and I ran again. So without a word being said, I was grinding my way back to the group. Then the Gods smiled. Two things happened almost simultaneously. The DS ordered us to stop running and they brought out a dummy 105mm round. These shells are about two feet long and are shaped like an oversize bullet on steroids and weigh about twenty kilos. The deal was now we were going to play strength games and do some battle PT. One of the games was to launch this projectile by a combination of brute force and technique as far as you could. The DS wanted to see what kind of explosive power we had. In a very short span of minutes I went from woofing my cookies to launching the round about as far as they had seen in a long time. While D-lineman might not excel at running, it's a different story when you ask us to throw heavy objects requiring Brute Force and Ignorance! The nods of appreciation from the Sergeants was something to feel good about. Here in the warrior class there was a huge respect for brute force and physical strength. Your lives could one day depend on it so they were going to foster it.

Beyond the intense physical challenges that every single day brought, we getting hammered with tactics and equipment at a frenetic pace. How frenetic? In about 35 days we went through the following: FNC1 rifle, FNC2 automatic rifle, SMG (submachine gun), GPMG (general purpose machine gun) 50 Cal Heavy

Machine Gun, grenades, M72 LAW (light anti-tank weapon) and the "Karly G" Karl Gustav 84mm anti-tank weapon. Besides this frenetic pace of becoming familiar with weapons, we were learning how to "advance to and make contact with the enemy." We did that time and time and time again. We did O (Orders) groups, planned attacks, learned the principles of recce, and a host of skills that would have very little application to the outside world. But building a proper slit trench or what may or may not provide cover from various forms of enemy fire were important. Because the stakes were high, the DS were merciless. Any shortcoming was a reason for a royal arse reaming. Some of these guys were definitely not who you would be inviting over to the next white glove cocktail party. Not that they were not nice people, it's just that it would be so outside their realm of experience or interest, so too were their specialties viewed exactly the same way. The public did not know they would tear off your arm and beat you with the wet end if you were somehow deficient. These boys played for keeps. I remember that one of our DS from Basic Officer Training had a shirt that he wore to PT. On it was as large skull with a bayonet stuck in it, with the saying "South East Asian War Games: Second Place." That settled that. Sometimes your very best would not be good enough and that would be very unsatisfactory.

Thankfully, even though there was no shooting war going on at the time, the Cold War was in full swing and both sides were still pursuing the doctrine of MAD, mutually assured destruction, where the hopes of mankind rested on a strategy based purely on annihilation. Still, there was some hope that it would stay conventional, and conventional wars required conventional things like infantry on the ground supported by tanks and artillery and every other thing required to move the military machine. We were not so far removed from memory that lessons learned in Viet Nam, the Korean War and the Great Wars were forgotten. So it was that ships and aircraft of all sizes and capabilities, and all other manner of support trades came to one common objective. Get boots on the ground and control the terrain. If you don't think that is the case I offer into evidence the undoubtedly horrific experiences of Viet Nam. And do not for even one moment think this is an anti-American campaign about whatever failed social or geo-political policies ruled the day. Sorry, we will skip right on by and stop at the boots on the ground. Until you control the real estate, you do not control shit! Just that simple. The French found it out before the Americans and a job that coalition forces in Afghanistan found out after the Russians couldn't do it there either.

So the problem I had come to was a rather intriguing one. I had to go to Gagetown, spend the summer driving my body in a course that I genuinely did not want to be on, do well enough to appease the Squad Bomb, but ultimately not do too well. If I had aced the course, the Artillery would be even less likely to let one get away. So amongst some assuredly intense DS and against the threat of rotting in some genuinely horrible place should I screw up, I had to hit some imaginary bullseye on some scale for which I did not have all the parameters and details. I did know two things. First, I was not going to let anyone there know that I had an interest in being somewhere other than there, that would have been a sure fire fast track to the undivided attention of these absolutely intimidating CF motivational speakers. I don't for a moment want to entertain how miserable life would be if they thought you did not want to be there.

Like every other military course, you are ranked on just about everything you could imagine. Beyond the hard tests and performance objectives system, there was a chit system. Good Follower chits and Bad Follower chits and according to what you did or did not do you would accumulate them. Getting the Bad chits was a walk in the park as it did not take too much to hit someone's "shit list" when you had that many DS around. The insight gained when I hucked the dummy arty shell for all it was worth, and the look when I stopped, puked and ran some more, told me everything that I needed to know. Performance in the field would be everything. I decided that my strategy would be to drive the body hard and absolutely focus on the weapons and tactics being taught me. I needed an out. Daily inspections were the rival of anything that we had seen in Rook camp or BOTC. These guys had their watches wound way too tight for my liking and it was easy to catch bad follower chits for some crime against humanity, during inspections, real or perceived. No matter how well you had your stuff squared off, you were going to catch hell sooner or later. For me, I just assumed I might as well make it easy for them. A button undone here, a shirt in the wrong order there, and sooner or later the bad follower chits would arrive.

On one hand I was absolutely enjoying the thrill and the adventure of the big guns and the combat arms guys. On the other hand, I honestly did want to fly. These guys were a different crew. We had not had a day off in weeks and finally we were to have a free day. Our first in weeks. They forgot one little detail. They had signed us up for the 20 km Volksmarch. Spectacular. We get a day were we could actually keep our "crack in the rack" and we got to go for a 20 km stroll. So it was as the rest of the base was getting ready to enjoy a leisurely walk we showed up in our PT gear and ran. We ran and jogged the 20k, crossed the finish line, and went back and slept. Day off my ass, at least they weren't screaming blue bloody murder about something or other.

I had read somewhere in the distant past that if the words "left flanking" and "oh fuck" were not invented then Canada's military in the Second World War would have had no job or the words to discuss it. So was the case in Infantry Battle School. We were advancing to and making contact with the enemy endlessly, over and over and over again. There was a lot of us and they wanted to get as many views of what we could show. It became very apparent, very quickly, do it with more gung-ho can-do attitude than everyone else, and sure enough the DS would go find someone who obviously needed their attention more than they thought you did. So a couple of successful run throughs and sure enough, I am just muddling along, FDH. Fat, dumb, and happy. That was not to remain so for long.

In all the weaponry we had been exposed to there was a full auto version of the 7.62 mm. This bipod mounted rifle had a 30 round mag and the lucky carrier got to wear the bra, a God damned evil contraption that carried an extra four magazines. In the time that I was so privileged that seemed to be a lot. So rather than the sixty rounds you would be carrying if you were toting your FNC1, you got to hump an extra 120 rounds which may not sound like a huge difference, but when you are humping up and down the hills and vales near Petersville in the shadow of Mount Douglas and it was hotter than the hubs of hell it mattered, a lot. But it was not just the weight, not just the bra. The same scene played over and over.

Contact:

Contact 10 o'clock, yada yada yada

Inevitably that meant you would hear… "C2 group, left flanking, remainder covering fire, on my command go". Off we would charge, the C2 guy and his winger like some scalded cat to get far enough so that we could assume a position about ninety degrees to the left of the contact. Once established, the rest of the platoon would leap frog its way, up to and over the enemy position with our automatic fire providing cover. Somewhere about what seemed to be the thousandth time I started running this scenario. C2 group stand fast, remainder left flanking, on my command go. And please just keep going. The game was getting a little redundant. Sooner or later we must have gotten our collective shit together enough that it was soon to come to an end. If nothing more, the DS was great at driving a schedule. According to what we saw, Battle School was to end in about thirty six hours. We had been living in the field, hoochies and all, for about two straight weeks. We had been pushed, pulled, and driven beyond what we thought a lot of our limits were and had passed exhaustion so long ago, most of us were dreaming of three things: a hot shower, a cold beer, and a good night's sleep, and by this time the order was immaterial.

So right there, in the midst of battle school, we were told we were going to get a hot shower, two beers, and a chicken and chips dinner. True to their word, we got all three. They had a field shower set up and the chance to stand down (relax) for the next four hours was going to be luxury. Soon as we had all gotten the lion's share of the cam paint, bug juice, sweat caked crud off and into what were our cleanest (that actually being better phrased as least filthiest combats), we were rounded up by a couple of raging wood fires and each issued two cans of beer. We were rolling. Then came the DS surprise. Our chicken and chips dinner was served *au natural*, in so much as the chips were still a potato and the chicken was very much alive on the end of the string. One man, two large potatoes, one chicken, next in line. Being raised a small town country boy who had been hunting and fishing since a young age, this was going to be a snap. Skin the chicken like a partridge so you aren't plucking feathers forever. To some of the cities boys, and especially a couple who seemed to be wrestling with the violent aspect of the combat arms, this was going to be a real first. Could you have imagined if the DS overheard you asking someone to kill your chicken? I, for one, not for even the briefest of military moments would have wanted to have been that guy. Your foreseeable future, for as far you could imagine, would become an undying hell. You couldn't kill a damn chicken? What was going to happen if the question arose about something way higher up the food chain? So it was that I had my chicken wrapped in foil with my potatoes and an onion roasting in the coals while a couple of the boys were still not quite sure if they were going to wring its neck or chop its head off. In the end that decision cost them precious time. I figured I could cram in an extra forty-five minutes of sleep during my four hours down time. The DS were onto to that and were summoned for a fireside chat. A veritable barrel head, grass roots lecture about the business of the business that would not change things in the small picture. We knew we were going to get a new one ripped shortly for being one step to slow for something. Often times, they showed us things once and expected instant mastery. Lesson: sometimes we don't have the luxury of the time to explain things over and over, and especially if you screwed something else up in the interim. Do it right the first time because you sure aren't going to have the time to do it again.

If you think I am painting a picture of barbarians, they were not. Even in a simple act of doing your supper from scratch there were lessons to be learned. Everything was becoming some sort of lesson. True we still had our share of legitimately useless bullshit, but for the most part the lessons were everywhere and by everyone. Our most junior DS was a master corporal who had recently qualified as a sniper. He was a natural when it came to talking about cover and concealment. Observation was key. The attention to details that they were driving into us was not about whether the button was done up or not. Were things as they should be, and if not, how quickly does that register in your brain and cause you to take action? All that from a button. These men teaching us may not have ever been inside an institution of higher learning as we would know it, but they were scholars in things that John Q Public Civilian would for the most part never quite understand the importance of or the requirement for. The hallmarks of professionalism and the standards that they held themselves to was exemplary. They were not talking the talk. They were walking the walk. They understood you do not ask troops to do things that you would not do yourself. Leading from the rear sure as heck would not cut it on any repeat performance. You came to understand that for men to respect you enough to instantly react to whatever the orders were, you had to be as committed. To use a phrase from the wildly popular poker craze, you had to be "all in". They call it the chain of command for a reason. But I have developed my own thoughts on the chain analogy. You can pull on a chain and move great objects with it. Do not for a moment try to push a chain. Categorically it is a futile exercise. You can inspire others to greatness. Willingness to be committed as you expect your troops to be has to be seen. In this case it actually is a case of do as I do. Many years later I would get to feel the sting of how deeply that could cut if it was not the case. I digress.

We had suspected that the DS was saving up their very best for last. So there we were, dug in at the top of the hill on the long slope looking down on Petersville. We had patrolled, advanced to contact, and humped till we were blue in the face. Thanks to one particularly thoughtful idiot I got to hump the breach block and receiver of a 50 Cal up Mount Douglas. Not that this oversized pimple on the arse of humanity was anything genuinely huge. Overrun by nasty old growth forest and for those who know what I described as my load, along with an SMG this was not going to be a stroll in the park. My buddy with the tripod, barrel and a couple of belts was assuredly not having a whole lot more fun considering he had his rifle. Mount Douglas does have one thing that I do not think I have encountered very many times on the top of a mountain. A swamp. Who in hell puts a swamp on the top of the mountain? The aforementioned idiot that had us hump everything up the hill pooched it bad. The DS finally intervened and mercifully sent us back to the staging area. They certainly did not care if we sneaky snuck our way back to the staging area, but I still had the all the kit to get down the hill. By the time we arrived at the bottom word awaited that one of the DS wanted to see me. All I know was at that particular moment my motivation to be there any longer was diminishing faster than the limit as x rapidly approached zero.

Figuring that I was in for another arse reaming for some offence against humanity as the DS defined it I was greeted by a totally different scenario than I had seen coming. The final day is coming and we want to give a couple of guys a chance to shine. My first thought was that I was screwing up bad and I was getting cut from the herd. You will be 2 IC to Bings (Tim Billings), and we have picked your section commanders for you. The wave of relief was instantaneous. All the other names were guys that I knew were excelling and there was no way in my mind that I was somehow being set up.

What followed that night was literally a chaotic scene that would best summed up as a strange scene from Apocalypse Now. I do not know for sure how many para flares, arty sims, and thunder flashes the enemy force went through that night, but I do not want to hazard a guess. The premise I guess was to soften us up for the morning assault. From the vantage we had we knew it had to be made under cover of darkness on their part. If not, in the simulated exercise, our heavies, the aforementioned 50 Cal and GPMG would have made mincemeat of anyone trying that approach. We were learning, rapidly. But we had a pile to learn and they were trying to teach as much as they could. At just before first light, all hell absolutely broke loose and it escalated into what could be called an all-out fire fight. Unbridled mayhem erupted that puckered your arse tight and caused adrenaline to course thru your body. At some point the DS ended the whole affair and then it was time to clean it up and shut it down. Everything from filling latrines and trenches to breaking down a hoochie city that we had lived in prior to the luxury trench accommodations.

As Bings was writing up his orders for the march, some twenty-five klicks in full combat order back to the base, I had a vision of my Dad pop into my head. Check their feet dummy. My Dad had taught me to keep one pair of fresh grey army issues socks in a plastic bag in the top of my ruck. No matter how bad it got I always had a clean pair for a real emergency. So as I was getting debriefed on my performance and doing my foot care, I took a brief break to order all the section commanders to do a foot inspection. I knew we were humping everything back and I knew some of us actually had bad feet by this point. The march would kill us, but if we could put some of the extra gear on the best feet, then maybe we could get more of us and more of the gear back to base. I remember the Warrant officer asking me what I was thinking. I thought I was going to get a new one ripped for daring to question weakness. Don't assume, never assume. It does not turn out well. Another good follower chit and I returned from battle school with several and things were on track. In my mind I was a few dust bunnies and a button or so away from being on target with my "Get out of Gagetown plan, the honourable way."

After we finished infantry battle school and had demonstrated enough proficiency in advancing on and making contact with the enemy, things certainly got interesting. We then spent the next couple of weeks running our asses up to the Gun Park. Here we were introduced to the heart and soul of the artillery, the C1 105mm Howitzer. For those of you who have not seen one, think light artillery ideal for work supporting the infantry.

Even though we had experienced some awesome adrenaline rushes so far, nothing would compare to the day we went to the range for our first live firing exercise. We spent an enormous amount of time digging in the trails, the combination tow bar and spade brakes for keeping the gun firmly in place when it was fired. We hung the camo nets and went through several exercises in making sure we had our gun aiming point and drill down. Finally, the first live fire mission came down over the Tannoy (field hard wired phone system)

Fire Mission Battery

HE – (High Explosive, ammunition type)

Charge 7 (the number of bags of powder that would be loaded in the casing before it was rammed home up the breach) of the big gun.

As the rest of the orders came the various numbers on the big gun sprung to life and there was a flurry of assholes and elbows moving in a well-orchestrated rhythm.

So the number 1 on the gun had heard the on and ready, which meant his gun was aimed where it was supposed to be.

One round, fire for effect on your own time, fire.

No sooner had the Tannoy crackled, the anxious voices up and down the line could be heard barking out fire. At that exact moment I do not believe I have ever witnessed anything quite like what happened next. Now I look back and joke about it being

Marvin Martian from the Bugs Bunny show. "The Kaboom, the earth shattering Kaboom, where is the Kaboom!" Well we had it in spades!

The roar of the big guns and the fire and smoke they belched and the recoil driven into the trails was a sight and sound that you will carry to your grave. You thought the Karly G 84 mm anti-tank weapon was something? Here to tell you, that 105 was an instant hard on. When the gun flashed, recoiled and the crash of hellfire and damnation let loose a million thoughts raced through your mind. The vision that stuck with me was what the hell must of have been like in the mud of France and Germany in the First World War. If memory serves me correct, it took about two days for the adrenaline to leave the system.

When the "battlefield smoke" cleared, I stood at a very interesting crossroads. I had survived "Battle School", had excelled in the field, and was now qualified as an infantry section commander and qualified to run a 105 gun crew. But the desire to be an aviator was stronger. Having successfully passed my Aircrew Selection Boards and armed with a great course report out of Gagetown, I was able to reclassify to become an Air Navigator. A myriad of hurdles and challenges still stood between the airplanes and myself, but I was now in the career stream to become "Light Blue", the traditional colour of the Air Force. I had escaped the "Dark Green Machine" but I would carry with me lessons that to this day have not faded.

Rook Races & Motivational Lessons
September, 1982

Every year, just before Ex-Cadet Weekend, the first year class' last major obstacle is exactly that, the Obstacle Course. It's a course that traverses far and wide over the college grounds and is designed to test your limits; physically, emotionally, and mentally. Most of the course has places where successful passage requires the co-operation and teamwork of your classmates. In essence, co-operate and graduate, go it alone and perish. To be an individual would leave you languishing on the course in a unenviable position. The obstacle course has had some common elements probably since the very first days of its inception. The natural obstacles and terrain of Fort Frederick provide too many options to be ignored for having cadets show their mettle. In my time, their Recruit Orientation Camp could be best summed up as "welcome to my nightmare". Even though our class had finished nine weeks of Basic Officer training in Chilliwack, British Columbia, and had a short but intense welcome into the Military life, we were not ready for "Rook Camp". I hate to sound like one of those grumpy old bastards railing about how things were different, but the absolute truth is they were. The final days leading up to the running of the "Rook Race" were affectionately known as "doggy days." Truth is it didn't matter what it was called, it was going to be hell. Most everyone was running the daily max of eight circles at circle parade at ten p.m. One circle was one lap of the quarter mile track around the football field so everyone was running an extra couple miles just for good measure just before bed. Each day the amount of time between wakey and inspection was decreasing rapidly. What they had once given us thirty minutes to do was now down to twenty and decreasing by five minutes a day. In the beginning we could not make thirty minutes but as the first few weeks wore on we got much smarter and much faster. But the fourth years were in fact waiting, patiently, since they knew we would soon be pushed. Now lest one think that I am describing a scenario of some sort of brutal torture that was senseless and pointless, I am not. Doggy days were designed with two things in mind, to forge the bonds of us against them (we had us), and to bring us to the point of physical exhaustion. Doggy Days would culminate in Hell Night, the night before the "Rook Race". Truth was that the Fourth Years had done a pretty good job of breaking us down. We had run, pushed, pulled, drilled, ironed, been yelled at, and doubled all over the college. But by the time we reached the square for the Rook Race, we were all ready for it to be over. All turned out, squadron by squadron, work dress pants, CF Cripplers (the affectionate name given to the most God awful athletic footwear ever designed, and thus their name), squadron t-shirts and a belt. At the end of the course stood the end of rook term. In between was a couple of hours of hell and misery. There would be "nothing fun" about it. We were going to get wet, get dirty, and be tested to the ends of our limits. Failure was certainly not an option.

For good measure, before we even started we were hosed down by Second Years with fire hoses to put us all on a wet damp and cold footing before the race started. So it was in my first year and so it was to be in my fourth year. Fourth Years did not run the rook race. They had certainly been there and done that. The drill was actually that a fourth year cadet ran along with each First Year as kind of a one-on-one motivational coach, and even more importantly to ensure that your rook made it into and out of each obstacle. Sadly, years before our time, a recruit perished during the race. His legacy was a good thing for the race and it would ultimately prove a valuable learning tool for me.

I was in Cadet Wing Headquarters but I had the luxury of having been a Frigateer since day one at RMC. In our time, the cadet wing grew each year as a number of Third Years would join our ranks from Royal Roads Military College, Victoria British Columbia and College Militaire Royal de St Jean sur le Richelieu. To break down cliques that had been forming since rook camp, some of the "purebreds" were shuffled between squadrons to give each squadron somewhat of a new look and feel. A few got to spend their entire college career with one squadron. I was on the fast track to that fate until by someone's weird sense of humour I wound up in Cadet Wing Headquarters. There is an old saw about being promoted above your pay grade, but there I was in Wing HQ. So at the time the list went up in Hudson Squadron to sign up for a "rook" living on the other side of the square in the place affectionately known as the puzzle palace, we were out of the loop on a lot of the day to day running's within the squadron. Traditionally, the Recruit camp staff got first pick. Like it or not, favourites happened for good and bad reasons. You excelled or you were on someone's personal shit list. In other cases the choices seemed to be as scientific as first empty line. In my case it was a chance to select a Lady Cadet and watch first hand with my own two eyes what she was honestly made of. Another learning opportunity presented itself. Since I was willing to learn, the lesson soon became apparent.

Up and down, over and around, the First Year class of 1986 was slogging their way through another grueling test on the grounds of the College. My rook was certainly showing her mettle. She was giving it her all, but somewhere out by the Commandant's house on the sports field, she looked like she was breaking. Not physically, but mentally. Not in any serious way, it is just that I could see that she was running the "Why the hell am I doing this. I could just quit and go to Civvy U or something, anything but here," thoughts through her mind. After the mental beat down of recruit camp and the physical and emotional exhaustion from Doggy Days, her will was at its limit. Somewhere I mustered the shortest motivational speech that I could. "Quit and you will never know." I absolutely wish that I could claim that it was original. But it wasn't, it came as the part of the lessons I learned at the college. In my second year, one of my classmates who had seen me spend the summer between first and second year in the gym at CMR getting bigger and stronger in the weight room while attempting to master the French language had first given me that speech. The weight room project ended as a success and we will leave it at that.

I actually had no previous football experience. My high school didn't even have a football program. All I knew about football was that there would be the chance to channel some of my aggression and to compete. Truth be told, I was a game day player who succeeded with a big motor and very little athletic ability, especially compared to some of my contemporaries. But I did learn some harsh brutal lessons that first football season. I was destined to become an interior lineman. Think of it as a combination battering ram, fire plug, and whirling dervish all rolled into one and you kind of get what it is like to play the interior line, the trench, the hunk of ground from inside one offensive tackle to the tackle or end on the other side. Generally five or six big bodies played the offensive line. Most times we played a four man defensive front. So not only were we out manned on every play, but the offense knew what they were going to do and what the snap count was that they were going to move on, which gives a big advantage to offensive linemen. This clearly begs the question of who would want to show up every play with deck stacked against them like that? The answer is probably best answered by guys who were just a little bit over the top. The other thing you learned real quickly in the trenches is that there is nowhere to hide. If you screwed up, you wore it and everyone knew it.

So it was the afternoon practice and we were running drills full speed and full contact during the later stages of two a day practices. For those of you who did not have the luxury, two a days are an intense period of training where the coaches try to take an undisciplined mob and turn them into some semblance of a football team. Problem is that we also got whipped into football shape. Trust me, there is very little that success on the CF fitness test had to do with football shape. The other issue? Genuinely one does not know how strong you are, since it is how strong you are tired.

I was getting tired. We all were. But some of us were sucking more wind than others. Coach was running plays back-to-back-to-back to simulate game conditions. So it was that several plays in I missed a read at the start of a play and moved into a hole in the controlled chaos where a guard had been a fraction of a second ago. Immediately you had best check right behind him for if he has pulled you can bet that there is another pulling guard who traps you and it springs the first pulling guard to create a mismatch of numbers, size and strength as linemen tend to be bigger and stronger than outside linebackers who tend to be much quicker than linemen. But in this case the offense was doing this on a running play with the intention of smashing the ball down your throat and exploiting that mismatch to the fullest. In terms that military men could absolutely understand, the problem was being solved by BFI, Brute Force and Ignorance, it's the sole solution. In this particular play, I was the ignorance. The brute force was a very talented offensive "There are cases where BFI is actually the best solution" guard who would become an OCFL All Star. He drilled me so far into the next week I had to back up three days to get to tomorrow. He de-cleated me. I was sitting there, arse on the turf wondering what had just happened. I was seeing stars and certainly questioning my sanity. Coach came over and looked me square in the eye because he knew I was thinking the same thoughts that my rook was thinking. He took one look at me and said "we are going to run it again, and keep running it till you get it. Quit and you will never know." At the exact moment a fire was ignited. I would show him. Not only would I get it, I would make the team this year, start next year, and make the OCFL All-star team in my fourth year. Lofty aspirations for a guy who was getting by on heart and very little natural football ability. Quit was something that did not enter into the equation. The fire of the passions that were ignited on the football field would burn within in me for a long time. Though in time the fires almost were extinguished by an invisible enemy to whom I had yet to be introduced, and from whom Thai would rescue me over and over.

Football Lessons
November, 1982

The football field at RMC came to define a huge part of how I saw myself. I played with passion and fire. What the coaches could not get out of me in practice came roaring out like a lion on game day. What I learned about commitment, teamwork, desire, and never quitting was shaped in huge part on the football field. The more I learned, the more I understood the need for contact sports at the military college, not that I had ever shied away from those. I loved to play hockey when the off season came. The weight room became my friend. I had left BOTC and arrived at RMC at about 160 pounds. By fourth year I was playing at 210. A few things had changed.

Just as I was starting to genuinely understand the crucial role that sports play in the development of leaders, the atom bomb was to hit the college in a way that made the decisions to include women in the cadet wing pale in comparison in my world. By my fourth year, I loudly championed LCWB not as point that would exclude women from the college --for me, the issue had come and gone— but for other reasons. Just like there was the last dinosaur at some point in history, LCWB would soon join that fate. Do not get me wrong. We had huge potential. The world was our oyster and there were those among us who were headed for greatness. The statement was made many times in jest that LCWB also defined us as the last class with boxing. In our first year, Gentlemen Cadets, like those who had gone before, stood in the square circle and had someone try and knock their block off. Once again, the lesson was the same. For reasons known exclusively to the "grownups", the advent of women at the college also sounded the death knell for boxing. I am sure that there were a myriad of reasons for the cancellation of the program, but from our position it was one of the changes that came with the arrival of the women. Not all cadets were natural boxers. Far from it. But anyone who has ever competed in a martial art, wrestling, boxing or any other one on one contact sport knows that two minutes is a long time. For some the time is the ring was short, losing in their first match. Others went on to win their weight classes and fight against the best the wing had to offer just before Christmas time of our first year. The lessons learned included one that was not quite so obvious. People do not die of split lips, bloody noses or black eyes. God knows we had enough of those, but it was one more step in the process that was to help shape our class, like those that had gone before us. Being able to fight on after being rattled was a necessary skill. More than one "tough guy" who talked a good game ended up having a long hard stare into their internal abyss after quitting when getting hit in the ring.

Unfortunately, some realities were starting to broach the ramparts of the hallowed institution. Money was becoming scarce and a huge chunk of the varsity athletics budget was being consumed by the Football team. I understand economics and I understand that very unpopular decisions often have to be executed. So it was that the groundwork had been laid.

Many years after the fact, I came across an interview where Major General Frank Norman recounted a little of what it was like to have to be the bearer of the bad news. The war was over and we as cadets did not even realize it. At least I certainly did not. We had been taught that you do not give up and that is not over till it is over. In our fourth year we played a game against one of our opponents who had a running back that would go onto to excel for the one season that his academics would allow. He was great. He was fast, strong and had a desire to win that rivalled that of any cadet. The game got out of hand and we were on the wrong end of what was to become a lopsided blowout. Some members of the opposing team had not learned the *grace in victory, humble in defeat* lesson. So it was that with just a few minutes left on the clock, the outcome assured with victory in their favour, some of their players started to chant, "It just doesn't matter!"

What happened next is something that I actually know that I did and that I have carried with me for a long time. For any that know what a lineman's three point stance is, you know that it is designed to allow for maximum thrust combined with maximum agility. There is another stance, the four point stance, where you dig in with both feet, grab two hands full of dirt and when the play starts you drive forward with all of your might. There's no agility and reacting, its brute force applied for maximum effect. It is a play that is usually reserved for short yardage defense or goal line stands. We were around mid-field and the opposing center broke the huddle and came forward to the ball. We were playing a three man front and I was lined up over him head-to-head. He reached down to bring the ball on point to get ready for the snap. I didn't care what defensive play was called. To me, at that exact moment, I could have cared less. I had more important concerns. Somebody was about to get a lesson and I saw myself as the avenging angel of wrath that was going to deliver it. He rolled the ball up and I dropped into a four point stance and coiled up for what was about to ensue. I had steam coming out of places you ought not to have steam coming out of and I was seeing red. Disrespect for a fellow competitor was something that was not on.

The moment that he flinched and started the ball in motion, I drove out of my four point stance with all the fury I could muster and drove my opponent backwards through his backfield and viciously slammed him to the turf. For good measure I gave him a wicked upper cut to the chops on the way. "Do not ever tell me it does not matter!" I screamed. What happened on the rest of the play I have no idea. I do know that several people got a lesson on why you respect your opponents, even if you clearly have the upper hand.

Another lesson came in that fourth year on the football field. When the offense punts the ball, generally one of the interior linemen will be in charge of setting where a wedge punt return will be set. Here is the deal, the two defensive lineman are the point of the wedge and the object is to blow open a gap that a fleet footed back can hopefully spring through. If you have had any experience with this concept, the point of the wedge is going to take a beating. Additionally, if not done right, the back is going to run headlong into the opponents who are waiting to tee off on him. So it was at Erindale in the fall of 1982. I am about to describe that play as it unfolded. A rook was supposed to set the wedge with me and we should have been able to reach out and almost touch each other. I set the wedge and the whole thing was going exactly as planned except for one small detail, my wing man had gone off the reservation and figured that if he took out some random guy he would be helping. That was not to be the case and our back got chewed up and spit out after I lost a three on one contest that was supposed to be more even, but for my wingman. I lost, no contest. The punt returner got drilled. My responsibility. I came off the field and I was pissed. Not the garden variety pissed off. I am talking about one step short of being an intercontinental ballistic missile. I headed over and grabbed the center guard of the rook's face mask and took firm hold. For those of you who do not understand why face masking is such a serious penalty, you just need to see the forces of physics at work. I proceeded to give him a reading from the "Good Book" and each verse was punctuated with a slap to the side of his helmet for emphasis. I remember somebody coming over and explaining that this guy's father was there watching me. My response went along the lines of "if coach calls a wedge and he isn't there next time, it will be much worse." Knowing the intensity with which I played there was sure to be some vitriolic invective that also accompanied my diatribe. Some knew beyond a shadow of a doubt that I was deadly serious. Now, before anyone gets their britches in a knot, this whole incident had absolutely nothing to do with a Fourth Year hammering on a Rook. I would have hammered on God himself if he was the guy pooching the dog. It wasn't about him personally. The issue was his failure, his conscious decision to do something that ultimately hurt our team and certainly did not help our back who had gotten flattened. I am sure his teeth rattled for days.

But God has a sense of humour. Later in the half we held on defense and were about to turn the ball over to our offense and another wedge return was called. I stared down the rook and growled two words… "Be there." What unfolded next was a thing of beauty. I picked the spot and we set the wedge. Sure enough my winger was there and he was fired up. I called the go, and we shot forward and split the opponents wide open. What happened next was poetry in motion. One of the fastest cadets in the wing was Tim Haig. He was blazingly fast. He could pick them up and put them down faster than anyone I personally knew. Sure enough, a few short seconds later the referee was signaling touch down. The nod between my winger and I said it all. Lesson learned on both parts.

A few moments later before I was back on the sidelines, and while there, my winger's father walked over. I had not up until that exact second thought what I would say if this moment arrived. I was spared. The gentlemen took the initiative and said just one thing. "He needed to hear that!" My response was simple. "Thank you sir". There were a lot of lessons learned on the spot. Commitment to the objective of the team has to surpass any thoughts of individualism.

Not every lesson I learned came on the football field. Truly though, one of the largest lessons was a byproduct of the football field. There was a group of players consisting of three fourth year players and a third year who was to be the Captain of the team next year. We were summoned to the Commandant's office. We knew what was coming, but we were not prepared to accept it. There had to be something we could do. After being put at ease, General Norman very calmly laid out why our team was to be the last. There would be no more. The RMC Football Redman had played their last game. A tough loss on the fields at Sheridan College in the playoffs that year was to be the last. I knew the moment I walked off the field that I would probably never again don a bucket (helmet) and do what had become the bastion of sanity in my life. I did not realize that for those who came behind me, they would never have that opportunity. Somebody had ripped my very soul out. I know that the feeling in the room was not mine alone. I remember thinking to myself that maybe we could have varsity basket weaving or some other such meaningful exercise. How could the Royal Military College of Canada cancel Football? Seriously? Did they not realize that the crucible that was shaping us was for some propping up by the very values we were learning on the field? How was it possible that just three short years removed from winning the College bowl and becoming Champions that the program would be gone? I was also smart enough to know one thing, once they dismantled the program, it would take a Herculean effort to ever put the team back in place. If asked to sum up what I felt, it was one word. Betrayal.

If you remember, I said that I had my sights set on making the OCFL All Star team. Success as that year six Redmen- got picked for the team, which was picked by your peers, the other players in the league. The recognition of making it was cause for great celebration but we were also saddened because two players that we thought were the class of the league came up short in the balloting. It was bitter sweet to be an all-star when others I felt deserved it too were left out. I was bent and twisted, going out on such a high personal note even as the team was being terminated. Three years in the weight room, pushing, heaving and grunting, and the job was done. Made the team, made it as starter, made the All-star team. What should have been an immense shot of testosterone and pride felt more like a wet fart in a paper bag. It honestly did not seem to matter a "pinch of coon shit" what I had done personally. The team was about to vanish, a victim of monetary constraints and other issues that admittedly went beyond what we as players were thinking. I learned an expression that would remain with me for the rest of my life, "please do not obscure the argument with the facts." The fact remains that it is categorically impossible to reason with an emotion, and trust me, there was enough emotion attached to this issue for us to blanket the college in a wave of outrage.

In the meeting with General Norman, with the door closed, he gave us the opportunity to speak freely. For some strange reason, I knew at that moment that the man delivering the message was actually just the messenger. Shooting the messenger would have been a decidedly bad idea. And so it was that a relationship was formed with a man so many pay grades above me that it seemed surreal. The fact that a flag rank officer cared enough to ask what I thought and felt seemed to be a legitimately hard pill to swallow when all I wanted to do was vent and rage. The issue wasn't that he had been made, the issue was watching a large part of your self-identity fall victim to a budgetary onslaught. Mostly in large part, the sum of our military experience had been on the ass end of the beloved shit accelerator. Shit comes screaming downhill at an ever increasing rate of knots until it lands squarely at the lowest levels of the org chart. For most of our military experience that meant us. Though we had survived multiple years in a system that had horrific attrition rates, we were honestly qualified to accomplish very little. We had been earning our degrees, getting fit, and having drilled into us at every opportunity the lessons of Truth, Duty, and Valour.

The Molding Continues

My first term of fourth year saw me leave my beloved Stone Boat for the lofty heights of Wing Headquarters. At the end of third year, when they announced the fourth year barmen slate, I was recovering from a double whammy. The previous week I had my wisdom teeth removed and four days after that I contracted Salmonella. Trust me, at one point there were well over 250 Cadets who were affected simultaneously. The MIR was getting cases of Kayopectate shipped in from CFB Kingston by the case and eventually just left them outside the door of Sickbay. There was no way on God's green earth that they were keeping up with the demand.

So on the appointed day I was glued to the rack. My door flung open and one of my buddies stuck his head in.

"And?"

"Wing HQ… Public Relations Officer (CWPRO)."

"Congrats, I am happy for you!"

"Not me, you."

And with that the door slammed shut and laughter headed down the hall. Now I am going to have to head over to the other side of the square and check the sheets for myself. This assuredly had to be somebody's idea of a sick joke. This time was pre ubiquitous photocopiers…… hell the wing newsletter that the CWPRO put out still used a Gestetner and the stinky chemicals. The college had a mainframe computer that cadets learned to program FORTRAN with punch cards. Yes times were very different. Sure enough my buddy had not been jerking me around. IV MLR Cousineau – CWPRO/RELA. OK. It might be true because it was on the paper. But like I had said before, "way above my pay grade."

So it came to pass that I spent a lot of time in the General's EA's (Executive Assistant) office. I was learning about soft military skills. Diplomacy, subtlety, form, function and God forbid, politics. Every bit of hellfire I could muster for the football field was offset by some of the more genteel aspects of becoming a gentlemen cadet. So, from dinners to cocktail parties I got to watch firsthand the art of diplomacy when required. I could see its point, it just lacked the appeal of "kicking butt and taking names." I was good at the latter and would later be described as being as subtle as a brick through a window.

On one particular occasion, the guy who turned into my best buddy that term and I had a very late night at Bill and Alfie's, the cadet pub. I am sure we had solved all the world's problems. The next morning there were two very distinct problems facing us. We could not remember the answers but even more pressing was that there was a "full riggers" morning dress rehearsal parade for the lining of the arch ceremony. Scarlet's, Swords, Boots and Gaiters and seriously hung over. So in a moment of brilliance a plan was launched to somehow "deke" the parade and not get punished. Here was the deal. If we skipped the parade we would be AWOL (Absent without Leave) and would be charged. Even though we were in Wing HQ, Squawks and Cous had nailed down more than their fair share of extra duties for various crimes against humanity. "Yes Sir, I do believe I did in fact eat ice cream with my hands in the dining hall. Yes sir, I do realize that gentlemen do usually use utensils and a bowl. Yes sir, but it was just football players in the dining hall. Yes Sir, two extras as Base Duty Officer will be just fine." So in a pure flash of brilliance we figured out how we would be at the parade and not get charged. We just had no intention of stomping out to The Arch with a God awful hellish hangover.

The sight and sound of the full wing marching by with colours flying, pipers piping, and the scarlets as far as the eye could see was a damn impressive sight. When the CWC called eyes right at the dias that had been set up outside the Commandants house , there sat the General, his absolutely elegant wife Anne, Squawk and yours truly enjoying morning coffee. With a toast of the coffee cup, we watched the entire wing parade by. The brilliance of our plan was brutally simple, we would invite ourselves for morning coffee at the general's house. Presumptuous? Damn straight. So it came to pass that we were not technically AWOL, and since the General and his wife did not seem to mind, we managed to skate. Perhaps the best part though was the look on the face of the CWC and the CWTO. For some things there are Master Card. Others, just priceless. This was genuinely one of those things.

So it was that it came to pass that the last all male class, LCWB, marched off the square on that sunny Saturday in May as newly minted Second Lieutenants in her Majesty's Services. But we were not the sole grads that day. The graduates of Otter squadron marched off the square and most were now first lieutenants and captains. Otter squadron was the non-cadet squadron that formed the structure of the UTPM (University Training Plan Men) and UTPW (University Training Plan Women) program. This program was there for other ranks to complete their degrees, learn their lessons, and accept their place amongst the officer cadre having been CFR'd, commissioned from the ranks. For all of our bravado and machismo, the reality is that female officers marched off the square alongside us. There were three. Roxanne Rees, Myrna Saunders, and Mary Turkington.

Two of the three had studied English and Philosophy alongside myself and the other members of the Stone Frigate English Fellowship. I know that any attempts to uncover the storied traditions of such an august sounding organization would be futile. During third year final degree selections would be made.

In our time, cadets spent a common first academic year. After that, in second year, there were actually three choices: to continue in the Engineering based studies, to transfer to applied science (Apple Sigh, Rack and Kye!) or to enter the Artsmen stream. By third year the Gears were selecting their discipline, the Applied Slack guys plugged along, and the artsmen chose which of the disciplines from History to Military and Strategic Studies (MIlstuds) they would follow. A very few cadets chose Honours English and so it came to pass that of the five 3rd year cadets who chose to pursue a degree in English and philosophy , three came from the Frigate that year.

What degree to choose to pursue was up to the individual cadet as long as it was compatible with the Military Occupation that they were in. Back to that whole artsmen not being an engineering discipline situation. But my MOC at the time was Artillery. (Lies my recruiter told me. I know I am the first in history of the military and I know that you are shocked and appalled.) By the end of my first year I can honestly say that I was not enjoying being a gear (engineer). So I gravitated to Apple Science. That did not help much. In the first term of second year we studied thermodynamics and the Carnot heat cycle engine. Brilliant in theory. On the last day of the term our prof made it abundantly clear that it would never work. Spectacular, I had just bagged it for the term learning about something that didn't work and I would not need.

Soul Dance

When your soul can't dance….

I have to confess that you will hear so many song references throughout my story you will begin to wonder if I ever did anything else but listen to music. In fact, at RMC, I got my stereo as soon as we were allowed. I came back to second year with my sound system and my album collection. Quite a collection it was. Built slowly and lovingly and over the course of a few years paid from the proceeds of Bingo.

As always there is more to the story. In the small town in which I spent my high school years, there was an expectation that by about age fifteen the young men would join the Wednesday night cadre helping with the Parish Bingo. I, too, assumed my place, but having been blessed with a deep clear voice, I became a natural to become the Bingo caller, which came with one serious perk. The Caller was the sole paid position and I received $5.00 per week. In the mid-seventies, single albums were $4.99 plus tax and doubles ran under ten. So Thursday lunches were spent in a record store on downtown Front Street in Belleville, Ontario. Trust me, I had more than one lecture by various Nuns about my tardiness and apparent disinterest for my studies. Oh how I wish I could have communicated that it wasn't that I was disinterested in academia, I was just more interested in being a teenager and feeding a serious music addiction. So my album collection grew and as luckily, one of my buddies in the Frigate who was in my platoon in Chilliwack was also a serious music fan. When we got united with Kenn Rodzinyak during our "Rook term" we had a plethora of music trivia in our heads and we were good at playing name that tune. So good in fact that the "Portsmouth Inn" kindly asked Rodz and me to bow out of the Friday night music trivia games, but not before we had scored another handful of albums.

In some ways my room became a refuge of "Coffee and Music". As an underclassman, you did not want to be seen as "idling about", for most assuredly someone would figure you had spare time and they would have or make a way to fill it. It's just the way it was.

High school dances, parish hall dances, and later the dances and formal balls at RMC, gave me the opportunity to dance. Music is good for your heart and soul. You can change mood with music and I had learned to do that by the fourth year of university really quite well.

When playing defensive line in football you can rest assured of two things: You are going to get hit every play, and you will be out numbered, usually six on three or four. So to get prepared for what was to come on game day, I would use music to push me into a very aggressive violent state. Some of my favorites were Number of the Beast by Iron Maiden, Deep Purple's Smoke on the Water, Ozzy Osbourne's Crazy Train, and Rush's By-Tor and the Snow Dog. Just like tribes have used drums to psych for battle for centuries, I too would work myself into the kind of internal frenzy that was required for the trenches. There are some who will have views that differ from mine and I can expect some flak and I can deal with that, but I hold steadfast in my resolve that all officers, regardless of classification or entry program, should be required to play contact sports. It is one thing to say you can hold up under pressure, but add a punch in the mouth and a shot to the head and then try. Football, Rugby and Hockey are three sports that have it in spades. There are so many lessons to be learned out there. Perhaps the one that strikes closest to home is trying to address the Rugby Ref as anything other than Sir or Madam, without words like "Please and thank you". You will find out how rapidly you can wind up in the "Sin bin" and hurt your team. In football you play the whistle, toggling between on and off again aggression. Failure to do so can result in penalties and ejection from the game. I will not talk about fighting in hockey. Not that I necessarily condone violence, but fists are better than sticks. I refuse to believe that the cultures of violence that surround rugby and football cannot be brought into hockey. Last year's World Cup of Rugby game between New Zealand and France was some of the hardest hits I have ever seen. The referee would have no foolishness. But I digress...

A Military Family

"I used to love my mother until I found out she was a civilian." It is an old saw that has been bandied about various military recruit schools for decades. The military is different and your indoctrination into military life and the way of doing things starts from the moment you show up. Drill, discipline, overcoming fears and limitations, and developing a self-confident "can do" attitude were things that were drilled into you from the moment you stepped off the bus at whichever recruit school you happened to attend. Does not matter what element, does not matter officer or enlisted, as the Drill Staff will start their immediate quest to break you down so that they can mold you in the image of what they need.

But I can't tell that joke. My mom served. My father served. My kid bro served. I served. Got us all."

My mother served as a Naval Reservist with HMCS Malahat in Victoria in the mid 1950's and my father joined as a Royal Canadian Dragoon, (Armored Corps) who remustered to RCEME (Royal Canadian Electrical and Mechanical Engineers). My father served tours in Germany in the early fifties and then a full year with UNEF Egypt in 58/59. From there he spent four years in Whitehorse doing Vehicle Recovery and Heavy Equipment Maintenance as the Alaska Highway was being finished up. My father was the quintessential "Mr. Fix it" and I have serious doubts if there was anything he could not fix. If he couldn't fix it, it was more than likely not worth fixing.

While I was in Winnipeg doing my Wings training for Nav School, my kid bro had informed me of his decision to enlist and join the Navy. In one of the funniest "lies my recruiter told me stories", my brother had thought he had joined the navy to be a Firefighter. Genuinely, once he was on the parade square at CFB Cornwallis having sworn in and showed up did he find out he was going to be a "Fire *control* Man". He would be responsible for guns and missiles and eventually his trade would evolve into a trade named "NESOP" (Naval Electronic Sensors Operator). Mildly ironic in two ways: The first was everyone shipborne in the navy learns to fight fires as part of Ships Damage control, and secondly, after I had completed my Electronic Warfare Courses we had similar training, different platforms. To this day my brother still tells a funny story about that fateful night he found out what his true MOC (Military Occupation Code) was.

For those of you who are familiar with the Irish Rovers tune "The Orange and the Green" we managed to have our own very family version at every subsequent family gathering. "Me mother she was Dark Blue and me father he was Green..." Throw in my kid brother's Dark Blue affiliation and my tri-service, Former Dark Green, gone Light Blue going to sea with the Dark Blue and it was always sure to generate some good natured "my service is better than your service" rivalries and humour. But not always. Sometimes the conversations took on very serious tones about the business of soldiering, or in many cases keeping the peace.

Dad's experiences in both Post Second World War Germany and then later in Egypt, made him a staunch advocate for peace. He was committed to it and right up until his death was very active in the UN Peacekeepers Association. I used to listen intently as he shared his impressions of the Nazi Death Camps that he toured just a few short years after end of the Second World War. I think everyone who deploys with the military has experiences or moments that go onto to shape their being, their thought processes and in some cases may cause them to question humanity itself. Those death camps were certainly that for my father. If he was not completely convinced of our need for peace then, his yearlong tour in Egypt certainly cemented those views. Peace at all costs. But there comes time that Peace can only be obtained or maintained by force and the willingness to use it. A look back through history can assure one of that. Events like the Holocaust and fascist Nazi rule were clear in the history books. Sadly though, we talked of other more recent conflicts. Ethnic cleansing in the Balkans, mass genocide in Rwanda and the War on Terror were but a few examples.

Commissioning Scroll
May, 1983

The words on the page cast a huge shadow of obligation. I had done it. I had survived the crucible that was known as the Royal Military College of Canada. I had graduated with my degree in Honours English and was now staring at my Commissioning Scroll. From enrollment on the first of June in 1979, to leaving for Basic Officer Training later that month it had been one hell of a journey. The daunting issue was that the journey was just beginning. All of us, all my classmates of the class of 1983, still had to complete our various phase training to qualify in our branch and Military Occupations. For me, that meant, more French language training and then off to CFB Winnipeg to attend CFANS (Canadian Forces Aerospace & Navigation School) where I would hopefully earn my Air Navigators Wings. I was unsure what sub specialty I wanted to be upon completion but I would have plenty of time to make those choices in the coming months. For now, I was trying to absorb the weight of the words on a singular piece of paper that carried a huge obligation and commitment.

Elizabeth the Second, by the Grace of God of the United

Kingdom, Canada, and Her other Realms and Territories Queen,

Head of the Commonwealth, Defender of the Faith

To

Medric Leo Robert Cousineau

HEREBY appointed an Officer

In Her Majesty's Canadian Armed Forces

With Seniority the 1st day of May 1983

We, reposing especial Trust and Confidence in your Loyalty, Courage and Integrity,

do by these Presents Constitute and Appoint you to be an Officer in our

Canadian Armed Forces. You are therefore carefully and diligently to discharge your Duty as such in the rank of Second Lieutenant Or in such

other Rank as We may from time to time hereafter be pleased to promote or

appoint you to, and you are in such manner and on such occasions may be

prescribed by Us to exercise and well discipline both the Inferior Officers and Men

serving under you and use your best endeavor to keep them in

good Order and Discipline. And We do hereby Command Them to

Obey you as their Superior Officer, and you to observe and follow

Such Orders and Directions as from time to time you shall receive

From Us, or any your Superior Officer according to Law, in pursuance of the Trust hereby reposed in you.

In WITNESS whereof Our Governor General of Canada hath

Hereunto set his hand and Seal at Government House in the

City of Ottawa this 2nd day of May

In the Year of Our Lord One Thousand Nine Hundred and

Eighty-Three and in the Thirty Second

Year of Our Reign

BY COMMAND OF

HIS EXCELLENCY THE GOVERNOR GENERAL

MINISTER OF NATIONAL DEFENCE

I was struggling with the weight of the words on the page before me. I had graduated. I was not the smartest, the fastest, biggest or handsomest member of my class. But I had mastered the lessons that four years at RMC had set out to teach me. I had been instilled with the virtues of the Colleges motto: Truth, Duty and Valour. I was committed to fulfilling my obligations as a Commissioned Officer and the requirements for Loyalty, Courage and Integrity. I knew of my Obligations to Duty.

I also knew that if I set a goal, I would work damned hard to accomplish it. I had learned attention to detail, team work and co-operation.

In time I would have my name inscribed on another piece of paper that bore the Governor Generals signature. I did not know this at this point, nor would I have any idea of the ramifications for my life for the decisions I would make in honouring my commitment to the Queen.

Part Two:

The Rescue

Duty

"NOT FOR FAME OR REWARD

NOT FOR PLACE OR FOR RANK

NOT LURED BY AMBITION

OR GOADED BY NECESSITY

BUT IN SIMPLE

OBEDIENCE TO DUTY

AS THEY UNDERSTOOD IT

THESE MEN SUFFERED ALL

SACRIFICED ALL

DARED ALL — AND DIED"

RANDOLPH HARRISON MCKIM

*This is the inscription on the North side of the Confederate Memorial, the Arlington National Cemetery, Arlington Virginia.

Prelude to the Rescue

Today I feel a profound sense of guilt. I know I have wrestled with it at so many levels. Today I feel the guilt when I think of my wife, my sweetie, my bride and one of the ladies who has been short changed the most on the face of the planet as far as military spouses go. Do not for a moment think I am going to go anywhere near the magnitude of the losses of those whose loved ones who have made the ultimate sacrifice. Theirs' is a pain I hope I never know. I genuinely have nothing but the deepest of admiration. Nope, my dearest falls into a different category all together.

Let me explain. You have heard about my ascent up the hill. Truly, she is either in love or crazy. I know crazy, and she is not that. Must be love.

Why in the hell anyone would hang around after my injuries is another conversation? A relationship is one thing if the building is on an undoubtedly strong foundation but a completely different story if the foundation is anything but. I am not going to try and speak to my wife's thought processes, her emotions and her decisions. That is her prerogative. Those are her rights.

But just for a moment I want to take you on a little adventure. I am going to tell you a story of love. A young aviator, military officer, married to someone in the nursing profession. I sometimes think that nurses and military members wind up together for one simple reason. Both can respect the demands of "crappy" scheduling and having to work on holidays, and trying to wedge in family obligations amidst work demands. Nurses wind up working some variation of one in two. Every second day they work, it may be in clusters of four on and four off, or some such variant. In so many ways, they are us.

As a young seagoing aviator, new to the squadron, something as simple as getting married could be a logistical nightmare. For starters it is actually a good idea if the bride and groom are in the same place at the same time.

Life as a young aviator on an operational squadron was busy. We were either getting ready to go to sea, at sea, or coming home from sea. How crazy was the schedule? In the first 298 days that we were married, I was gone a total of 117 days. I was gone for stretches of 51, 18, and 48 days. Longest stretch home: 77 days. The others: 43, 21 and 37 days home. So in the mayhem before this we had planned a wedding and were having a house built. One partner works half that time and you get about 80 days that she is off when I am home. The deck was stacked against us.

Keep in mind in the months previous to this she had lived through the "he is gone and we can't tell you or we would have to kill you" trip. There was a night when I left for an overnight duty watch on the ship and was deployed as part of the ready duty ship on a classified mission. Jocelyn got a call stating I was safe yet there was nothing else they could tell her. She was glad to see me twenty one days later. I thought life on the squadron fun. We worked hard, partied even harder. Honestly, sometimes it is hard to imagine having the kind of life when we were back home at the squadron. During the week we honed our craft as aviators. When the weekends came it absolutely was a grand time.

Given the aviation rules about "bottle to throttle", you could not drink unless you were grounded or for some other reason unavailable for the flying program. Once you had time expired, and your crew day had run out, well it was game on. By Friday afternoons, things often went sliders and it found us in some form, closed up in the mess having a few beers. Then TGIF. The first couple hours the pace was hot and heavy. By about seven the wives and girlfriends would show up. The Snake Pit, the back bar, was off limits, and a place where we could pretty much discuss whatever. In fact there were several cases where wives and sweethearts chummed with their "messmates" while we solved the world's problems or at least solved the next Anti-submarine problem, or just drank more beer.

The late night cab rides, pizza runs, and "red alerts" --spontaneous parties that went from house to house in the patch (The PMQ`s- Private Married Quarters) -- these were a real blast. We came, we saw, we partied. Our wives and girlfriends in some ways for their own defense became like us. They developed bonds, camaraderie, a reliance on each other. Saturday mornings were that brief period before we started all over again, this time in public. We would slowly congregate at a watering hole called the Split Crow.

Maritime and Irish music, pub grub (wings and skins) and darts. Starting in the morning, or thereabouts, by three in the afternoon the party was in full swing and it was time to make our move to Peddlers. Wall-to-wall craziness, students, military, and us. We were a crowd all by ourselves. At some point the party would turn into dinner plans and then an evening of continued merriment. Live hard. Party hardier. Sundays we re-grouped, with exactly five days till we could do it again. And we did. In many ways Halifax was an extension of Kingston Ontario. Colleges, Universities, military, wine, women, and song. The Carpe Diem lifestyle was our way of dealing with the harsh realities of naval aviation. I was barely five months removed from basic wings training when two C130 Hercules had a mid-air crash that claimed the lives of pilots whose names were in my log book. Before much longer, T33 pilots from VU32 Squadron. Aviation was thrilling, challenging and relentlessly unforgiving. We would often dismiss the Grim Reaper with a shrug, and dismiss it as CBD: Crash, Burn and Die. The reaper would always claim someone else. Our bravado part of our self-defense mechanism.

If someone asked though, it was indeed a glorious time. Young, vibrant, so full of life and so much to live for. I wish I could say that it would remain so forever.

On the 298th day of our marriage, I set sail for the fisheries patrol that would change the course of my life forever...

The First Launch
October 6th 1986

I hung out the back door of the Sea King staring into the black abyss below. The knot in my stomach grew and tightened with each unsuccessful attempt to get the helo into position over the Sea Hawk. The fisheries officers had been right. The only free space would be on the stern. What we, the helo crew, had been unaware of, was the myriad of guy wires and antennae overhead along with all the fishing gear on deck that would leave us with a scant six foot by six foot area to access. How in the fuck were we going to do this? The question raced through my mind and caused the knot in my stomach to turn into a vice like grip of anguish.

Usually in a situation like this, we would have a stable deck and a larger unobscured area from which to effect the transfer. This was as far from usual as you could get. The sixty eight foot vessel was being tossed about like a hanky in a hurricane by eighteen foot waves that combined with swells to hit thirty feet in places. The fifty five foot whip antennae on the vessel were fifteen feet above our normal hover height. They sliced through the air, whooshing dangerously close to the belly of the aircraft, threatening to impale and disembowel us with an assured catastrophic outcome. CBD: Crash, Burn and Die.

Ken was struggling to get the helo in a stable position using the hover trim. The hover trim system locked the aircraft vertically, and all the horizontal movements could be controlled by a joystick located near the cargo door of the aircraft. A steady hand with lots of practice was required to maintain a steady hover with the inertia created by ten tons of helicopter beating the air into submission. The problem was that usually we had a fixed spot to work over. Tonight that was not the case. The vessel pitched, heaved and shuddered as it was pounded mercilessly by the North Atlantic.

"Goddammnit all!" The usual calm cool crew demeanor was starting to fray at the edges. Ken's frustration was starting to show. He had tried yet again to get us close enough to maintain position when the shipped was tossed twenty feet out of position.

"I have control." Han's voice was clear over the intercom. Hans Kleeman was the crew commander, flying right seat and clearly he had seen enough.

"You have control," Ken replied as the red light indicating engagement of the system was extinguished.

Hans moved us out of harm's way and we backed off to reconsider the options and to collect ourselves.

"This clearly is not working." Hans's voice, calm, cool and confident. Trying to instill the air of professionalism that governed our crew co-ordination. No Shit Sherlock! An absolutely penetrating glimpse into the obvious. Was thinking it, but certainly was not voicing it. Such sentiments would add little to the tense air that filled the chopper. Every attempt to get close to the stricken vessel ended in the same result. The ocean tossed the vessel hither and yon with complete disregard for what we were attempting.

"OK, Ken. We are going to try again. This time we will use Voice Con." Voice Commands. Ken would use a series of commands, Ahead, Back, Left and Right with modifiers like easy and steady to try and position the helo where he wanted it with Hans controlling the aircraft trying to get in his mind's eye the picture that Ken was describing. This was a procedure we had practiced many times, and we would give it a try. Due to the lack of visual references, we did not usually ever attempt this at night since disorientation and vertigo could rear their ugly heads with catastrophic consequences. CBD.

"Pilot. Vessel is at our two o'clock at fifty. Ahead, forty, thirty, twenty, ten, easy ahead five, four, three, two, one. Steady Ahead." We did not try to move the Helo in more than one axis simultaneously. We were now dead abeam the heaving vessel.

"Pilot contact at our three o'clock sixty. Right sixty, fifty, forty." The big grey behemoth moved in the direction Ken was describing. "Pilot easy right, fifteen. Pilot steady. Left fifteen. Contact now at our nine o'clock." The vessel was now on the port side of the helo, partially obscured by the helo.

"Pilot easy left ten, five four. Steady. Pilot contact now three o'clock at thirty." I could imagine Hans trying to maintain the mental picture as being described by Ken over the intercom.

We tried, and tried again, yet all to no avail. Anytime we approached a position that was anywhere near close for insertion, the combination of the wind, and the sea state heaved the vessel and the Helo into some unworkable configuration. Our sole accomplishment? We succeeded in doing was tightening the knot in my stomach that was now squeezing bile into the back of my throat. If we couldn't execute the easy part of this evolution, I had no idea how I was going to get on the vessel and effect the Stokes litter transfer.

"Rescue One Nine, this is Charlie Two Delta". The radio sprang to life. The non-flying pilot was now in charge of the radios.

"Two Delta. Go"

"Rescue One Niner, be advised a bulk grain carrier, Angel Two, en route, and ETA your location about one hour. She has large motor life boat and will launch to effect transfer from Sea Hawk to the Angel. You can then do hoist transfer from the Angel."

"Roger that". The tsunami of relief hit me like a wall while the crew co-ordination continued.

"Pilot say fuel." Ken wanted to know how much gas we had remaining. Once the number was stated, Ken made his command decision. "Pilot, we are going to bingo fuel, and check out the Angel Two en route Mom" (the code word for the ship from which you launched). Ken was back on the radios calling the shots.

"Two Delta, and Nipigon, be advised we are Bingo fuel this time. Intentions are to do a flyby of the Angel so we can have her prep the hoisting area and we will return for fuel, relaunch and do the Cas-evac" (Casualty Evacuation).

There was not a happier man alive on the face of the earth than me at that very moment. I had just witnessed what Hell on Aviators Earth looked like from a back seat crewman's perspective and to say that "Plan B" had my whole hearted endorsement would be perhaps the most significant understatement that I could have mustered at that time.

About fifteen minutes later, we had the Angel in sight, and commenced our fly past to survey the situation. She was huge. Six hundred feet long and unaffected by the ocean even in the current fury. There were unobstructed deck spaces that were larger than the entire Sea Hawk. This was going to be "Easy Peasy" and clearly, my trip to the deck of the Angel to effect the transfer would be exactly what our training evolutions and briefings had been. Plan B: Simple hoist onto the deck, load the Stokes litters, do the transfers, hoist back up and return to Mom. It could not or would not be simpler under the conditions. The knot in my stomach eased and the bile in my throat subsided. At least I was not going to have to die trying, and that option had clearly been in play a few minutes earlier. The images of what I had just witnessed while hanging out the back door of the helo were already showing up uninvited in my stream of consciousness and causing me to question my sanity. The voice in the back of my head played three simple words: Truth, Duty and Valour. I would need them all.

I sank into the passenger's seat and eased the straps on the Double Lift Harness. I was trying to take deep breaths and erase the memories from my mind of what I had just witnessed. It is said that Hell hath no fury like a woman scorned. Clearly who ever penned that had not seen the North Atlantic in the midst of a raging gale and most definitely never considered what we had just attempted.

The Second Launch
06 Oct 1986 (Later in the evening)

On our first launch we had gone airborne with both of our detachment crew commanders but it was becoming apparent to all that the work was far from being over. Bill Ropp had already flown this morning DFO (Dept. of Fisheries and Oceans) Fishpat (Fisheries Patrol) sortie, so Ken was planning to swap him out and bring in LT (USN) Brad Renner, our US Navy exchange officer and a skilled pilot in his own right. The remainder of the crew would remain the same and we would just hot fuel (Rotors and Engines Running Refuel) and launch ASAP.

The anguish in the voice of the Captain of the Sea Hawk as we had tried to effect the transfer on the first launch was clear. We had to stop him from setting the injured crewmen over the side of the Sea Hawk in small life rafts so we could pluck them from the ocean and get them to medical attention. In my mind, if this was a course of action he was considering, the seriously injured must genuinely be in serious distress. I know it sounds more than condescending, but it wouldn't have been the first time we'd have Medevac'd someone whose "injuries" though severe, were not life threatening. I was getting a real sense that whatever had happened that morning on the long liner must have been catastrophic if the insane course of action of putting someone over the side in 30 foot seas whipped by gale force winds seemed to be viable. How bad had it been?

Hot fuel completed and pilot swap executed and we were ready to launch for the next sortie. The blackness now complete and the rains intensifying, we were ready to head off and effect Plan B, the clearly superior option from my point of view.

"Two Delta, request vectors to Angel". The Sea King's notoriously suspect antiquated Navigation system was no match for the modern precision of the CP140's Inertial Nav system.

"One Niner, Two Delta, steer…" I was lost deep in thought. Introspection? Contemplation? What I had witnessed in the previous two hours would cause anyone to question what they had considered doing and I was absolutely ecstatic that this option was now off the table. The Angel Two was bigger than a couple of football fields and rock steady in the ocean, the antithesis of the Sea Hawk.

We traversed the distance in silence. I was not the only one lost deeply in reflective introspection. Thirty minutes into the transit, Ken started working the radios.

"Angel Two this is Rescue One Niner we are twenty minutes back. Confirm you have the two souls ready for the Medevac?" No sense arriving without as much prep work being done as possible.

"Rescue One Niner, this is Angel Two, negative." The Captain's thick Germanic accent cut the silence like a cleaver in a butcher shop. My stomach tensed and I could taste the bile starting to form again. "One Niner we are unable to launch life boat into the seas. Sorry. I repeat we are unable to launch." The implication of that sentence both knocked me flat on my ass and took the breath out of me. Holy Mother of God. We are back to Plan A. The elation I had felt an hour earlier was gone. Erased. Shattered. In its place? Fear.

Gripping.

Terrifying.

Paralyzing and all mine.

Somehow, some way we were going to need to get me aboard the Sea Hawk. Our previous attempts were nothing more than dismal failures highlighting not the deficiencies in our crew and gear but a set of environmental conditions that were outside our or anyone's normal envelope of operations. The knot grew and tightened with each mile we flew closer to the edge of Hell I had witnessed from my back seat perspective. I was gripped by something I'd never experienced.

"Rescue One Niner, we will attempt to take station to the lee of the Sea Hawk to provide a break from the Sea. Over?" The Germanic voice was trying to help however he could. I intuitively knew that he was aware of what we were facing.

"Roger that… Sea Hawk and Angel, Set course heading…." Ken was giving orders to set up the relative wind and ships motion to give us the optimum chance of success. He was also trying to have as much ready so that we could maximize our time on station since we now knew what we were up against, our "Can Do" Bravado replaced by a stark reality. If they say that Ignorance is bliss, I could now attest to that. The first launch, I had no idea what we were actually facing. The second, I was clearly in the dragon's jaws. I silently prayed the aviator's prayer over and over. "Holy Mother of Horsepower do not fail us now!" I somehow knew we were going to need it all.

This time when we arrived on scene I was already hanging out the back door in the double lift with Ken on one side, Al Smith, my Aesop, on the other, both secured to the helo by long straps called monkey tails so they would not fall out of the chopper. We were going to try the hover trim again, which would be operated in conjunction with the rescue hoist by Ken, while Al tried to thread the needle with the guideline.

"You have control." Hans voice clear over the intercom.

"I have a light, I have control". The helo was now being maneuvered in the horizontal plane according to Ken's inputs into the joy stick. The huge wind and sea break provided by the Angel Two was helping but just barely. The Sea Hawk was still being buffeted about and the stabilizers were not doing much in my mind. In fact, all I could see was that the guide wires from the aft rigging to the outboard pontoons were having little effect on stability while adding yet another element of danger to my world. Something else to cut me in half with. The Sea Hawk continued to pitch erratically in the churning ocean and we continued to be all over the sky attempting to get close while Al worked to get the guideline in that six foot by six moving foot window and into the hands of the crewman.

Slow motion. Surreal. They say that time stands still and your life flashes before your eyes. I can attest that it does. The guideline snagged in the overhead wires and one end was now firmly attached to the Sea Hawk, the other end to my chest on the double lift harness. The slack in the line was disappearing faster than I could process. When it hit taught I would be ripped from the helo to fall to the vessel below.

But Al was faster. He reached over and unhooked me a fraction of a second before the rope snapped like a giant snake that slithered towards the ship's rigging. Holy fuck! That was beyond close. A half a second slower and I am a dead man. The violent motion of the vessel, combined with the lag of the hover trim system just demonstrated why we were in such a precarious position, and I was at the leading edge of that. This would not be the only time that I would escape the Grim Reaper's grasp in the next hour.

"Pilot, you have the con." The light extinguished as Hans took over from the right seat in the front.

"I have the con."

"Let's back off and rethink this boys. This clearly is not working." The second great *Aha No Shit Sherlock* moment in as many launches. The executioner's axe had swung, come whooshing by and I, thanks to Al's quick reflexes, and had the chance to once again ponder the very precarious situation I was in.

Hans maneuvered the helo back up out of the way and took a look at the whole situation again. Clearly, in his mind, and ratified in ours, was the problem of keeping ten tons of lumbering helicopter behemoth on station over a point that was all over the ocean like a seismic needle dancing a jig during an earthquake.

After a couple of minutes of reflection, while I was still trying to get my heart out of the burning of my throat, Hans proposed a solution.

"Here is what we are going to try…" Everything that was in the AOI's (Aircraft Operating Instructions) had clearly failed so if we were going to get this to work, we needed to try something new and untried. The challenge of doing it in the middle of a black ass night in a raging gale would unequivocally exacerbate the difficulty and erase the already thin margin of error to nonexistent.

"I am going to fly this sucker in a manual hover…" Well there goes the AOI's … Flying a manual hover at night was dangerous. The pilot had no references to guide him so he would genuinely be flying by the seat of his pants. "Brad, I want you to keep an eye on the bulk carrier. It'll become our artificial horizon. Keep us off it and ensure we do not crash into it. We are going to have to be quick so do not waste any time." The last command directed at the back seaters, and more specifically me. We did not need to be in this precarious position any longer than need be.

This bold decision bordered on insanity but it was the best plan we had, in fact the only plan we had. So Hans put his seat full back, full up, and opened his window to allow him an unobstructed view of the vessel below. He slowly started to maneuver the Sea King into position when the flashes of light caught my eye. Lightening? Fuck No…

"The lights, the lights, they are blinding me. The flash cameras. Knock off the lights." Brad's voice, pleading, intense and more than a pang of desperation. Here we were, trying to pull off something that had never been done before and the crewmen of the Angel II thought it was a great time to take flash photography. Spectacular. Brilliant. I could not be more sarcastic if I tried.

For the first time that evening the Gods smiled in my mind though. Once the flashes stopped Hans had gotten us to a position where Al could use the backup guideline and it proved to be what we needed. Our traditional guideline has a three pound monkey's fist on the end for weight but the wind and rotor wash had been blowing it all over Hell's Creation up to that point. The jury rigged backup made by the Bosons in the Ship's Deck Department was weighted by the head of a ten pound sledge hammer and this made all the difference. Hans had gotten us close enough that Al was able to let the guideline virtually free fall, laser beam-like, to the deck below. In about three seconds we had gone from nowhere even close to having a guideline on the deck.

I did not have time to think. I unplugged from the intercom and in an instant I swung out the door into position and with a knowing nod shared between Ken and I, found myself now swaying wilding between the end of the rescue hoist and the guideline, descending into Hell and praying to every God I could think of. If I was going to die, I did not want to piss off whoever was manning Heaven's Ops desk that night. I had a greater chance of meeting them than not.

Death Smells
07 Oct 1986

The wind was howling and the deck was pitching on the Nipigon. The weather had not improved overnight and if anything the seas were rougher. The plan as we had briefed it was to launch when we got within 200 hundred miles of the Bow Drill 3 Oil Rig. We would land on the rig, hot fuel, and disembark the casualties and return back to Mom, while the Labrador helicopter with the doctor onboard would retrieve the casualties and fly into St Johns.

We had the chopper fired up and were "turning and burning" when they escorted the ambulatory casualty from the hanger to the Crew Door. The AESOP (Airborne electronic sensors operator) was securing the patient in the passenger seats and I was opening the cargo door so that the Stokes litter could be loaded safely into the back with the other casualty safely secured. I looked at the hands carrying the load and the grim looks on their faces told the story. We were now heading to the oil rig with One Red, One Black. The code words for one seriously injured, one dead. In reality, we were not able to call it but the facts were what they were.

Death has a smell that is overpowering and even drowns out the smell of burnt jet fuel. We might not have been allowed to pronounce the most seriously injured as deceased, but there was no doubt what has happened. The realist, the pragmatist in me knew. The idealist wished it were not so. What if we had been successful on the first launch? Would the outcome be different if he had received medical attention those two endless hours sooner?

The knot in my stomach was forming again and I felt like I would wretch yet again. I'd had enough dry heaves the night before on the trip back from the vessel that I was sore. The smell of death was doing nothing to help the situation.

Nothing we had ever trained for or heard about had prepared me for what had happened in the previous twenty four hours, the beginning of the descent into hell on earth, and its ongoing traversal. In fact, decades later, I can tell you that it was just starting.

The night before, when I had seen the first casualty, the thought had crossed my mind to just get him in the helicopter and book it for Mom. I would deal with the other casualty onboard. Panic had momentarily taken control of the rational side of me. I know that would have accomplished nothing in light of where we are, but the horror of what I was staring into could make you second guess anything and question everything you had ever believed. How he could be alive and if he was I sure as hell hope he was feeling no pain. What if? Two precious hours and the doc's morphine syringes would have brought relief, maybe. Maybe it would have shut him down quicker? Who knows? Woulda coulda shoulda as the pilot pulled collective to get us off the deck.

I puked again.

Rotor Rumblings

Rotor Rumblings. The 443 newspaper column that appeared in the Shearwater Warrior.

Provided courtesy of Flying Officer Manwell Dip.

Rescue on the North Atlantic.

The seventh day of our Fishpat started out like the rest. Plans were made for two flights in supports of the Fisheries Organization. Just prior to the first launch, Nipigon was alerted about a developing SAR situation that involved a sword fishing vessel 550 NM south east of St Johns, approximately 395 NM from us. The first sortie went as scheduled but the second was cancelled when Nipigon was dedicated to the SAR and was now steaming at up to 26 knots towards the Sea Hawk.

The helo crew was designated and preparations made to launch as soon as the ship was within Range. The Sonar Dome, reeling machine and receiver and any unnecessary internal stores and equipment were removed. Two Stokes litters, extra blankets, first aid kits and an extra guideline rope were prepared and in the aircraft. Finally, the crew briefed for the upcoming drama on the high seas.

The 68 foot American Sword fishing vessel the Sea Hawk had had an accident onboard. Two of her crewman had been injured when a wave broke over the stern section of the boat. One had a crushed knee, deep chest and throat wounds and a broken jaw. The other had lacerations, broken clavicle, and broken arm. Both men were in various degrees of shock.

Rescue 107, an Aurora, was on station and gave us vectors to the SeaKing. The 160 NM transit was uneventful and the crew of Rescue 19 arrived with enough fuel to stay on station for 30 minutes. The bulk carrier Angel II was 1 NM away and ready to give assistance. The TACCO talked with the Seahawk's captain, ensured all loose gear was stowed, and explained what was going to happen during the upcoming guideline transfer. The Sea Hawk, making one knot into the wind, was pitching and rolling erratically with no steady period. Conditions were: Night, ceiling overcast, occasional light rain, wind 270/35 g45 sea 18-20 ft. (Editor's Note: Winds were from the west at 35 gusting to 45 knots)

The SeaKing crew made several approaches to the Sea Hawks port side using both voice conning and hover trim procedures. The pilot had no outside references and positioning was further hampered by horizontal stabilizers ranging out from the Seahawks beam and a variety of antennae wires and ladders both amidships and on her stern.

None of the standard procedures worked. The aircraft could not react quickly enough to the Seahawks violent unpredictable motions. After 35 minutes of frustrating effort, the crew was forced to abandon its attempts and return to mother to refuel. On departure the Seahawk and Angel II were discussing the possibility of transferring the two casualties by lifeboat. A pick up from the bulk carriers' open forecastle would be relatively routine.

After hot fueling on the Nipigon the Seaking was back on station about 2 hours later. The discussed boat transfer never occurred, when Angel II was unable to launch her lifeboat in the high seas. Seahawk was now about a ¼ mile off the lea of Angel II to block the excessive sea motion. It didn't! Again some standard hover trim/voice con procedures were made and each time, Seahawk elusive deck pitched and rolled violently away. At one point a line was lowered but got entangled in the stern ladder and antennae and was ripped violently from the aircraft when Seahawk pitched forward.

The crew took two minutes to back away and rethink their approach. Seahawk was directed to snuggle right up to Angel II about 60-80 ft. off her beam. The helicopter went into a manual 40 foot hover 90 degrees to the Seahawks stern, using Angel II as sort of artificial horizon. The pilot kept his concentration on the heaving wheelhouse and forecastle of the Seahawk. The co-pilot checked instrument and aircraft position relative to Angel II 60 feet away. The TACCO kept continuous voice con keeping a close eye on the two high antennae amidships. The AESOP continuously adjusted the guideline position, ready to drop it immediately that a good position was attained.

For 10 to fifteen minutes the crew jockeyed and dodged obstructions to slowly move into a good position over the 6 by 6 foot hoisting area. The aircraft at times approached to within 20 feet of the Angel II where crew members taking flash photographs temporarily blinded the co-pilot and at one point the Seahawks two 55 foot swaying antennae's passed two feet under the aircraft. The intensity in the aircraft was reaching its limits.

Finally the guideline was lowered to a good position on the stern and was retrieved by a Seahawk deckhand. The aircraft was in a good relative position and the extra TACCO was lowered to the deck. Strange aircraft attitudes including over 20 degrees of bank and pitch were necessary to maintain Rescue 19 near the Seahawk. The crewman reached the deck safely after having once been flung into the sea when Seahawk bucked unpredictably. The two stokes litters followed shortly thereafter and quickly prepared for the casualties. The two men were secured in the litters, one at a time and lifted to the helo. At last the SeaKing crewman was on his way back up and the Helo departed for Nipigon. The two casualties were being treated by the Ships Medical Assistant while the exhausted crew experienced unspoken satisfaction and relief that this difficult transfer had come to a successful, safe conclusion.

The two men were cared for overnight in the Ship's Sick Bay, while Nipigon closed the oil rig Bow Drill 3 where it was planned to transfer them to a doctor's care and for onward transportation by a Gander Helicopter to St John's Hospital. Unfortunately the more seriously injured of the two young men did not survive his ordeal and he died on board Nipigon during the early morning of 7 October. The planned transfer took place without further incident and with Rescue 19's arrival in St Johns, Nipigon's part in this saga ended. To the aircrew involved, the night's events will never be forgotten. Then men and equipment were extended to the limits and valuable lessons learned will be passed on the HS community.

To the reading public, I'm sorry that Manwell's usual levity is lacking in this story, the situation was too real. To Hans, Brad, Bill, Miles, Vic, Ken, Al and Al, F/O Manwell Dip send s his best. Nipigon has proved herself to have one HEL-UV-AN-AIRDET.

Phone patch
25 November 87

We were flying a routine training mission out over the dip sectors, areas 20 to 40 miles south of Shearwater, over the ocean. An area where Sea King crews could hone their Anti-submarine Warfare Crew skills and the myriad of over water back door utility skills including everything from moving cargo via slings, various hoisting operations, and flying the Helicopter from the back door using the hover trim system. Aviation is a very unforgiving game, and remaining current on the myriad of skills are part of what was required to keep up your "operational efficiency and combat readiness qualifications." Routine flights, practicing skills that could be called on at a moment's notice if the mission changed at any point, are the backbone of aviation.

"Savage One Zero?" The call sign used that day. Savage indicating that the crew operating aircraft CH124410 was from HS443.

"Ops, Savage One Zero Go." They knew at ground control that we could hear them. Sometimes when low in the hover at forty feet over the ocean and forty miles out, comms could be weak and broken. Not today.

"Savage One Zero, switch to ops freq and check in."

"Ops, One Zero, Roger, out!" For some reason they did not want to clutter the main frequency that was used for tracking all the aircraft training that day.

"Pilot, switch freq to Ops". Certainly a strange request but not completely unheard of.

"Ops, this is Savage One Zero, checking in"

"Roger Savage One Zero, confirm you have one Captain Cousineau airborne with you."

"Ops, One Zero, Affirmative, you are talking to him." This had just gone from strange to a whole new level.

"Savage One Zero, please climb and maintain comms while we establish Phone Patch with LCol Mackinnon."

"One Zero Standing by." The Squadron Commander was in Winnipeg at the Air Commanders conference. If he wanted me via phone patch, immediately, all I could think of was I had done something to absolutely piss off the command structure and he had gotten a new asshole ripped, and keeping in the finest of military traditions he was about to turn on the beloved "Shit Accelerator.". Since shit flows downhill and rapidly, I was about to get an even larger anal orifice ripped.

"Savage One Zero, phone patch established, go ahead."

"Skipper, this is Savage One Zero standing by." Voice recognition was a huge part of working in our very small community and I knew that LCol Mackinnon would recognize my voice.

"Cous," he started. I breathed a huge sigh of relief. If I was getting a new one ripped it would have be "Captain Cousineau" not "Cous," the nickname that everyone on the squadron knew me by. "The Governor General has just informed the Commander of Air Command that you are to be awarded the Star of Courage."

"Roger that." Hell I did not know what the appropriate response was but I was rapidly losing it.

"Cous, hard copy message traffic to follow but I wanted to be the first to congratulate you on your amazing work on the Sea Hawk SAR."

"Thank you Sir," I was awash in conflicting emotions.

"Cous, I am signing off now, again, Bravo Zulu". Bravo Zulu, a naval signal that could be transmitted using two flags, the Bravo and the Zulu, meaning "Well done".

"Roger out." I was a mess. On one hand, recognition from the highest levels, on the other racked by guilt and fear. The crewman had died. The images from that night jammed their way in to my stream of consciousness yet again. I could taste the bile in the back of my throat, see the images burned into my mind, and smell the sickly sweet odor of death.

Death.

Death does not smell pretty.

Many equate death with funeral homes and those that they have waked. Clinical, embalmed and very sterile. That is not the death I am talking about. Traumatic Death, hours old, has a smell. The smell is so thick it has a taste. Sickening, and if I had to put one word on it, "coppery." The sickening smell of traumatic death floods my sense of smell and taste.

I did not feel like a hero. I felt like I was going to wretch, the knot in my stomach every bit as large as that night. The images as clear as that night. The line between the past and the present obscured in a mixture of intrusive thoughts and feelings.

The neck gasket on my immersion suit, affectionately known as our poopy suits, was cutting off my airway. I could not breathe. I wanted to get out of the helicopter as badly as I had wanted to get off the Sea Hawk that night. Holy Mother of Horsepower do not fail me now. The Aviator's Prayer. God how I wished I could be anywhere else. How I wished I could make it stop. The sights, the sounds, the smells, the tastes and the nightmares. Invasive and ever present.

Star of Courage Citation

(Taken from the Governor General's Website)

Decorations for Bravery

Lieutenant Medric Leo Robert Cousineau, S.C.

Eastern Passage, Nova Scotia

Star of Courage

Date of Instrument: November 23, 1987

Date of Presentation: June 10, 1988

Lieutenant Medric Leo Robert Cousineau, S.C.

Star of Courage

On the night of October 6, 1986, Lt. Medric Cousineau, a member of the crew of a Canadian Armed Forces Search and Rescue helicopter, risked his life to rescue two seriously-injured crewmen from an American fishing boat. At the time of the rescue it was dark and weather conditions were terrible, with rain, strong winds and heavy seas; and the deck of the boat, which was pitching and rolling continuously, was obscured by antennae, fishing apparatus and machinery. Fully aware of the hazardous conditions, Lt. Cousineau volunteered to be lowered to the deck of the vessel in order to move the injured men from the boat to the helicopter. On the first attempt he was thrown overboard when the boat pitched violently, but on a second attempt, although he fell into the sea, he managed to scramble aboard. He was able, despite the flying spray and the tremendous noise of the large helicopter hovering close overhead, to quickly organize the preparation and evacuation of the two injured crewmen. Had Lt. Cousineau not willingly put his own life in jeopardy, both of the injured men would certainly have died.

Citation for Hans Kleeman

(Taken from the Governor General's Website)

Meritorious Service Decorations (military division)

Captain Hans E. Kleeman, M.S.C.

Lazo, British Columbia [Canada]

Meritorious Service Cross (military division)

Decoration awarded on June 1, 1988

Captain H.E. Kleemann, M.S.C.

443 Squadron

Canadian Forces Base Shearwater

Meritorious Service Cross (military division)

On the night of 6 October 1986, Captain Kleemann was the Crew Commander and pilot of a Sea King helicopter launched from HMCS NIPIGON to rescue two seriously-injured crewmen from the fishing vessel SEA HAWK. Due to the vessel's small size and configuration, a mere 2 meter by 2.5 meter stern deck area was suitable for a hoist rescue. Weather conditions were deplorable, with 6 meter seas, winds gusting to 45 knots and very poor visibility due to darkness and rain. Despite using the lee of a nearby large bulk carrier to gain some protection from the seas, the SEA HAWK continued to pitch erratically, and standard rescue procedures repeatedly failed. Captain Kleemann then boldly maneuvered his helicopter lower and perilously close to both ships under such arduous conditions that the slightest error would have been catastrophic. With exceptional skill and the finest of crew coordination, he achieved a hover just above the SEA HAWK's wildly pitching stern from which the rescue was completed.

Captain Kleeman's outstanding professional performance of his military duty at a rare high standard has brought great credit to both himself and the Canadian Forces.

Investiture
10 June 1988

Some days one has to be thankful for everything that they can get. Today it comes in the form of a clear and sunny day. One could not have wished for a nicer day. Cloudless skies and sun drenching everything in sight with a warm blanket of Vitamin D therapy. For me, the sunny day was what I needed. Not that everyone couldn't use more bright sunny days, but what I did not need was a wet, stormy, black skies day that was dark and foreboding. I already had that except no one else could tell. My own personal hell was tearing my insides apart. I felt like I had swallowed some caustic substance that was threatening to eat its way out from my insides.

Today should have been a great day, full of celebration and congratulations. For my parents, for my kid brother and sister in law, for Jocelyn in the company of our two month old daughter, it most likely would be. Yet I stood on the precipice, staring into hell, hoping I could get through the day without incident.

We were all assembled at Rideau Hall for my Investiture, along with all the other recipients of Bravery Decorations. We were going to meet Her Excellency, Madame Sauvé, the current Governor General of Canada, to formally be presented the decorations for Bravery we had all been awarded. There were a couple dozen individuals who were going to be awarded the Medal of Bravery and a few of us to receive the Star of Courage.

The Director of Protocol was briefing us on the procedure to be followed and the etiquette for dealing with the Queen's Representative. After all would be seated, except for Her Excellency and her aide, we would be paraded into our seats. Then the formal ceremony, full of pomp and circumstance would begin.

The entire audience was there in support of one or another of the recipients, and there were also several political and military dignitaries in attendance. This ceremony was to honour those whose actions had clearly placed other's lives and the interests of Canada ahead of their own to save or in some cases attempt to save other human beings. Altruism in its purest sense, sacrificing oneself for the benefit of others.

The ceremony began and my thoughts drifted. We were in a large, well-appointed room in rock solid Rideau Hall but I was back in the mosh pit of the pitching helicopter. The smell of burnt jet fuel and death overwhelmed me and added further fire to the blaze that raged in my gut.

One by one, we were called in turn to stand before Her Excellency as the Master of Ceremonies read out the formal citation. Upon completion of the reading the Governor General would pin the appropriate medal on to a hanger that had been prepositioned on our chests to ensure that the medal pinning would go smooth and flawlessly.

"Captain, then Lieutenant, Medric Cousineau." I knew my parents and family could not have been prouder of me than at that exact moment. Fortunately there were no thought bubbles above my head betraying my thoughts. Fear, gripping, overwhelming and paralyzing had taken over my thoughts.

The irony is that most will never know how they will react until they are put in the situation that requires the kinds of actions that were required to land one here before the Governor General. But that is the easy part. What becomes problematic is the litany of second guessing yourself that accompanies the thought process, "Could I do it again?"

"On the night of October the 6th…" The narration began and I stood with clenched teeth, my tongue hard pressed against them, to tighten my abdomen in hopes that I would not lose the contents of my stomach. The waves of nausea swept over me and I felt very much like I had that night, adrift and awash in a sea of conflicting emotions. I cannot remember the rest of the citation as I was lost in a jumble of images straight out of the depths of Hell.

"We are so proud of you." The sentence snaps me back into the present. Madam Sauvé, was hanging the medal on the aforementioned hanger. I don't know how many times she said it. But there was something in her eyes that told me perhaps she understood something from the narration.

"Thank you your Excellency". With that I bowed and returned to my seat and began thinking of how soon I could get a drink, a real stiff drink, and several more of them. The country seemed intent on remembering and I was focused on forgetting, trying to drown the images in the bottom of a bottle.

The Governor General's Speech
10 June, 1988

Her Excellency The right Honourable Jeanne Sauvé

Governor General of Canada

Address at the Presentation of Awards

For Bravery

Ottawa, Ontario

Friday, June 10, 1988

Distinguished Recipients,

Ladies and Gentlemen:

Today's ceremony is Canada's way of recognizing those of its citizens who, through their courage, demonstrate their concern for their fellow citizens. This is always a pleasure for me and a moment of intense emotion. Each time that I preside at such occasions, I ask myself what motives inspired these acts of bravery. Although I cannot define them precisely, I can nevertheless recall the virtues of those who demonstrated uncommon courage and put their physical and moral resources at the disposal of others.

Gathered together here, the recipients once again look like ordinary citizens. Their humility, however, cannot obscure the magnificence of what they have done. There is an obvious contrast between the official character of this ceremony and the events that occasioned it. Let them be assured that the Stater has not forgotten them and that it wants to stress the exemplary nature of their conduct. By choosing them to receive the admiration of all Canadians, the State wishes first of all to honour them and, in this way, to give prominence to the qualities that must not pass unnoticed, because they reveal the value of the men and women who form our nation. Canada was built by the daily efforts of its citizens: it benefited from their talents, efforts and creative spirit. Our nation requires constant effort and unflagging perseverance from all Canadians, past and present. A common will united us and from out united effort arose a personality which identifies us.

That personality emerges in all its splendor at moments of danger which require and uncommon affirmation of those qualities that distinguish us. This is what came to the fore when these heroes performed the actions which we are honouring in this ceremony today. Their actions show that Canadians are capable of deeds far above and beyond the requirements of ordinary conduct. This latent force manifests itself suddenly, for no one could predict the accidents that the citations recall. In such circumstances, one must draw on internal resources and altruistic feelings that are part of individual character and personality. Heroes are not born; they are created by circumstances. One cannot train to be brave in the way that athletes train. Confronted by tragic situations, the heart, and mind incite heroic actions. That is what happened to the sturdy souls who display the qualities that they have developed and the depth of their sense of common humanity.

I want to thank those who brought these acts to the attention of the authorities, thus allowing us to publicly reward there heroes. I salute their families and the citizens who were the beneficiaries of or witnesses to their bravery. Our history, already filled with noble deeds, now has a new page, and it is with great pride that all Canadians sign it along with me.

The Question

The Question I could not answer, and the moment I knew I was done.

That is one hell of a question and when I could no longer answer it with certainty, I knew I had to stop flying. I could easily have gotten innocent people killed if I could not perform. Collateral damage is one hell of a euphemistic term for the innocent. What if? What if I had not been as fast as Al? What if I could have been as cool under fire as Ken was? I was losing it. The nightmares, the flashbacks, and the anxiety attacks had become so common that the only place I could find refuge was a blackout. I was done as an aviator. I could not fly at night; the anxiety had gotten to the point of literal paralysis at the back door. I looked out into the darkness, the flashing taillights flickering off the wet rotor blades and I was back there.

Again.

Again.

Again.

The macabre dance with the Grim Reaper left me with a few reminders that may be of some use to future military officers. The British colonel was prescient in ways I would come to know. The horrors of war, or serious personal trauma as evidenced by the crewman of the Sea Hawk, leave marks. These things do, and if they did not I would be genuinely afraid, for that takes me to a place where humanity turns to the inhumane.

Sir Charles Upham knew. He knew it in spades. The only combat soldier to earn the Victoria Cross (VC) and bar. The two citations of his actions make me shudder. Perhaps what the world will never know is what racks you between the first and the second times you are called on to find whatever it is, deep inside you, that gives you the strength to do what is necessary. To do your duty. No, I am thankful that most are never called to answer it once, let alone a second time. There is a side to citations for Gallantry that I now know with firsthand experience. What is written on the citation by the Chancellery Committee scratches but the tip of the iceberg and I still am angry that no one ever talked to me? Why?

Quite simply I know what happened in my heart of hearts out there at sea that day. Quite simply, every man airborne on both sorties to the Sea Hawk, deserves the Meritorious Service Cross, to then Capt. Ropp and Ordinary Seaman Gillis, the Meritorious Service Medal. For every airman and sailor afloat the CDS commendation. You see, I know what I did. I know what they did, and nobody ever asked me. If they did ask, trust me, it is gone in a blackout or flashback.

What is not evident in the citation is that we did not get it done on the first sortie. Hanging out the back door of the Sea King in an overhand monkey grip, I watched us unsuccessfully try everything in our arsenal to get it done. We were unsuccessful, and during our refuel trip there was a plan to move the injured to a huge bulk carrier and our inspection en route turned this into what should have been a walk in the park. I was the happiest man on the planet for I had no stomach for what I had just witnessed. I didn't want any part of what we'd just escaped. The knot was as big as a grapefruit. My mouth tasted like glue and I could not spit if I tried. When Plan B failed because the huge bulk carrier could not launch a 55 man life boat, we were back to Plan A. Fucking Plan A. Hanging out the back, looking into the abyss, again.

Again.

Again.

Again.

At that singular moment, that was when the die was cast, and my fate sealed. There are those who will wish to argue I had a choice. For those who genuinely know me, for those who knew what shaped and molded me, for those who know the crucibles of where I speak, No, NO! I did not have a choice. For if I believed what I knew was in my heart, mind and soul, and listened to anyone of them, I knew what I had to do. I knew that which my duty was.

Truth, Duty, Valour. They're not just words. Not in the back of a Sea King that's the sole hope for men dying quickly on a long liner on the angry North Atlantic.

There are times when I am wracked with horrible anxiety attacks because of the guilt I feel. To know that you have looked into a man's eyes and lied with your heart and soul, maybe trying to convince yourself, that he was okay, when the rational side of you knew that not to be true. For those who wish to debate whether I am playing God, let me tell you what I know about that subject with great certainty. There is a God and I ain't him! When I was out there that night I swore solemn promises to every God and Deity I could name, and a few I made up. When you are staring at what may very well define the end point of your life, you have to get right with whatever God or Gods that you believe in, and there comes a point when you have less than about point three seconds to get square as you prepare to meet whomever it is that you just swore to or at!

When you are standing at the precipice, the abyss, knowing how close you had been and you hold in your arms, someone who is clinging onto his very life by the faintest of threads, it changed me. So many things happened to me that night, I still do not understand them all. Maybe sometime in the fullness of time I will get my wish. Maybe the God that I swore a solemn oath to will consider my part paid in full, my debt retired. Maybe I will get to enjoy nothing but long walks by the seaside, as I watch the coming and the going of the seasons, and measure life not by the race of seconds in society, but the natural rhythms of the seasons of birth through to death and rebirth again. Maybe I will just keep calm and walk the dog. That is my solemn hope.

I have paid dearly with my mind and body and I get that part of it was what I signed up for. I knew going in what the stakes were. At least I should have if I understood any of the lessons that I had learned. Names in the Books of Remembrance are poignant reminders when they were you friends, mess mates, squadron mates, shipmates and others that you have served with. Perhaps my deepest respects for the fallen comes in the brutal reality of how close it was for me. You think that would leave you with an insatiable thirst for the fruits of life. In reality, it left me racked with Survivor's Guilt and anxiety and panic attacks. The images have not gone away. Nothing I have tried to date has worked. That statement was true until Thai. You often hear talk around various "recovery rooms" for addictions about life in the "Before Time" the demarcation point being the anniversary of dealing with the addiction. My before time had been marked by the 6th of October, 1986. Nothing and I mean absolutely nothing went unchanged in my life. I have had so many nightmares I have lost count.

Panic Attack
The 1990's

I have been awake for forty-five minutes and have already had two panic attacks and the rage. I am pacing like a caged tiger and the raw energy courses through me. I need to scream. Deep, primal. JUST GO AWAY! Leave me alone. Directed at the images, ever present.

I am trying everything I know, everything I have learned, and relief is not there. My resting pulse has shot up from seventy five to over one hundred twenty. I wish I could hard wire the switch to the off position.

I reach out and there is no one there.

Alone.

Again.

Still.

One day maybe when I reach out there will be a touch, a nod, a word, a look of knowing. Most will never understand the blessing they have. Those who are not so blessed, cursed indeed, are the ones who get it. Some, like me, hanging on to reality with tenuous grasps that can slip away in an instant.

There are fine lines. Life and Death. Good and evil. Truth and lies. The calm and the storm. Sometimes one has the luxury of examining those dualities at their leisure. Other times the entire world comes crashing into the front of your consciousness with no warning. Sometimes the images and the emotions can be controlled. That is something that mostly escapes me.

Rage.

Fear.

Guilt.

Shame.

Doubts.

After all these years, the questions are still there. What if...

The dry heave twists my stomach into a knot. What if....

In so many ways, solitude is a sanctuary. If I can cut down the external stimulus, maybe, just maybe, if I am actually lucky, I can grab one small piece of reality and hold on tight. Maybe if I am really lucky the thoughts of suicide and homicide will be replaced by something, anything.

Images of the Reaper, beckoning and patient, ever present, whirl through my mind, a combination of death and destruction. He is not happy. I cheated him what he thought was his due. Death was shortchanged. He wanted his due. He wanted me. He may get me yet. I do not know.

Therapy Session
Early in Two Thousand and something

"Can you feel the soft breeze blowing over you? You breathe in gently... Soft, soothing ...almost melodic. Gently let your breath out from deep inside...... slowly feel the breath leaving you."

Holy fucking Jesus Mary Mother of fucking God!

The vision.

Out of the black, the horror. Howling winds screaming like a banshee. The harsh knives of North Atlantic salt spray cut my face. The noise of the large ship on the lee, the vessel and the helicopter made anything less than a scream unintelligible. Deafening...

Gut shot. A psychic punch to the solar plexus, doubling over and retching. Fucking dry heaves. Fucking visions. Fuck..... Fuck...Fuck.... Help me... please... somebody... anybody....

In the darkness I can see me. Not from my eyes. I am outside again. I reach out. Gone.

The panic crashes in like a runaway freight train. I am a caged tiger. I begin to pace. I can feel my heart rate accelerating and I cannot get it to stop...I stop pacing and the clenching and unclenching of my fists continues. Coiled. Tense. Ready to unload in a moment's notice. The muscles of my traps ready to snap from the tension.

"Notice the calm as it courses down your body..."

The soft voice. They have no God damned idea. At this exact moment I have crossed the line. I will tell them whatever they want to hear. Just make it stop...

Later, the door opens and the therapist gently raises the light level.

"How did that go?"

Marvelous. I haven't been so relaxed... I think I might be making some headway. Right down the highway to hell.... Yeah it was spectacular....... Was it good for you? Could not have been better.... Panic attack... anxiety... racing heart and suicidal thoughts replaced by homicidal thoughts... I can't remember the last time I had this much fucking fun. It has been a real slice.

"Shall we do it the next week at the same time?"

Oh for sure... I will be here. Can hardly wait! Sure I will get right on that let's see... next Tuesday we have our morning panic attack followed by our afternoon run and hide before the nightmares. I still got today's feelings of isolation and loneliness, before the nightmares. Fuck me. It is hard to imagine having all this fun....

The conversation drifts as do I ... what we talk about on my way out I can't remember... I very rarely do. I certainly don't remember them longer than an hour or two... these are the people I am supposed to talk to. I would talk to them ... if I trusted them... ain't going to happen... there was not a snowball's chance in hell of that ever happening... If they knew what was inside my head they sure would not be in such a great big hurry to get in there... today, no one dies... maybe.

"You know I think that...."

"Stop that. I do not want to know what you think. I want to know what you feel." The look of resignation crossed his face. He was relentless. We had been at this for weeks. He wanted me to share what I felt.

Good luck with that, let me know how that is working for you? Point. Counter Point. Thrust, parry, jab, block, counter. He would try and get inside the defenses. I was dug in deep. Entrenched. Years and years of hurt had cemented a near impregnable fortress. Nobody gets inside. Nobody. I was safe in there. What ya thinking? Do you think I am just going to lower the drawbridge across the moat and let you waltz right in? Seriously? Just paint an oversized bull's-eye on my ass. "Bummer of a birthmark, Hal." Bad reference to an old Far Side cartoon.

"What?" He had that look of being mildly perplexed and slightly intrigued. Where was this going? Had to be his thought. I was on the move, the elusive Jell-O under his thumb. Where was I off to this time?

"I was thinking about an old Far Side cartoon and at this exact moment, I feel it is amusing."

"You feel?"

"Yes I feel." I feel it is pretty amazing that you are actually thinking I am going to let you in. Don't think he would want to hear that. I wonder if anyone has ever told him how messed up this interview room is. A window to outside would be nice. Anything more than a broom closet on steroids…. Claustrophobic… the darkness of the ship. The sounds of the machinery, the ever present mechanical noises against a back drop of structural creaks and groans. Truly one of the blackest places in the world… below decks on a ship. Water tight means light tight. Couple of decks down below the water line blacker than coal. I leave my cabin at 0430 to go down to sick bay to check on Doc. He must be smoked by now. I know that whatever I was trying to pass off as sleep wasn't happening. I was still wound tighter, way tighter than I ever should have been. I was going to have to do the medevac to the Oil rig. So we are going to launch in a genuinely foul weather and fly 225 miles or so, hit an oil rig in the middle of the Atlantic, refuel and swap the injured to a Labrador helicopter and then return to mom. After last night's little adventure this was a walk in the park. Even if the navigation system was a useless piece of antiquated crap straight out of the 1950's. There is no life like it!

I liked the breezeway much better. A big open cross passage on the steamer. Cross passage, breezeway, open air and capstan to sit on. Do not lean on the stanchions. They break and you could have a man overboard. Those do not always turn out so well.

We were coming back from Bermuda and one of the ships had a man over board in the middle of the night. All the ships were brought to rescue stations and we had a helo "turning and burning". At first light we launched. The minutes we waited till we could see anything seemed an eternity compressed into minutes. There was a lot of time spent that day looking. At night fall we shut it down. The search was over. After identifying pop cans and other bits of trash all day long, I was convinced if he was afloat we would have found him. The sea claimed another. Relentless and unforgiving.

"Are you with me?" His voice calm, reassuring, trying to ground me.

"How long?" I am sitting dead still. My heart now racing. I want to run. My fists are clenched. "We gotta get out of this place if it's the last thing we ever do." I know I can blow him out of the way. Knock him half way into the middle of next week, come back three days to get to tomorrow. Run. Run for the Hills.…..

"A few minutes."

Fuck. Space time dilation. Lost. Where did it go? Away. Probably the one guy who gets me and I don't think he gets me, but he is closer than just about anyone else alive. I got a wife I won't tell the story too, and a world I can't. I can't tell anyone. Not a single soul. At least he lets me be me. I was gone again. Away…

Here but not here. "God Grant me the serenity to accept…" the words melt into a voice. "Doesn't say anything about liking it." Short version? Fuck it, fuck it, and fuck it!

I don't remember much about the next couple of sessions.

I had gone way deep again. He was trying his damnedest to get me back on track. I was out there.

"You remember when we talked about classic rock?"

He had dialed in on my love of music. My best musical ability is turning the stereo on. I can't play a single note on any musical instrument and my singing is worse. Much worse. Doesn't mean that you can't love the oldies. Sometimes I try and use the music to take me back to happy times and my happy place. Dissociate. Trigger it. Works for the visions. Problem is that I go there so I don't have to be here.

"Yep was listening to the Who's Behind Blue Eyes on the way here today, classic."

He started humming along and then started to sing it from the top. "No one knows what it's like to be the bad man to be the sad man behind blue eyes."

I was that. The sad man. I could not remember happy. Faked happiness for a lot of people. If I pretended to be happy at least they would not try and figure out why I wasn't. Then again, they probably were not going to find out which one of the "Pooh" characters I was. But they would ask, and want to gain access to the fortress, access right to the inner sanctum. "Like that is ever happening."

I had one guy, the one who I actually made some headway with, he saw me shut down. Mid-session comatose. Bunkered down and not coming out. By now I am dissociating and going out of body a lot. Descriptions are hard while watching your life at arm's length as not much more than a disinterested bystander.

I drift back into the room and find myself humming along.

"But my dreams, they aren't as empty, as my conscience seems to be. I have hours, only lonely, my love is vengeance that's never free."

"What are you feeling?"

Most of what I felt was nothing. Vast tracts of teenage wasteland "Out here in the fields, I fight for my meals, I get my back into my living. The Who, Baba O'Reilly. Who's Next..." Me, please let it be me. A few minutes, free from the anguish, the guilt, the shame, the hurt, the betrayal. Perhaps the one that cuts the deepest is the betrayal. How fucking dare they.... "I don't need to fight, to prove I'm right. I don't need to be forgiven."

"Lost and I want to run." I want the anonymity I want to go where no one knows my name.

"Why do you run?"

Spectacular. I can see this is going to go really fucking well today. "The simple answer is I don't like being here. I would rather be somewhere else, in fact anywhere else."

He sat there, the tick of the tape recorder breaking the silence that now hung heavy in the air.

"Guilt? Shame? Both?" He did not say it in an accusatory manner that would imply some serious baggage. He said it soft, a kind of catharsis in its tone alone. If he could get me to admit even a small slice, then he would have his beachhead. We had fought over this piece of real estate for a long time. I did not like him. But I was starting to develop a sense of respect. Intense feelings of anger, resentment and anguish, triggering my flight or fight response.

"Guilt." A barely audible whisper.

"Where are you? Right now where are you? Tell me so I can help you."

"The helicopter. I am on the damn helicopter and shit is really hitting the fan."

"Why do you feel guilty?"

"Because I am alive."

"Survivor guilt is a very normal reaction amongst rescuers who lose a person."

I don't think he was prepared for what happened next. I know I sure as hell wasn't. I went from steady state to an all-out rage attack in less time than it takes to blink.

"Jesus fucking H Christ lord love a fucking popsicle stick. You mean to tell me you been sitting here for the last however fucking many months it's been, thinking I am carrying survivor guilt about the guy we lost? Seriously? You have no fucking clue. Oh I feel guilt. I am alive and he is dead. I was not there for him. He was there for me. Without him I am a dead man."

I drift. I am about to go and he knows it.

"Help me understand. You said he was so seriously injured you could not believe he was alive. How did you think this happened?"

"Not the dead guy. Al. Al my Aesop. Al is dead and I was not there for him. If he had been one second slower, less even, I get torn out of the helicopter and onto the ship seventy feet below. I would be dead. Deader than dead. No hope. My life was always in my crew's hands, theirs often in mine. But never like this."

"In what way?"

"Look doc, it is like this. I do not know if you have ever looked someone squarely in the eye and know that everything that had to be said or would be said between you about what just transpired was covered in that look and a nod. If I have to explain, you would not understand. Recognition that he had played God or God's Hand. I knew it. He knew it. In either case, He had saved me. I live, he dies. Hardly seems fair." I am shutting down and I feel myself crossing my arms over my chest. I hear him talking. Nothing registers. I am out on the North Atlantic. The darkness oppressive and I begin to shake. I shudder. I heave.

At some point I hear the doc…. "I think we will stop here for the week."

I walked down the hall and out to my car. I wanted to kill someone. Take me to the edge and leave me fucking hanging… "For another ten minutes please deposit…" I wonder if any of these docs treating PTSD are going to ever get that the chances of me getting to where we get me to open up next week is actually unlikely. Note to self: next time he brings it up, about Al, I will let him have the rest of the story, both freaking barrels. In so many ways, I feel cheated. I feel I betrayed him. I feel I did not have his back, like he had mine. I feel guilt. I feel shame. I feel anger. I feel I want to run…. I know that I am not going to "share". It's my world. Sad this is how I feel most days. I drift.

Lost.

Alone.

Very, very, very lonely.

Truly the ones who would understand, the brothers and sisters of the military cadre, I cannot tell them. Them especially. Decorated hero my ass. I want to run…. I need to be anywhere else. "You want me to feel? I feel you should go fuck yourself." I drift.

What Do You Feel
Sometime around 2005

I hate this room. It's too small. Way too small. It's the size of the micro quad on a steamer. Whoever thought it was a good idea to do therapy with someone who has serious issues about space in a room where I can touch all four walls should seriously rethink their approach to this whole therapy game.

The micro quad is a four bunk cabin on an Improved St. Laurent Class destroyer. Four bunks, four lockers, one desk space, and four junior officers crammed in for weeks at a time while the ship was deployed. Rumour has it that someone once sent a request to the Department of Agriculture to find out how many pigs you could raise in a space that size and the answer was none. Brilliant, can't raise a pig in there but it was good for four Subbies (Sub Lieutenants in the Navy). Space on board is always at a premium and every available space is used for something. Wasting it on luxury accommodations for junior officers, untrained ones at that, was never going to happen. But it sure helped develop a phobia of enclosed spaces.

"How are we today?"

"Lovely, just frigging lovely". Sarcasm dripped off each word, the tone unmistakable. How the frig did he think I was? I was heavily medicated, my life was a shambles, my relationship with my family a train wreck, and I felt like killing myself more often than not. How did he want me to answer the question? I had been meeting with this guy for a while now. Every single week, week in week out. Mostly the sessions followed a similar pattern and I think we both just wound up frustrated. He was frustrated because he couldn't get inside my defenses and I was frustrated because he kept trying.

It's like we were watching the same episode of a bad show every week. The dialogue went something like this.

Him: I do not care what you think, I want to know what you feel.

Me: What I think…. (He had a no chance in hell of getting me to talk about my feelings. Most of them were medicated into oblivion or I just did not give a shit!)

Then it happened. After months of therapy, the dialogue took a different turn. I don't know if he got pissed off or what. But he raised his voice. Bad idea.

"I don't care what you think! Tell me what you feel!" he insisted.

"So Doc, you really want to know what I feel?"

"Yes."

"Okay, today I feel like I will not kill you." Each word was measured.

"Don't say things you don't mean."

"Look Doc, you crossed Robie Street at about 8:37 with a gray rain coat draped over your left arm. If I wanted you, I had you. So just be thankful that today I do not feel like I will kill you."

The tension in the air was clear, palpable, and electric.

He stared at me in stunned, shocked silence.

"So Doc, you still interested in what I feel?"

The session finished.

One of us was clearly rattled, and I didn't feel like it was me.

The Beast

Woe to You Oh Earth and Sea

For the Devil sends the beast with wrath

Because he knows the time is short

Let him who have understanding

Reckon the number of the beast

For it is a human number

Its number is six hundred and sixty six.

> Excerpted Number of the Beast-
> Iron Maiden

I do not know the exact date, though I am sure some research will dig it up, but I have no inclination to do so. Not that it would matter.

"… We do not believe that…." It does not matter what came before. It does not matter what comes after. Whoever we is, had the nerve, the unmitigated gall to tell, in this case me, that they did not believe me. I do not care what it was that they didn't believe.

Snap. At that moment, that instant it was over.

I dropped the phone on to the table. I walked away as it still rattled off the hardwood of my dining room table. I would kill myself. I was done. I was completely spent. I had no more anger. I had no more resolve. I had nothing. Everything I believed I had learned, everything that I believed I stood for. Everything from the top of my head to the tips of my toes, every thought, every action, my very essence was being questioned by some nameless, faceless bureaucrat. I was a shell and I would rectify that very soon. Death was honestly the solution. My death. Not that I hadn't dealt with suicidal thoughts before. If practice makes perfect, then by that train of thought, I was pretty damn good at it. In my case to have the internal discussion meant that there was the smallest glimmer of hope. Now there was none.

I had no emotion left.

They had won.

I had no will.

They had done it. They finally accomplished what had never been done. I quit. I was broken beyond all repair. No more than you could retrieve a shattered crystal vase and return it to its former self, would that work with me. I am not talking about a stress crack. I am talking about thousands of shards of broken glass, certainly not resembling anything like its former essence. Definitely not functional.

Shattered.

Complete and total devastation.

I was broken. Every ounce of will that I once had was gone, drained from me. No more, I could not take any more of anything. What happened inside of me in that instant I am not sure if I will ever recover from? Definitely they had shattered the very last shred of trust that I had, I felt one thing: betrayal.

Whoever they was they had finally succeeded in doing what had never been accomplished before. I QUIT!

They were victorious and just like a cold wind can suck the warmth out of a room, a darkness unlike anything I had ever felt descended upon me. The death wish came racing in from everywhere at once. I was going to die, and I was going to do it. I would die by my own hand.

All the years leading up to my military service had been spent learning lessons about not quitting. Then some of the world's best, BOTC, Rook camp, combat arms battle school, the football field, the remainder of my time at RMC, years spent learning to become an operational Naval Aviator, the fleet, all had pushed my limits. They had bent me. They had tested me. Some of the struggles much easier than others, but I had not quit. I would always find the resolve somewhere deep inside me. The passions, fury and joie de vive that I had once felt were gone. A man who had cheated death so many times, been to the very edge of the abyss, was going to kill himself. I was that man. They were VAC (Veterans Affairs Canada).

I had stood beside my oldest daughter and watched her fight. What I thought I knew about bravery and courage was nothing compared to her. She embraced everything that I was not. She had faced and beaten cancer three times by the age of thirteen. She defied all odds and graduated (if there is such a thing) from the palliative care unit. Her back was so messed up that they had grafted her fibula into her back as a strut graft. A year in a body brace and learning to walk again were just some of the challenges she faced. She had what I did not have. She had a will to live. When she was ten she was told, in a very kind and loving way, what the outcome was, the march of the inevitable. That is something that no one should have to face, but older in life you should have a better skill set to help cope and bring it into perspective. Ten years old and being told cancer would claim your life, probably within the next year, is something that goes beyond the realm of human comprehension and experience. She did not want to die and willed herself to be better. For me, living in the darkness was so horrific that I was going to do it. I would kill myself. The daily thoughts of doing it over the course of years had allowed me to formulate a plan that would work. This time was different. In my mind, all those other times, there were always some nagging doubts and unanswered questions. This time there was resolution. I did not care if I had shaken hands with the Reaper before. This time I would embrace Death with a huge hug. Death would not have to wait long.

I had long since removed any firearms from my home. Not that I was violently opposed to weapons and what they may or may not have stood for. The brutal reality is that there were more than enough times that I would have, if I'd had access, used them. I had been trained. I would pull the trigger. In this case it would be my twelve gauge. There would be no mistakes.

The absolutely scary part is how fast all this can explode from somewhere deep inside you and instantly and immediately take over your thoughts.

As I stood looking out over the ocean from my living room, the only thing I heard was my wife. She was seriously laying into it someone with everything she had. I can actually not ever remember seeing her being this angry. She was pulling words out of the "military lexicon" that would have made some of the Drill Sergeants and Directing Staff grin.

"You idiots. Do you have any idea what you have done to him? Can't you fucking read? Who do you think you are? He has had specialists for years trying to tell you how bad it was inside his body and you, who would never stand up for anything, question them. Even worse, you are questioning him. You will never know. But I do!"

What followed next was the phone being slammed on the table for emphasis and then my wife gave it to them some more. As Alice Cooper would say, "Welcome to my nightmare." They heard, first hand, her version of what had transpired for almost twenty years. The events were not pretty and in some cases the cuts of just listening to her unload was almost as bad as the hell I was in. She had her own hell, and it was worse than mine. Someone was the guest star, the main character in "Welcome to my fucked up world." I was that person.

My wife is a strong person like no other. Now she was as mad as a wet hornet and someone would feel her sting. Remember she had put up with crap that comes with being a military spouse and she was great at "sucking it up." She was repetitively taking one for the team. Direct hits amidships. The ship that was our marriage should have gone down for the count. Somehow she had managed to keep it afloat but she was running out of options real quick. She was like a cornered animal and she fighting mad. She had become me. The will, the desire, the fire and the passion was all hers.

To those of you who live with someone like me. You, know exactly what a tempest it can be. Most of the times I was numb. I would tell the joke that "I had an emotion once, but it died of loneliness." I was absolutely spent and there was not one iota of gas left in the tank. When I did show any emotion it usually started at anger and most times rapidly accelerated to rage. I was very much like the Incredible Hulk, who once angered could not control what was happening, and genuinely, most of it was actually not good.

Anti-psychotics, anti-depressants, anti-convulsants, and a whole pile of other medications had absolutely rendered me a chemical zombie. I was dead man walking with no desire to live.

I had huge gaps in reality and memory even though I may have appeared to have been functioning and coping. I was really in trouble, not that I cared anymore. I had family all around me who cared. I could not reciprocate. They say that one is the loneliest number and that I shall never dispute that.

By now things had deteriorated to me hiding in my room. Some days the simplest of questions by my kids were enough to finish me. If anything, even the slightest irritation, set me off, then Dad would lose it. The expression walking on eggshells barely scratched the surface. I was actually a time bomb with a really short fuse that had no control.

One thing happened though when the missus had her go at VAC. Even though I knew it, I never felt it, and not because I did not want to, I could not! Somebody had my back. Somebody was laying it all out there for me. My wife was doing what nobody else was. There was a spark. Not of drive, not of will, not of passion nor fire. The tiniest of sparks was just a little bit of trust. I had spent years pushing her away and trying to protect her from the horrors of my mind. Now I know this to be a huge mistake. Back then that was all I had. The images and the thoughts were ever present and decidedly not helping me, they sure as hell weren't going to help her.

Failed Attempt

The pain of today makes it simple to wish for no more tomorrows. No more night terrors. No more disappointments. Not having to deal with the anger or the rage. Not having to stare into the depths of despair racked with self-doubts. Second guessing yourself... what if? The woulda coulda shoulda's... what if I had not... It's so easy to glance at life through the retrospectoscope and wonder how things would have been different if only...

The feel of the rope in one's hand is heavy, but there is a purpose. Simple, wrap up all the anguish and make it go away. Wrap it up and finish it, once and for all. No more pain. No more self-doubts. No more anguish. How many times had I gone to therapy and came home feeling worse? Trying to explain the warring negative emotions that rule each day. How is it that the most positive thing you can think of is to end your life and the rest of it goes downhill from there?

Thirteen turns in a rope. The Hangman's Noose. The rope has some serious heft to it. Its purpose is to snap one's neck as part of the hanging process. Quick, painless and over. Over... no more. I just can't take it anymore. Looking into the abyss of darkness, no happiness, no joy – just more of the same. SSDD- same shit different day. Sinking into a quagmire of desperation. Nothing, absolutely nothing feels good.

What would have happened if... Your mind wanders off on tangents trying to second guess your actions. How would the story be right now if only... and then you start running the countless scenarios through your head. So many decisions, so many different branches on the decision tree that could have led to a different outcome. But they didn't. You are stuck with what happened and how it has affected you. Damn. Woulda coulda shoulda all shaped by the reality of "did".

In therapy, the two sides square off over and over.

"You know Doc, the rational side of me tries to compartmentalize and deal with what happened and frame it all in some logical sequence guided by the framework of what should be a rational thought process. You know what sucks? Sucks large? All of that gets swept away in the flood of reality of what actually happened out there."

"So what did happen?" The question, honest, sincere and yet one more attempt to get inside the walls of my defenses.

"What happened? Shit happened. Really bad shit. You ever stare into the depths of hell?"

"What do you mean?" An attempt to frame the question and put it into perspective.

"Look Doc, I am talking about something so horrific that the very thing itself makes you question everything you think? Challenges you. Rocks you. Shakes you to the very core?"

Once again, the probe about to come. "Can you give me an example?"

"Doc, I turned around on that deck and I stared at the first injured guy. Buddy tapped me on the shoulder as I was kneeling on the deck trying to get the Stokes litter rigged. Doc, I have never ever seen anything like that…"

The floor falls away beneath me, the certificates on the wall, the walls themselves disappear, and I am gone. Back into the shit, the dark, into the place that swallows me and drags me down and holds deep. Maybe this is what it would be like forever if the rope holds.

I have no idea how long I am gone … Lost in space and time, immersed in thoughts and images.

"Are you still with me?" Gentle, guiding and trying to get me back from wherever I was. He wanted to know. I wanted to run.

"Fuck this shit Doc. I'm done. I have had enough." I am beat to a pulp and I can sense that one more time he thought he was going to get inside, to get a glimpse of some of the things that were in fact tormenting me. Not today. I don't think so.

Radar Love

I've been drivin' all night,

My hand's wet on the wheel

There's a voice in my head

That drives my heel....

The lyrics to Golden Earring's Radar Love and its hard driving beat scream from the car speakers with the volume maxed out, the windows down, and the sunroof wide open. The cold wind whips in and yet I feel nothing.

I glance over at the dash clock, 4:55. The needle on the speedometer is climbing fast. Too fast. Who gives a flying fuck? Posted speed limit my ass. Eighty, ninety, one hundred and climbing. The line between life and death blurs and I keep my foot on the accelerator. One twenty, one thirty and climbing. I can't feel anything. Nothing. I am completely ambivalent. One fifty heading for one sixty kilometers per hour.

I hammer the brakes and steer through the middle of the corners, flattening out the line and bleeding off the speed as the tires shriek and burn. Damn... nothing... my heart rate remains unchanged and I feel completely disengaged. I am a stranger in my own body. Detached, I watch from somewhere outside myself as I go through the motions of driving. How is it possible to feel nothing? How is it possible to ignore the forces of gravity, the cold, and the pounding beat of a favorite song?

This disconnected nothingness could not be more different than the 4:30 night terror wake up call.

I jump with a start. My heart pounds like a jackhammer and I need to run, to get away. I am soaked, covered in a clammy sweat that has soaked the bed. I am disoriented and I need to be anywhere but here. I don't know where, just not here. I look over at my wife, who once again is going to awake to an empty bed. I slip quietly from the room, trying not to wake her. I slink out of the house and into the car. Maybe today I can feel something other than the sheer terror that has shattered my sleep? I don't need an alarm clock. The images will crawl from deep out of my subconscious and present themselves on the big screen of my dreams. No, they are not dreams. Dreams imply something pleasant. There is nothing pleasant about a panic and an anxiety so severe that you believe that this time you are going to die in your sleep, trapped, shrieking, and unable to wake up, unable to feel. The intensity of the sleeping horror is the flip side of the waking moments when I do not feel at all. Even at a hundred and sixty klicks in a tight turn. Heavily medicated, nothing seems to register. No positives. Detached indifference. Complete ambivalence to living or dying.

I push myself to the edge to see if I can jumpstart feelings. Today, once again the sensation of speed fails to do it. Perhaps the pin. A long seamstress pin. I reach over and disengage it from the seat beside me and stab it into my leg. Nothing. Is it the meds? Or something else? What it is, is nothingness.

I eventually make my way home and sit in the car listening to music. Maybe tonight is the night, the night I get to sleep through without the visions from hell shattering my sleep and beating me up with the mental two by four. I would not bet on it though.

How many times this scene has played out has blurred. I have tried other methods to jump start an emotional response. They too have failed. Nothing works. I am a shell with an emptiness so deep and dark that I doubt anything can live in the shadows. The stream of nagging what ifs and woulda coulda shoulda's haunt me as I search for answers. None appear. Logic is blurred and beaten into a form that is barely recognizable. I have a strange premonition that the doctors are going to jack up my meds again. Our conversations about my complete indifference to life, *particularly my life*, will precipitate the next in a series of increases in the meds that has continued unabated for years. I don't sleep well. I can't find peace when I am awake. Nothing interests me for more than a few moments. It's wrong, and I know it, and there's nothing I can do about it.

Part Three:

New Beginnings

I have stood.

I have stood at the gates of hell,

On the prec'pice of the dark abyss,

Shadow boxing the Grim Reaper.

Glimpsing Horrors of bottomless well.

I have stood at my Heaven's Gate,

To glimpse the views of Paradise,

Only to tumble further downward,

Wracked with Anger, Rage and Hate.

I have stood at the gates of hell,

On the prec'pice of the dark abyss,

Swearing solemn Deity Filled Oaths,

While praying for my Eternal Soul.

I have stood at my Heaven's Gate,

To glimpse the views of Paradise,

Only to know, my life, my work,

My service dog, my destined fate.

Cous -Jan 2013

Dilligaf
Approximately September 2011

Big, burly, looking every inch the "Biker" stereotype. Long flowing hair held back in a ponytail, and a huge beard to match, black leathers and a vest adorned with patches and pins, and a cane in his hand. He moved with pain, it was in his essence just as the tattoos that adorned his massive forearms would be there forever. Judge the book by the cover and what you would miss was one of Canada's best living military historians and a man who in the past ten years has ridden his motorcycle and sidecar across Canada fifteen times using it as a vehicle of outreach.

Paul "Trapper" Cane is a legend in the Veterans' motorcycling community, and to those who know his story, a man with very few equals. Trapper's injuries are the result of a night time parachute jump gone horribly wrong. He had tangled chutes with another jumper and when he cut away to try and function his reserve, the one hundred and eighty foot free fall to the ground was about sixty feet short of the required height. He hit the ground at "one hell of a rate of knots" and shattered pretty much everything.

Twenty two surgeries later and he was left with a constant reminder of how life can change in an instant. Many would just pack up their toys and spend their life living in the spot on Desolation Boulevard between resignation and despair. Not Trapper. His motorcycle kept him sane and he realized that there were many smashed up veterans who could use the camaraderie of the military that had been lost when they left the Forces, many of them unwillingly and nursing their own injuries.

That was exactly how Trapper had found me. I first met Trapper at the Digby Wharf Rat Motorcycle rally. As is the norm with veterans, we started to play the "where were you and who do you know" to establish bonafides. In our case, it was real quick. I had spied the white maple leaf on his jump wings, indicating active service with the Canadian Airborne Regiment.

"Do you know Pete Kenward?" My opening volley in the game.

"That I do, I served with him several times." Trapper went on to recount a story about an exercise with then LCol Kenward. Trapper was a former Patricia (PPCLI), a pathfinder and a sniper.

"Captain Kenward was my platoon commander at Basic." We had nicknamed him Captain Canada; all those who have ever served with Kenward knew him as a man of uncompromising standards and as a man who commanded respect out of the extreme levels of personal performance that he displayed. The image of him launching into a freefall swan dive off the mountainside in Chilliwack the day we went rappelling for the first time is not something one ever forgets.

From that initial who did you know where and when, the beginnings of a friendship were sparked. In time I heard the story of Trapper's accident and the founding of the CAV, the Canadian Army Veterans Motorcycle Units. I have to admit, it was comforting to know someone who was as crazy as I was.

In the next two years, I ran into Trapper out on the road a few more times, and in each encounter both of us learned something about the other. A mutual respect deepened. Then came the night when Trapper came and spent the night at our house. Trapper was on the East Coast swing of one of his cross country jaunts and we provided R & Q. (Rations and Quarters).

We sat up late into the night and we talked and shared. He knew I was hurting. He knew that there had to be something that had driven a former aviator to the point where he had lived his life by the "Dilligaf" motto. Dilligaf: Do I look like I give a Fuck? I undoubtedly did not. I had pretty much given up on most everything, including myself. I really did not care if I lived or died. I hoped death would be a liberation from the night terrors that haunted me, the twisted sights and sounds of torment.

Trapper, a natural born leader, realized that I had no reason to live. Something or Someone had squashed my soul and extinguished the fire of life within me. But he knew better than to give me a "pull yourself up by the bootstraps and get a grip on yourself" lecture.

Very late that night, my wife got out one of the newspaper articles and showed it to Trapper.

"You want to know what happened. This! And how he was treated afterward, or more specifically, was not treated." Trapper read the article and responded with his characteristic "Man Oh Man."

"Sounds like it was one hell of a night out there…." I could see him trying to construct the images of what the article had described.

"Yeah, it was one hell of a shit show."

In the next two hours, Trapper asked leading questions and gently probed, trying to flesh out the story.

"That is how you arrive at Dilligaf. You arrive at a point where you have been so far in the abyss that you really do not care anymore."

"I do know." I believed him, for Trapper was a man who had been to his own version of Hell and back.

In time, the Dilligaf patch on my vest was replaced by a new one that Jocelyn had found.

"I survived Shit Creek." I was on the road to recovery.

Reid's email.
December, 2011

I stare at the screen and I blink several times. The knot in my stomach rises and I find myself drifting back to a place that I have visited so many times before. I am out at sea, thinking about so many aspects of what had happened. Today was very different though. I had worked up the courage to ask a buddy a huge favour.

Reid "Reid-O" McBride had been in our wedding party, he was with me at RMC for the last two years, at Nav school, a teammate with the Shearwater Flyers Rugby team, at the Seaking OTU, but he was one who had washed out and went on to become an Aurora Nav. No shame, just the reality of the job in a SeaKing. Being a TACCO was intense and demanding and not everyone thrived in the chaos that was Helicopter Anti-submarine Warfare. But Reid also has another linkage. One that I had very rarely, if ever mentioned to anyone else other than Jocelyn. Reid had been airborne the night of the 6th of October 1986 except he had the luxury of watching the events from the CP 140 Aurora that was flying top cover for us. Since he had been at the SeaKing OTU and passed the phase one Utility flying phase, he was more than familiar with what we were attempting that night. I had never discussed that night with him. Same went for the other crew members airborne, except for the now deceased Doc Hagey.

I had finally, after decades reached out in December of 2011 to ask him if I could get a scan of his log book, any photos of that night and a synopsis of his recollections. I figured that years from now, the kids might like to have this stuff for their benefit. Perhaps I was seeking validation of the events and the craziness. In January of 2012, I got his response. His reply follows and the impact that night had on him was not inconsequential.

Hi Medric,

Here is my logbook scan, as well as a better scan of the photo of the vessel that was in my logbook.

I am trying to get the Mission Report (Purple) for the flight pulled, but it has been a long time, so am not sure if an electronic copy still exists.

Anyway, my crew was tasked with a Type 9 mission (fisheries patrol) when we got a call from RCC about a Sword fishing boat that had 2 guys badly injured after falling into the reeling machine the hauled in the line. We were tasked to find the vessel and then provide top cover for the Nipigon Sea King while it did the rescue. Due to the distances involved, the Nipigon was still outside helo range, so she was making flank speed to a location where the helo could launch. As the helo would be on a max range profile, there wasn't a lot of time for the helo to effect the rescue and get back to the ship to refuel, before continuing on to St Johns. We gave you guy's direct vectors to the *Sea Hawk* where the hoisting was extremely difficult due to the limited amount of deck space and the large amount of masts and other obstructions. The Sea State didn't help, as the vessel was bobbing around pretty good, so you got dunked a few time and knocked around against the boat until you finally made it on board and brought the first injured crewman to the helicopter, with the process repeated a second time for the second fellow.

As I recall, one fellow died enroute to St Johns, possibly on the Nipigon while you were steaming to get within helo range of St Johns, and the second fellow died in the St Johns hospital.

As can be seen from the logbook entry, we recovered in St Johns and spent the night after a 13.8 hr flight, flying back to Greenwood the next day (doing Bag Stuart's Instrument Check Ride). JP Germain is listed a Crew Commander, but he was really Pilot Standards, along to make it legal as Kevin Lasher, a USN exchange officer, was just finishing up his upgrade procedure. We also did another coordinated T9 with the Nipigon later in the month, so Nipigon was obviously out doing a Fishpat/WUPS type patrol.

On a personal note, after that I decided to go ahead and buy the new RX7 I had been on the fence about for the previous 2 years (When Roots and I rolled the 260Z on Caldwell Rd). While it wasn't a great investment, I was a young single Captain and could afford it. You only go through life once and after seeing this event, you realise that life is pretty fragile and can end at any time.

If I get the Purple I will send that along.

Best of luck with your project.

Reido

"You only go through life once and after seeing this event, you realize that life is pretty fragile and can end at any time."

The words leapt off the page and into my cranium. If that was what he was thinking from a few hundred feet in the air, I guess it sure explains my thoughts and feelings.

Bullseye.

New Beginnings
06 August, 2012

I am a caged tiger. I have been for the past couple weeks but now the nervous energy, the anxiety and the symphony of self-doubts have hit a crescendo. The church hall is cool, large and spacious, neat rows of tables with a few chairs at each and a clock on the wall. I stare intently at the clock, having picked out a seat that will allow quick access to the exit and allow me to sit with my back covered and keep an eye on everyone in the room. Old habit or self-protection mechanism matters not. I am not going to have anyone approach me from behind without me knowing it. I swear the hands on the clock are going backwards.

We flew into Kansas City, Missouri on Saturday afternoon and we are now in Concordia, Kansas. I would probably never have made it here ever, except for one huge thing. My service dog was coming from a School called CARES (Canine Assistance and Rehabilitation Education Services) located in this sleepy, small town in the middle of the Midwest farming and cattle country. On the drive here we'd passed several herds of cattle, lots of range space, and all kinds of crops, most of which had either been harvested or burnt to a crisp under the hot summer sun.

In about twenty minutes class would start, and it could not come too soon. I had been unable to fall back to sleep after my usual four thirty visit from the horrible images in my mind. I tossed and turned and started second guessing my decision. My biggest fear? What if the dog didn't work? What if this was just another in a long string of failures in trying to make peace with my past and getting help to move back from the brink? Not that many months had passed since my last serious run through with the plan to ensure no tomorrows. I could not take the stress. PTSD sucked the life out of me and I could not find pleasure in anything, anywhere, at any time. Darkness, desolation, and isolation had become my constant companions.

"What if…" There were a lot of those. I could second guess myself to death and at times nearly had. The death part. Freedom.

Liberation from the relentless onslaught of the darkness that gripped my soul.

I swear the clock is going backwards even as the room begins to fill with other families, all of whom are there to obtain their service or therapy dog as needed. All I know is that I am drowning and need a life preserver and fast. I'd asked for a German Shepard on my application. My thought process was that maybe the dog would help keep people away from me. I should have told them flat out I did not want a poodle, a doodle or any other froo-froo dog. That wasn't me, but it was too late. In about an hour, we would be meeting our new partners and Joc could tell my anxiety meter was pegged. I was a bag of jangled nerves and was having serious trouble focusing.

"Good Morning, Ladies and Gentlemen." Sarah Holbert's voice was kind, and inviting, but still had an air of authority. "Today you will meet your new dogs and we will commence your team training immediately. First we need to cover of a few administrative points."

My mind checked out completely. Jocelyn was here to take notes and I was lost in the quagmire of the previous two and a half decades of my struggle with PTSD.

I glanced up at the clock and it was now about forty five minutes from when I had last been aware of the time or my surroundings. Stress had pushed me way out there this time. I hate it when it happened but this time if it had, I am sure Jocelyn would have said something.

"Megan and I are going to start bringing in the dogs and one by one we will introduce them to you and tell you a little bit about them." With that the first of the dogs appeared. A yellow lab, then a golden retriever, another lab and yet another yellow lab.

This fourth dog bolted from Megan and tore the leash out of her hand and I disappeared in a flurry of slobbery wet kisses. This dog was genuinely excited and I hoped that the owner could handle this little fireball.

"I see you have met your girl Thai. She is yours. She is part of the hot litter. The weather was smoking hot here in Kansas when she was born, so all of the litter was named after hot things." Megan continued to talk but I was lost in a sea of elation. She wasn't a

Shepard and she sure as hell wasn't a Poodle and she honestly seemed to like me. The tears flowed freely down my cheeks as I stared into her big brown eyes.

"Thai. You are such a sweetie. I hope I do not frig this up."

The rest of the class received their dogs, one by one, but I was oblivious. I was too concerned with Thai. She was now my responsibility. I could not get over the calm disposition of all the other dogs except Thai. I had gotten the class clown. Only later, weeks later, would I come to understand her initial behaviors, but for now she was my goofy little girl. In the coming days I would learn the skills I needed to come up to speed on what she had been taught.

The CARES program matches dogs based on the interviews and arranges the pairings. I was not sure I was up to Thai or if they had gotten the pairing right. In time both would be proven right.

Night Terror Intervention
Late August, 2012

I awake with a start from the dreams, from the nightmarish images. My heart is racing and I want to run. This time, however, it is different. Very different. I feel something licking my hand and a presence in the bed.

What the…?

Then as my head clears and my heart rate slows and the hammering in my chest subsides I become aware of Thai's presence on the bed beside me.

"Hey Joc?"

I whisper gently at first.

"Joc?"

My voice becomes a little louder, the tone more insistent.

"What is it?" she mumbles. She is still mostly asleep and clearly unimpressed by being awoken yet again in the very early hours of the morning.

"You are never going to believe this. Look beside me." I am hoping she is going to roll over and witness what I am feeling. Thai, the little lady yellow lab who has been paired with me is up on the bed having left her bed beside ours, and is licking my hand and nudging me. The big brown eyes and floppy ears are a welcome relief. She is right there with me and was trying to wake me up. I glance over at the clock.

It is 4:25.

The impact of the time hits me like a freight train. Thai has been trying to wake me before 4:30, the appointed time for the night terror to take control.

I don't know how she knows, how she does it, and I don't care. What I do know is that after decades of night terrors and broken sleep, I have just awoken to Thai trying to wake me up before things escalated into a full blown night terror. Four thirty in the morning. Alive, awake, with the screaming shrieking over the yawning abyss short circuited this time by my dog. By my beautiful dog. By my fully trained up loving dog.

The darkness of the cabin on the frigate can swallow you. Below decks there's no natural light. Inside of a ship are dark recesses where all light is artificial. It's a place where sailors and airmen sleep as the noises of the ship blend to form a dull melody that drifts you off to sleep. In this case, my cabin is shared with the Ships Diving Officer and Senior SAC (Shipborne Aircraft controller). I quietly slip from my lower bunk and don my flight suit. I cannot sleep. I am a bag of jangled nerves and even though I have to brief and launch in a couple of hours to take the injured crewman to an oil rig where they will be transferred to a Labrador Helicopter with a doctor on board, I am too stressed to sleep.

I make my way down the passageways over to Sick Bay. I open the door and stick my head in. "Doc" Hagey, the Ship's Senior Medical Assistant looks like I feel, and that is not good.

"How they doing Doc?" Having risked my life to get them this far I was emotionally committed to them making it. I, we, all of us had risked so much to get them to safety and medical treatment.

"Not good." Doc was being brutally honest and sharing what I had suspected. "The trauma is so severe, the blood loss and shock are not good." I knew which of the two he was referring to. "I suspect the other has massive internal injuries and his vitals are unstable." I nod knowingly and look over his shoulder at his assistant who is trying to bring comfort to the men. I don't know what to do, what to say, and I struggle to make sense of what has happened. I am haunted by the thoughts of what could have happened if we'd got them on the first attempt. What if we had gotten them medical attention two hours earlier? I am lost deep in thought.

"You ok?" Doc is asking about me this time. He'd seen what had transpired out there and heard the intercom chatter as I had been smacked off the back of the vessel and crashed into the wheelhouse.

"Doc, I am stiff and sore. I got the feeling back in my right side, but the worst is my stomach." I didn't need to finish the sentence.

He knew. He also knew that I was about to go flying and therefore he couldn't medicate me. We sat there in Sick Bay, both of us, lost in thoughts. I know mine were trying to come to terms with things I had never seen and done. I suspected the same for Doc.

"When you get back after this sortie you come and see me." I think he was worried about me. Hell, I was worried about me. I told him about the aches and pains from the physical battering on deck, but there was nothing I could tell him about the knot in my stomach and the lump in my throat from the thoughts and doubts and scary movie that had already begun to play on its endless loop.

"Doc, I am off to the ops room. See ya later."

Back in my bed I ponder the powerful unknown complex mechanism that is the mind. How it puts things together in its filing system is a mystery. All I know is that this morning, just before 4:30, for the first time ever, the entire nightmare array had been interrupted and it was a furry, four legged wet nosed savior that had done it. My faith in Thai is growing by leaps and bounds. There is an old aviation adage that you have got to trust your instruments. In this case, I need to trust a dog who is showing she could become my emotional early warning system.

I reach down and rub her ears.

"You are such a good girl." Her otter tail wags excitedly and thumps against my leg. I don't have the nerve or inclination to kick her off the bed after she's just pulled my ass out of the fires of night terror Hell. Instead, I choose to let her snuggle in as I try and drift back to sleep. Could it be that after decades of struggles, help has finally arrived?

Down By The Sea
September, 2012

The slow rhythmic crash of the waves onto the shore is a constant reminder of the ebb and flow of the ocean. Constant, unrelenting and ever present, the ocean serves as a reminder of how big the world is and, for myself, just how small I am.

I often take Thai for long walks down by the ocean and try and make peace with her. After all these years I still struggle with the events of that night.

There is a point in the sequence of events, after I stepped out of the helicopter and into the darkness, that I was launched about thirty five feet through the air to land at the base of a moving wall of water as high as a house. Looking up into the black night, neck deep in the ocean, one can absolutely understand miniscule. The relative motions of the fishing vessel, the helicopter, and the waves choreographed a complex dance of intricate movements that were chaotic and uncontrolled. Mathematicians contend that they can describe these types of complex motions with a set of equations. No definition could bring order to this jumble.

To me, it was like being tossed about like a nut on a string. Powerless, hanging on for dear life, shadow boxing the Grim Reaper, realizing how helpless I was. The sequence of events that first set up my "aerial ballet" quickly reversed themselves and before I knew it I started skipping across the waves on a path that would inevitably intersect with the vessel's stern.

As I flew across the wave tops I can confirm that the adage about your life flashing before your eyes is true. I can also tell you that in the split seconds it took, I knew the impact was unavoidable and would hurt. My right side crashed into the transom, hard. The pain exploded in an instant, even as I watched the wake and screws in the roiling ocean beneath me. This perspective was momentary, for in the next instant I was launched upward into the overhead wires and rigging, some taut, straining against the shrieking wind, others broken and useless, except as lashes for whipping the sky and SAR crewman. The skills honed as a D-lineman on the RMC football team were immediately pressed back into service as I tried to disengage from the ropes and wires.

I am brought back to the here and now by Thai. Once again she pulls me back into the moment, somehow knowing that my thought process was a runaway freight train of emotional dysfunction that would result in a crash causing me to shut down and withdraw. Her body check on my left leg is unmistakable and comforting as I walk along the trails.

The trails.

Where one foot goes in front of the other, over and over, and where Thai is always ready.

"You are such a good girl."

I reach down and gently rub underneath her ears. It's one of her favorites and she needs to know when I am happy with her actions, which makes a positive re-enforcement necessary.

My thoughts drift off to another distant place. I wonder if those in the medical community who dismiss the use of Psychiatric Service Dogs in the treatment of PTSD have an explanation for what just transpired. The Law of One Sixty Eight is in the forefront of my consciousness. There are certain rules that are immutable; there are the same number of days in a week and hours in a day available to each of us, one hundred and sixty eight. The dilemma, the conundrum that faces all who struggle with the ever present monster of PTSD, is that the beast rises up and attacks on its own schedule, relentless in its onslaught. The problem remains that if one is lucky they get an hour a week with their mental health care professional. One. If they're lucky. What about the other one hundred and sixty seven hours? That's where Thai comes in: as my constant companion standing ever vigilant to deal with the issues that arise. Perhaps most disturbing is that in many cases I was unaware when the issues were transpiring. But Thai knows. Her acute sense of smell detects the changes in my bio-chemistry immediately. She picks up on the pheromones released by my skin. Thai is my emotional early warning system and can alert me to problems as they fire up, before they get out of control, before the freight train gathers momentum. Her body check short circuits the process. I put one foot in front of the other. Thai takes up station on my left.

I continue my walk, struck by the beauty and solitude of nature. The call of the seagulls are a staccato punctuation mark in the stillness, their shrill calls a reminder that there is a huge world out there. For years I couldn't enjoy simple pleasures like this because I was cut off and isolating myself. The panic and anxiety attacks were bad, the dissociative episodes were worse, and my coping mechanism was to avoid any situation where I thought they could occur. Eventually that place became everywhere and I was a bag of jangled nerves in any situation. Now, thankfully, with Thai's assistance, I can make it back out into the places from which I had cut myself off. Do I make it everywhere? No, not even close. There remains certain places that still push me to the edge and Thai helps drag me back and keep me grounded. I often find myself asking a very simple question: what would my mental healthcare team do in this situation to head off my issues? How would they alert me to their onset if I am completely unaware of their presence and impending interruption of my day?

I don't have an answer but I do know one thing- with Thai helping me I have made more progress in the last few months than I have made in the decades preceding her arrival in my life. The rope in my hands is a leash, and a lifeline, to Thai. It's no longer that noose I tied all those years ago.

Coming Out
October, 2012

Thai and I are walking along in the company of someone who is prepping us for some media work. They are trying to get as much background on Thai and me as they can so they can decide how the segment will proceed. They want to know what is pertinent and what had shaped my journey.

"How did you get paired up with Thai?" The question is earnest and honest, pure in purpose, with no hidden agenda.

It is a beautiful day, and I for one am just enjoying the moment and Thai's company. She is such a gift and in the few short months we have been together, she is already having such a huge impact.

I recount the process of going to CARES and how that had come about, and more importantly what a mess my life had become before Thai, the "BT", the before time.

"I could easily have been the mayor of 'Dysfunction Junction'. There was not much, if anything that was not being negatively affected by my PTSD and categorically was not a pretty place to be or operate from. If anything, it could best be described as a Reign of Terror."

We continue to walk on and share moments that helped give a better view of the complexity of PTSD and the multitude of negative effects and consequences that accompanied such a devastating mental injury. I prefer injury to illness since it is about something that happens to you, some event or sequences of events that is so far outside the realm of "normal" human experience that the result is the beginning of a group of symptoms that will leave the injured changed, shaped by consequence, and in some cases, perhaps destiny.

"Are you okay with telling your story?" This question hit hard and made me stop and think.

"Truth be told, I am nervous and a bag of jangled nerves, but yes, I will be okay. In many ways this will be a huge public "coming out" party." The reference to coming out was traditionally used for those who stepped out of the "Closet" and openly addressed their sexuality. A deep secret, shielded from society's view, to protect and guard both anonymity and those surrounding the individual.

"I get that. You realize that once we do this there is no chance of going back?" Again, honesty at the forefront.

"I crossed that bridge already. That happened on the sixth of August. One of the biggest struggles I had with getting a service dog would be my inability to hide. Before Thai, I suffered, mostly in silence, with an invisible disability. Some had their suspicions, very few knew for sure, because I was not inclined to share my past. But the day I got Thai, I turned an invisible disability into a very visible something. We are all familiar with guide dogs for the blind, and I am clearly not blind. Many assume I am training her for someone else, a visually impaired person, but I will not perpetuate that misconception. My stock answer is "she is trained and she works for me. I am the one with the issues." I generally let it go at that. If I get a sense I am talking to a veteran, a military member or a member of the First Responder community, Police, EHS, Fire, and 911 Operators for example, then I may be a little more forthcoming. So if I was worried about the genie getting out of the bottle and never being put back, I should have addressed that before the sixth of August."

Awash in a sea of emotions, we continue our walk and I am now introspective and contemplative. I could easily just walk off into the future, and I doubt anyone would begrudge me or my family our privacy and our space as I attempted to heal. But there were the voices, the voices inside my head, and in my heart.... "What about the others?" I knew that if I was ever going to have any peace in my mind and in my heart, I needed to find a way to help others get some of what I had got. I did not yet know how I would do that. The "how" would come in time. The answer would appear. All I knew currently was that there were countless others struggling with their demons, the beast, in their own private Hell, watching their families be destroyed. No, if coming out could help save another it would be worth it. Anything more than one would be an absolute bonus.

Hitting The Deck
October, 2012

The crow's sharp caw shattered the morning's tranquility. Thai and I were taking a leisurely stroll along a section of the Trans Canada Trail. Heading out from Caldwell Rd. to Bisset Rd. there is a five km section of trail that is ninety-five per cent woodlands and marshes. Though technically within Halifax Regional Municipality, it could be in any section of wilderness. By the time you get away from the trail heads, the noise of the roads and the cities are lost to nature's symphony. The wind in the trees, the running water, the complex diversity of birds and insects combine to drown out the stress of the city noise.

Peaceful, at least until the Crow.

I looked up into the tangle of branches and the overhead wire that runs alongside the trail. Wires and entanglements overhead. In an instant I am sucked into the vortex. Suddenly I am twenty feet in the air, the wires and rigging of the fishing vessel are right there. The wind is howling, the ocean is pounding, and I'm right back in the midst of my worst nightmares come true.

The complex forces of wind and wave conspire to hurtle me down onto the hydraulic line hauler and I am doing a pommel horse straddle to keep from being impaled. This is somewhere I do not wish to be, though unsure of how I am getting off it or what is next. My answer comes in a heartbeat when I'm airborne again. But this time I am swinging over the deck of the fishing vessel. It's as close as I've come to getting onboard and from a height of about twelve feet I work the quick release mechanism and free fall to the deck below. The coating of hydraulic fluid from the Sea King combined with the six inches of saltwater washing across the deck serve as the perfect slippery combination to launch me into the wheelhouse of the Sea Hawk.

Mercifully I hit starboard side to, the same side that hit the transom a few seconds before, so I felt nothing more. Agony is agony. I am on the deck. The noise of the gale, the vessel, the nearby freighter, and the helicopter combine to a where all I can do is scream and hope to be heard by the deck hand.

"Go get the most seriously injured first," I shout. He disappears from view and I set about the task of getting the Stokes litters onboard. Earlier in the day the decision had been made that we would send them both down at the same time so that once separated, we could load the second casualty while the first was being sent up to the helicopter. The litters are being buffeted and jostled about, swinging wildly in the air. Somehow, I still don't know how, we manage to get them onboard. I draw my Russell Belt knife and start separating the two litters. I am kneeling on the deck, awash in water, when I feel the tap on my shoulder.

Turning, I stare through the gates of Hell and see one of its tortured residents. Nothing, and I mean nothing, has prepared me for this. I want to puke. My stomach wretches and I heave. I am trying to remain calm and cool, trying to instill confidence, yet wondering how the apparition before me can still be alive. Mother of God Almighty, how has he survived? Guilt blossoms instantly. What if we had got him on the first launch? That would have been two hours ago. If nothing more, Doc could have slammed him full of morphine.

Something…

Anything…

Thai is up on me. Her paws hit me just above my waist. A physical reminder that my mental train of thought was derailing and heading somewhere very dark, very black and so counter-productive.

"Easy Girl. I am back with you." Once again, she knew when I did not. I had been dragged into a thought process that I have wrestled with more times than I ever care to remember. That is the problem. I do remember and I wish I could forget. I start back down the trail trying to enjoy nothing but Thai's company, haunted by the sights that never go away. That tap on the shoulder, the viscera and blood and gore. Don't ever tap me on the shoulder from behind. Ever.

Polaris Missile
November, 2012

The wind howls and the rain beats furiously on the windows and skylights. The storms are always more enjoyable from the dry side of the glass. The warmth of the gas fireplace takes the East Coast chill off the house. The staccato beat of the rain hammers off the patio deck just outside the glass doors. The darkness envelopes everything beyond the arcs of dull light escaping through the window. Tonight certainly is a night fit for neither man nor beast.

I am glad to be warm and dry and safe at home, and then in an instant I'm back at sea, back on the deck, back in hell.

The raindrops have become liquid barbs, driven by the fury of the gale augmented by the rotor wash of the Sea King hovering overhead. The wind and waves toss the deck and I marvel at skill of the hands-on flying miracle performed by Hans Kleeman who somehow manages to maintain station over the bobbing vessel. The same forces of physics that have launched me hither and yon like some human missile also threaten to destroy the Sea King and all souls aboard. At one point, a huge wave rolls by and I swear it is going to envelop the tail rotor. I wince and believe the helo is doomed. But the fishing vessel pitches and the optics change and the huge grey helicopter goes from an apparent tail stand in the ocean to hovering overhead while the Sea Hawk's whip antennas hungrily seek to disembowel the Sea King's fuel tanks. Absolutely nothing about this whole damn evolution is going anywhere near things for which we have planned or trained.

I struggle to get the most seriously injured into the first Stokes litter. He is a big man, solid, hard from years of work on the ocean. But he is shattered, torn apart from the violence of the accident earlier that day. I am lying through my teeth. I am trying to assure him that everything is going to be okay, and that the ship's Doctor was onboard the helicopter, ready and waiting to help. I knew that it probably didn't matter, but I was not going to tell him and I was shocked that he was still lucid. He could respond by squeezing my hand. His devastating injuries made speech impossible. I try to remain calm. My insides are like the ocean, churning and threatening to spill forth at any moment.

I finally get him secured in the Stokes litter, and then the deckhand and I maneuver the litter to the vessels edge to get him ready to head toward and into the safety of the helicopter. In a guideline transfer, the helo is at a forty-five degree angle and will climb in altitude to keep the Stokes litter and its precious cargo out of the water as it swings clear of the overhead obstructions of the guy wires on the vessel's stabilizers. That was the plan, and that is how we had executed it hundreds of times in training.

Just as we got the litter up on to the vessel's gunnel, the ship pitched violently and we were hit by another large wave. The Stokes litter disappeared under the wall of water and the guideline pulled through my wet hoisting gloves so violently they began to smoke. I know Hans was pulling collective as hard as he could to try and gain as much altitude as quickly as possible when the Stokes litter shot out of the ocean like a Polaris missile launched from fifteen feet under a wall of water to twenty five feet in the air in a second. I was trying not to get dragged into the North Atlantic for yet another dunking. I was trying not to spill my guts on the spot. We had work to do, unfinished business with another casualty.

Thai is up on my lap staring into my face. Another trip to some mental land of anguish from which she has hauled me back.

"Thai you are such a good girl." Her big brown eyes stare longingly into mine and her thick otter tail beats on my leg. I am not sure if she understands what she has done. All I know is that I am so very appreciative that she has. No matter how many times I hear the voices in my head say that the Stokes going under the water was not your fault, the fact remains that it was me that was there. They talk about having blood on your hands, most often in some figurative conversation. In my case it was very real, and very literal. You begin to question yourself. The horrible second guessing dance of macabre "what ifs?"

Thai hammers into me with both paws. She is very agitated. I think she's not real happy that she has dragged me back from the edge and I am still there, beating myself up, questioning what I did. It is not so easy to come up with answers when somebody dies. The answers are never easy.

Transom Jump
December, 2012

The trail is morphing from stone to mud. The rain is falling in driving sheets that are whipped into a frenzy by the winds. It's hard to imagine that drops of water can sting like this, with the fury of a wasp. But they can and do. I continue walking down the trail, once again caught out by the lies the weatherman told. I think most people would like to have a job where they could be wrong as often as the "weather guessers". The water is starting to pool in the tracks left behind on the trail and soon it will become slippery underfoot. I am hoping to get home before I am soaked to the bone and start to feel the effects of hypothermia. It doesn't take much for the wind and cool temperatures to suck the heat out of your core and for the shakes to start.

And then I'm shaking.

Hard.

The knots in my stomach are twisting tighter and the taste of bile is burning the back of my throat. The first of the injured is now enroute the helo.

"Go get the other injured," I yell. I scream as loud as I can knowing that the deckhand likely can't hear over the wind and torment. But I think the deckhand knows what I want as much by intuition as actually hearing what I say. The noise is deafening. I kneel to prepare the second Stokes litter and get ready for the next transfer. With any luck, we will not get hit with another rogue wave at the critical juncture of the evolution. I sure as Hell have no desire to see a repeat performance of what just happened. Everything that could have gone wrong from an environmental point of view sure as hell had. The aft end of the vessel was still awash in the remnants of the waves that were pounding the vessel mercilessly.

This time I hear the hatch slam shut as the deckhand approaches with the second casualty. He is deep in shock. Nothing registers with him as I try to reassure him and brief him on what is about to take place. I keep talking on the outside chance that it is getting through, but in my heart I know it isn't. The first of many second guesses start to haunt me. Why couldn't the other guy have been in shock, oblivious? This guy looks so much better from the outside, but his internal injuries do not show. He too is in dire shape – but different from what I had just witnessed.

After securing him in the litter, we get him to the transom and execute the guideline transfer flawlessly. Fuck. Why the hell did the other guy have to go all Voyage to the Bottom of the Sea? Why the fuck did the waves have to swallow him up? In in a flash, Ken and Al are manhandling the second Stokes litter into the back of the Sea King while I round up our make shift guideline. The crewman asks if I am staying aboard. All I can think is that you have got to be frigging crazy. I don't want to spend ten more seconds on this boat, let alone the two days it would take to traverse into St. John's. I want to throw up. My stomach is knotted tighter than a coiled python and all I can taste is bile. No, I want off the damn boat, now.

I look up and Ken is holding the horse collar out the back door. I wave him off as I have already put the quick release mechanism of the double lift harness back together. I want my hands free to be able to deal with anything that is going to come up after I bail out from the vessel and into the ocean. My plan is legitimately as simple as it gets. Stand on the gunnel and time my jump so that I can swing well clear of the vessel's stabilizers and into the open ocean. The biggest obstacle we might face is if the hoist jams. If it does I will be at the mercy of the elements in the North Atlantic. Strangely, this is a better option than staying on the boat. I want nothing to do with this floating slaughterhouse that has been the scene of such human carnage. Already the images have burned into my subconscious. How could anyone be alive after an accident like that? How could he have survived? Why couldn't we have gotten him earlier? The haunting doubts have begun… little did I know they would last for decades.

I scramble up on the transom and jump and for the first time something goes according to plan. I am clear of the ship and in the open ocean briefly before being hauled skyward to the Sea King.

Rescue One Nine was heading back to Mom, HMCS Nipigon plus two souls (the rescued physical bodies), but minus mine. Something has happened out here. I have no clue what. All I want to do is sit in the Nav's chair and wretch. The heaves won't stop.

The Decision
January, 2013

Cool, perhaps even cold, with a brisk ocean breeze defined the day. I often make the joke that at Hartlen Point we get two types of days: windy days and really windy days. At the mouth of the Halifax Harbour on the Dartmouth side there is a peninsula that juts out into the ocean surrounded on three sides by the harbour, the ocean and a body of water known as Cow Bay. The wind swept terrain is home to the Hartlen Point Forces Golf Club and a lot of seaside wetlands, scrub and marsh. The course is a haven for wild birds and this year there is a flock of Snow Geese wintering on the course along with the flock of Canada Geese which have taken up residence in Cow Bay.

The snow crunches underfoot as Jocelyn, Thai, and I go for our walk out on the course that has been closed now for the winter season. The vast fairways and open spaces make for a great place to take Thai for exercise and she can chase her ball with reckless abandon. We make sure we do not let her anywhere near the greens and tee boxes being cognizant that we are privileged to share the space with those who maintain it.

Today's conversation centers around the changes that we have seen in my life since Thai walked into it on the sixth of August.

"You know Joc, Thai has been such a blessing. It has just been a few months but look at how far we have come." I knew that Joc would be in agreement.

"Her waking you up so the night terrors do not happen is my favourite part. I get to sleep through the night and I do not wake up to soaked sheets and know you are going to be there in the morning." Even though she is stating the truth it hurts. For too many years the night terrors had affected us both and I think she was honestly grateful to be done with the worst of them. Thai had figured out when they were starting and now was waking me up before they got into the real intense sequences.

"So how do we help others get what we've got?" The question was sincere and from the heart. "You realize that we could do nothing, continue on and life would be so much better for us. But what about the others? How do we get them help? Many have no idea that this is even an option and if they do they either have no idea how to turn it into a reality or how to afford it." Both of those problems were prongs on a pitchfork of dilemma that faced so many who suffered the ravages of PTSD.

"What about those who are living in their woodsheds, their basements, cut off from their families, battling their demons, hoping for the strength to carry on and not knowing that relief could be available in the form of their own version of Thai?" We continued to walk on down the second fairway at Hartlen Point, and we were going to cut across from the third hole over to the space by the seventh green.

"I'm not sure what we can do." Jocelyn was thankful that I was back from the edge, but at the same time I could sense her apprehension.

"You know I was talking with Kate and she is going to do another walk this year." Corporal Kate MacEachern is the young trooper who had marched from Gagetown to her hometown of Antigonish in full battle order minus a weapon in nineteen days. "Look at the profile she raised. The media attention was huge. I was talking with Kate and I have an idea. What if I did a similar walk? We could raise funds and advocate to help others."

"What do you have in mind?" Honest question to which I did not have an answer.

"Honey, I am not sure, but I have been giving it some thought. My plan would involve walking because that is part of my long term treatment plan."

Her next question was a natural. "Where do you start and where do you finish?"

"If I got to choose, I start right out the front door of our house and we end in Ottawa. I have to take it there because that's where the decisions on this are going to be made."

"Are you crazy?" As soon as she said it I could tell she wished she hadn't. My struggles with so many different facets of Mental Health were well known to those in my family.

"Sweetie, the doctors have different words, but I think there is no arguing about my mental health issues." Factual. Honest. The eight hundred pound gorilla was out of the closet and in the room now.

"So how are you going to do it?"

"I am not sure. I have no idea on the logistics but we could call it the Long Walk to Sanity because that is what these past few months have been. Every day, my walks and time with Thai have helped me come to terms with little pieces of the problems that have haunted me for decades. Do you want to know two amazing things about Thai?"

Joc nodded and heaved the ball. Thai was off like a shot running carefree, glad to be a dog and run and play.

"Joc, I can tell her anything and she never judges me. She does not care what I tell her. No judgment. The second part is that I know for a fact she is not going to tell anyone. Never, ever. I know this is going to take a lot of work and I am going to have to train for it, but we can help others. If we do, maybe the voices in my head go quiet." Once again, the reference to serious mental health issues, but in this case it was my own admission. I was slowly coming to terms with my injury, my illness, or call it whatever you will.

"Okay." That was it. One word. An acknowledgment, a validation, and the approval to start planning the trip.

We looked over and there on a huge boulder by the number seven green was an Inuksuk, a traditional Inuit formation that had two common meanings: "someone was here" and "you are on the right path".

If you believe in signs, this was clearly ours. We were going on a journey, a quest, and we had no idea how it was going to turn out.

Boot Plan
Late Jan 2013

"What you up to today?" Jocelyn's question was part of our daily routine. Even though she knew the answer would most likely be taking Thai for a walk, she still wanted to hear me say it.

"Different plan today. Going to walk later but after I drop you off I am going to see Luke MacDonald at Aerobics First. I need to talk to him about footwear for the walk. In all my discussions with Kate she reinforced something that I knew. Comfortable footwear that could stand up to the rigors of the trip were going to be an absolute necessity. If I develop serious blisters that I cannot deal with, the entire walk could be shut down before it even starts. Literally, my boots are going to be where the rubber meets the road, and there is no doubt in my little military mind how important proper footwear would be."

Aerobics First is in downtown Halifax, on Quinpool Road, and a friend who was a podiatrist and fit shoes for a living gave a glowing recommendation to go see Luke. If Sheldon had said so, then I would follow his advice and go see the man he declared to be "the best in Halifax".

"Can I help you?" The clerk in the store was trying to be welcoming but I could see her casting a furtive glance at Thai. I think she was unsure as to Thai's status and why I had her with me in the store. She was trying to read the badges on her vest and I could see a sign of relief when she realized that Thai was a Service Dog and she was clearly identified as such.

"I have an appointment with Luke to get fitted for some footwear." I was not sure how this was going to evolve and I looked around at hundreds of pairs of the latest "running" shoes and Gore-Tex outer wear. Not exactly what I was here for, but Luke had come highly recommended.

"Have a seat and Luke will be with you shortly." I plunked down on the designated bench and was still fascinated with the myriad colours of shoes whose brand names were foreign to me. This was not my world.

"Hey, Medric, nice to meet you." Tall, lanky and thin gave Luke away as a runner. Hopefully he was not going to be under the mistaken impression that was the reason I was here. "What can I help you with?"

"Luke, great to meet you, Sheldon says to say hi. What you can do for me is to fit me for some boots for a walk. I need something that will support my right ankle, I tore it up pretty bad last April in a motorcycle accident. I fractured the ALS bone and tore and stretched everything." I could see the inquiring look on his face, so I showed him the photos on my phone. The swollen, discolored shots of my ankle were angry looking.

"So my plan is to walk a half marathon…" Luke was nodding and I could see him measuring me up and I think he was arriving at the conclusion I could accomplish that with training.

"Every day for fifty straight days. One August to nineteen September, rain or shine, hot or cold, I walk." He could not hide his look of shock and disbelief. Here I was, a former D-lineman, by any standard a huge man, looking desperately out of shape, less than a year out from some very serious trauma to one of his ankles who was planning to walk more than a thousand kilometers in fifty days. I could easily concede the skepticism, it would not be unwarranted.

"Why do you want to do that? There has got to be a story." His question was not out of place. In fact they were just the first of many probing and professional questions that would ensue over the next two hours.

"Her." I gestured towards Thai who was curled up at my side. "I am going to do this walk to fundraise and advocate to get more service dogs for other veterans who struggle with PTSD, just like me."

"Can I ask?" The tone had gone from skeptical and incredulous to sincere.

So I filled him in on the essential elements of my story. What had happened, how Thai had come about, and why it was so important for me to help others?

"OK. Take your boots off and hop over here. Stand on one foot." Thus began a process of measurements and functional tests that were more complex than anything I had ever done before to get fitted for anything going on my feet. Clearly the recommendation was right on.

"You realize that there are several factors that will cause..." I cut him off.

"Blisters? Heat, moisture and friction. Any of those can, and if you get more than one, it is almost certain game over." Kate's word echoed in the back of my mind. We had spent several long talks about blisters, how to prevent them and what to do when they inevitably showed up.

"Exactly. So what I am going to recommend is an ankle boot, breathable, waterproof and fit just for you. But it doesn't end there. You are going to need boots for the morning and boots for the afternoon. By midday, after 20k, your feet will swell and friction will become an issue. The other thing is you are going to need to let them air out and dry out. The plan would be, even and odd days, morning and afternoon boots. Mark them EM: Even Morning and so on just so you do not get them confused. Make life simple on yourself."

"Simple is good. Keep it Stupid Simple." We both laughed.

"What I am going to recommend is a New Balance 978 because they are breathable, waterproof and have a sole that will stand up to the pounding."

"Luke, I am going to have to trust you. This is your world and I came for your expertise."

"Thanks. I will give you the boots at cost and I am going to see if New Balance will sponsor a couple of pairs."

"Now it is my turn to say thank you." Heartfelt and sincere.

"You know Medric, we have just spent a couple hours together and I am worried about you. Most people quit because of their mind and never get anywhere near the limits of their human potential. Do you know why I am worried? Those pictures you showed me of your ankle? You will not quit. You will physically hurt yourself before your mind says quit."

I guess I had been wearing my passion and desire on my sleeve.

"Hey Luke, you want to hear something funny? We have just spent more time fitting for these boots than it took me to draw all of my kit at basic training." I started to laugh, and Luke raised a doubtful eyebrow. "Shit you not Luke." With that we both started to laugh uncontrollably.

Crazy Physics

Thai's wet nose gently nudges me awake yet again. In the darkness and the stillness, her body presses up against mine and she is content to let me reach down and rub her ears. Another rough night and she has once again been on duty waking me from the tortured dreams. At least they are no longer the ugly, hideous full on night terrors that have haunted me for more nights and years than I care to remember. So many that they blurred into decades of awakening to panic attacks, heart pounding and soaked in a cold, clammy sweat so bad that my wife could wring out the sheets... on her side of the bed. Since Thai had assumed her night watch, things had gotten progressively better. Sometimes I was still haunted by broken sleep and visions in my subconscious that I wish I could erase.

Tonight I was struggling with the crazy physics of what had happened. A Sea King, whether over land or water, would hover at forty feet. The radar altimeter would adjust the hover height for the waves over water, but not that night, not in those conditions. That night required so much more. Hans and Brad were both flying with hands on the controls. Brad to keep us off the bulk carrier, Hans keeping us out of the water, over the boat, and safe from being impaled by the whip antennae of the Sea Hawk.

The Sea Hawk was sixty eight feet long and the whip antennae were fifty five feet in height, which is higher than our usual hover height, taking us out of the cushion of air caused by the down draft that also aided our hover. The waves and swell ran from twenty to thirty five feet and we were trying to deposit me in an area that had a scant six by six overhead clearance. Hanging out the back door, watching the wild swings of ship, ocean and helicopter in some macabre twisted dance did nothing to ease the knots in my stomach.

I had given up counting how many times I had replayed the sequence of events in my mind while I was awake. The night time visions I could not stop from coming. From getting launched through the air into the ocean, dangling like a machine nut on a string, tossed by the forces of nature, to skipping across the wave tops, crashing into the transom, fighting off getting entangled in the rigging to that necessary decision to function the quick release and free fall. Events that in reality probably last much less than two minutes. Two minutes that turned into an eternity of hell. The gateway to the prison of PTSD had been opened.

What I did not realize that night was that I had been handed a life sentence, completely unaware of the charges against me. "An eye for an eye, a life for a life…" I start to think about the vision of the Stokes litter and Thai becomes very animated and agitated.

"I know sweetie, time to let that go and think of something else." I wish I could. I never want to see those images again. Sadly, I know I will. Even worse, all too soon!

Looking For Heroes

When we go looking for heroes...

Today is a banner day... the frigid cold snap has eased and I can get Thai out for a long walk in the snow and sunshine. I am working on compiling quotes and background material on some of the people I call heroes. The list is interesting and varied and there are reasons why these people are there. The list as it unfolds is by no means exhaustive. Nor should it imply in any way, shape, or form that this list is anyway to be construed as your list, nor should it ever be. But I do know one thing, and this I know "as sure as God made little green apples," when the moment comes that we need heroes, we had best be able to find them.

We build highways, buildings, monuments, and other solemn places to reflect. Do we build a building for a hero only to honour them? I think not. I think the fallen will have made peace with their makers and God, gaining eternal peace in the worlds of their understanding. These material things are not for who the heroes are. No, these reminders serve as solemn cenotaphs of what they represent.

The question we then have to ask ourselves is what they actually represent. For me to get there I have to take a serious left turn and go to a topic that is sure to set some people off, so be it. It's my story and I have big frigging shoulders.

I am about to open a huge can of worms, one which has been debated by scholars far more brilliant than I for time spans that I cannot comprehend trying to prove the existence of God and the origin of the earth and so many other arguments that people seem to struggle with the big macro overview of the universe. I would like to put it out there that I am going to approach the problem from a different tack in my mind and one that works for me.

In hoping to prove that my entire undergraduate education was not a complete exercise in futility of little use to a military officer. You see I took Honours English with enough Philosophy courses to minor. That little feat was made possible by the professor who taught me second year history. He was acting department head and

I had to convince him to waive a mandatory history course for an optional philosophy course out of his department. You never get what you don't ask for, the records will show that I am missing a history course that all my classmates took. I am indeed thankful to that man for he taught me a huge lesson, and more about history than he ever realized. Although I have lost much to the ravages of medications, I still have some rolling around in there somewhere. Why philosophy? Why English? Nowadays I guess the buzz word is "critical thought." Think for God's sake, think.

Sometimes one might wonder how someone with such self-professed mental illnesses can think. The problem lies in that we can, I can. People who suffer from serious mental health issues often run into this conundrum. Diminished Capacity should never be mistaken for diminished capability. But rue the world those times when I have excess capacity and diminished capability. The problem is I no longer know from moment to moment which is going to occur. So for me the simplicity of "Keeping calm and walking the dog" works on so many levels. One of the greatest is that it may very well be those first few steps that lead to a walk. A short walk. A longer walk. A really long walk. A series of daily walks that you spend, day by day, 24-7 with your four legged furry canine partner who has your back. Some days she helps because I can tell her things, and I can tell her when I need to. I need to a lot. In this world, sadly there are a lot, and I mean a lot of people who confront mental health issues and that is taxing an already overloaded system. It is not just veterans, former or serving, who are developing mental health issues and very serious ones at that. Folks, a week is one hundred and sixty eight hours and if you are real lucky you get maybe an hour or two with your Mental Healthcare team. It is rough. I understand budgets and staffing and all the other good things. But I understand one thing even more than all of that. I know that one hundred and sixty seven hours is a long time to spend on the "dark side of the moon". People by nature have been afraid of the dark, and there are issues that surround just that item alone. Imagine having the dark in your head, so dark, so black, and so oppressive your world collapses. Mental Health, physical, spiritual. Everything goes, very much akin to developing a high speed wobble on a motorcycle and the only way out is power, and one day you run out. There is no more right wrist available. The ensuing crash is inevitable and not pretty.

So one day you are laying in the smoking wreckage and you are taking stock, and you ask yourself, who was I talking to? Trust me, when you are leaning out the back door of a Sea King at night in a storm staring at a fishing boat bobbing like a cork and your pilots and crew are doing everything humanly possible, whoever you are talking to at that moment before you leave the aircraft is God. Also, take it to the bank, I swore oaths to virtually every religious deity I could think of. I did not want to miss the one who might have been on duty that day. I needed all the help I could get.

I look at the numbers, the size of the boat, the seas, the freighter, and our helo and I try and recreate how we did it. The physics are not pretty. Divine intervention ... I had certainly talked to enough gods. Years later I come to know that we all pray, and we all pray to the same God for the same thing. How do I know this? How can I be certain? Walk the halls of pediatric oncology wards late at night and between the beeps of pumps, and soft footfalls, you can hear teardrops fall. All of us there, separated not by race, color, creed, but unified as one, praying, praying to a God that exists for all of us to spare our children. You see, it is there. That I know that the seeds of love are sown, and that in a place marked by such suffering and in some cases death, know too that there are other stories. Stories of Hope, Strength and Courage. I have been judged to have my actions deemed Courageous. I know what I did that night. Know too, what I am about to undertake leaves me with feelings that make that helicopter ride feel like a walk in the park. I have seen Courage. I have seen it in children who need to believe in heroes. They embody at a young age what the world needs to never forget. When you going looking for Heroes they had better be there.

My unwasted undergraduate degree. Descartes, philosopher and mathematician, drove his discourse to a starting point. That which he knew and could start the premises to form the foundation of his beliefs. Cognito Ergo Sum. Je Pense donc je suis. I think therefore I am. I have undertaken a similar exercise and I have arrived back at the point several times. When you believe you are about to die, whoever you are talking to at that exact instant is by definition, God. Years ago I learned a great line from my father, "it doesn't matter which team sweater you are wearing, as long as you are playing the game."

During those long walks with my girl, I wonder if the world could just figure out that we are all the same. Look at three lab puppies, black, chocolate, and yellow, my personal favorite. I defy you to look at them and tell me the real differences. You see dogs can teach us so much. But I digress.

What if a unified world where peace breaks out and we figure out how to unite against the real enemies? They are out there. Perhaps one of the most serious issues is mental health and the stigmas that surround it. Mental Health is hampered by the Stigma. There are huge issues. I have those who have been around me at certain points in my life that were hurt by my illness. I cannot change what happened. I am not proud of it nor can I deny it. My wife and children took it the worst. Sooner or later, my illness gets everyone because it gets me. So then you wind up praying to the God you know exists and you get an answer to your prayers. The world will come to know how that same God I prayed to out the back of the helicopter, and the one I saw others pray to in darkened corridors late at night, that God has set me on a collision course with destiny.

So what do I know? Well I guess I know there is a God, and since I was talking to a being that was not me, I by definition am not God. There is a God. I ain't him. (Please insert whichever name, gender, pronoun or label that makes you feel comfortable). Whatever floats your boat, just don't ask me to be admiral of the yacht club.

What else do I know? I know that trying to swear solemn oaths, and get right with the God that you may meet in the next few moments, may be a little concurrent activity overload. Might I suggest from first hand personal experience that you might be better served by getting right with God long before things get out of control? Trust me, at the point that things are going from bad to worse, it is very nice to know someone has got your back. Some people get hung up around belief and certainty. In my case, I am certain I am talking to someone and I got a belief that I need some serious help. The belief disintegrated into a wave to certainty as I crashed to the boat.

Concept of Ops
April, 2013

Today certainly would be a great day. I was about to meet face-to-face with Vaughn, my old Nav school course mate who agreed to run the administration and logistics for the Long Walk to Sanity. This would allow me to focus on the physical preparations and keeping my head in the game without becoming overwhelmed with all the details that would invariably overwhelm me. As crazy as it sounds, I was attempting to pull off a huge coup of advocacy, fund raising and awareness and yet at the same time could get overwhelmed when there were more than a couple items on the very simple "To Do" list that Jocelyn left me each day. Even more telling was the fact that the "To Do" list often included the simplest of things, like reminding me to eat.

"You should be called Tom Sawyer in the Adventures of Huckleberry Finn." Uncle Frank's words echoed true and the reference was one that we had discussed before on several occasions. He was alluding to the fact that I had this huge vision yet I had many other people going to "paint the fence". Guilty as charged. I knew what needed to be done, and I knew what the stakes were, I just was not capable of executing, and was so grateful that Vaughn had stepped up.

Vaughn had served tours in Afghanistan as an operational squadron commander of an Aurora squadron, and of a test and evaluation squadron. As a Lieutenant Colonel, he had the skills and the experience to handle the Long Walk to Sanity. He said he had the time. I was sure hoping, no, counting on it.

Each day my daily walks and time hitting the TRX and kettlebells as I prepared physically for the upcoming sojourn were becoming ever more demanding. I was feeling confident that I could be ready physically. The two biggest challenges that remained were the six inches between my ears and the logistics.

The car pulled up outside our house on a very nice spring day in the "Passage". Vaughn had arrived for dinner and we would have the chance to start and hammer out the Concept of Operations, the big picture for how I, we, the team were going to pull this off.

Over a great pasta dinner, Vaughn and I had caught up on the years we had drifted apart, and he filled me in on what our other Nav school classmates had been up to. I had lost track with most of them when I left the military in 1991.

"So, Cous, how do you see this unfolding?" His question was direct and to the point.

"Vaughn, I have spent a lot of time talking with Kate MacEachern, the young lady who marched Gagetown to Antigonish last summer. I have learned a ton from her about everything from the physical preps to lessons learned out there on the road. She walked every step of the way, and she covered a lot of long, lonely miles and I have determined a couple things. First off, Canada is huge, and there are some pretty vast spaces with nothing but miles of Spruce trees and wilderness. No matter how good a speaker I am the damn trees are not going to fund the service dogs for other veterans. Do you know who Willy Sutton is?"

Vaughn shook his head side to side. "The name is not familiar."

"Willy Sutton was a bank robber, and according to urban legend, when they asked him why he robbed banks, his answer was simple. *That is where the money is.* I plan on taking a page out of Willy's Playbook."

"Robbing banks is a bad idea Cous." He said it in a halfhearted, joking manner.

"Don't worry Vaughn, I'm not going to ask you to organize bank heists. I have no intentions of having either of us spend our foreseeable futures turning big rocks into little rocks. The plan is simple though. We will go where the money is and tell the story to people who will understand what it is I am talking about. We go from town to town, do our walk, and then pitch up at a Legion or other similar venue, do a fund raising BBQ and then I will do my speech. We just keep repeating the same basic plan, day after day until I arrive in Ottawa the 19th of September, fifty days after kick off on the 1st of August. KISS principle at its finest. Keep it stupid simple or something like that."

Vaughn pushed back from the table, and seemed lost deep in thought, coffee cup in hand.

"That is actually not a bad plan. The concept has a lot of merit." I could tell Vaughn was appreciative of the simplicity, yet potential effectiveness. Battle plans rarely survive first contact with the enemy.

"That is why the route I have chosen is what it is. Obviously we start in Nova Scotia, then into New Brunswick, a few stops in Quebec, then we jump to Toronto and work our way back to Ottawa. With this route, I will be in and around Shearwater, Halifax, Moncton, Gagetown, Valcartier, St. Jean, Borden, Kingston, Petawawa and Ottawa. I had served or trained at most of those locations. We added in visits to our Veterans Long term care facilities and places like Beechwood National Cemetery and we now have a framework. See and be seen."

"Cous, let me go to work on it. I have a couple ideas, and we may have to change the route some. But I get what your thought process is." I am glad I could convey my message clearly. I was hoping that the Long Walk to Sanity would not be "Diary of a Madman, version Two point Zero".

Woulda Coulda Shoulda
April, 2013

"Hey Doc, you ever hear of a kids author and poet named Shel Silverstein?" I was sincere. This was not some play on words or some sort of word trap.

"I can't say I am familiar." His answer was forthright and honest. I think he has long since figured out that I am not much on bullshit and skirting around the issues. We have been seeing each other for a little over a year. The first therapist I had in many years, the first since Thai and the first I did not feel like terminating with "Extreme prejudice".

"Doc, have you ever heard" and I begin to recite from memory.

"All the Woulda-Coulda-Shoulda's,

Layin' in the sun,

Talkin' bout the things,

The woulda-coulda-shoulda done.

But those Woulda-Coulda-Shoulda's,

All ran away and hid,

From one little did."

"Wow, what a great piece. Very appropriate for you." Again there was sincerity reflected in his tone and body language.

"Doc, I am going to paint you a scenario. You are confronted with a child soldier in some African nation. He is armed with an AK 47 assault rifle and he cocks the weapon and starts to bring it to bear on you. What do you do?" I count a mental thousand and one. I snap my fingers. "Too late Doc. You're dead. You just took longer than you had to make the required decision. It was a 'him or me' situation and you hesitated a fraction of a second too long."

He sits there quietly. He is lost in thought. I think the impact of what I described has just hit home.

"Doc, I call it the retrospectoscope. Twenty-twenty hindsight goggles. It is so frigging easy to second guess when you have the luxury of time. Unfortunately, we are all faced with operational decisions where time is a precious commodity. You have got to read the situation, formulate a plan and act. Live time. You can't afford the luxury of ever second guessing yourself." I am getting angry. My tone reveals my inner feelings.

"Does this make you angry?" He is starting the probe to get inside the defensive wall.

"You are God damned RIGHT it makes me fucking angry!"

The anger sweeps me back out to the Atlantic, on that night when all this started.

I swing across the deck, having just been astride the long line hauler and up in the rigging, I am as close as we have been all night. I am ten to twelve feet above the deck and I pull the quick release. The briefest window of oppourtunity and I am betting my life that I have timed it right, that the ship will not pitch violently in the fraction of a second it will take me to free fall to the deck. Luckily the vessel does not, and the grease and oil on the boots of my poopy suit combined with the salt water of the North Atlantic to make a deadly combination with a co-efficient of friction of zero and I crash headlong into the wheelhouse.

I feel Thai's paws on my lap. I try and snap back to the present. How long did I have to make a decision and act upon it? Less than two seconds. Thousand and one, thousand and two. Live time, real world, with seaborne and airborne things moving wildly in three dimensions from the freaky physics or angry sea and buffeting winds. Make a decision. Make the right one and you are brilliant, make the wrong one and the whole mission could go to hell in a very large hand basket in less time than it takes to read this last sentence.

"You know Doc, when we finally got to St. Johns, the next day when I was with the Newfoundland Constabulary as they commenced their investigation, I was struggling badly with the Woulda-Coulda-Shoulda's, but the reality is I was struggling with the I Did's." The struggles with the demons of decisions made decades earlier still haunt me.

"You know you were doing the very best you could?" He was trying to get me to be nice to myself, grant myself absolution for some sin, real or perceived, that I have been dragging around for decades, some mental piece of destructive baggage that has been weighing me down, and keeping me anchored to that night.

"You know Doc, I understand where you are going. I logically understand what it is you are trying to do. But we have an accountability factor in the military. You are accountable for your actions, and I woulda-coulda-shoulda all I want, but guess what? There is the reality of what I did. A man is dead, and I have more than had his blood on my hands. I had it on my gloves, my flight jacket, and my immersion suit and in the end I was the guy that was there. This was not some nameless, faceless, enemy who I was trying to kill if the balloon had gone up and the Cold War had gone live. I can make peace with that. This was someone we were trying to save. This is a whole different ballgame. Woulda-coulda-shoulda's my ass. I am struggling with the realities of what I did." My voice trails off and I find myself thinking about that night again. I have lost count as to how many times I have been out there, in the darkness, staring at the boat, wondering what I could have done differently, wondering if the outcome would have changed if we had done things differently. What if he had not been a Polaris missile?

Thai starts licking my hand. For the second time in the same session I am brought back to the here and now by my Service Dog. My psychologist, my "Spin Doc" as I jokingly refer to him, is trying to get me to be nice to me.

"Have you ever considered…." I cut him off before he can get there. There is probably not a place or thought process that he could try and take me to that I have not traversed a thousand times before.

"Woulda Coulda Shoulda and what I did!" I am struggling badly now. The intensity in the room has been clear, very present, and very out in the open today.

"Perhaps we should wrap it up here today if you are okay with that?" Spin Doc asks.

OK? Hell I would have been good with that if we had shit canned this about a half an hour earlier.

"Good by me Doc, till the next time…" I try and convey a sense of optimism and he rightly pegs it as thinly veiled sarcasm. I think he knows how much I struggle with these sessions. I know how much I do. I live with the "I did."

My New Normal
May, 2013

The sound of the arrow "thwacking" into the target after the whoosh of the bow string was a great sound. The fact that the arrow was just inside the yellow of the bullseye on the target brought a smile to my face. A nice tight grouping of three arrows. Two just to the left of the bull, and the third just inside. Off a little horizontally, but a good vertical grouping.

"Nice arrows." My buddy Chris and I were spending some time sending a few arrows down range. I was thankful to Chris for being there for me when I struggle. He can let me vent, and in a lot of ways he understands the challenges I face. He faces his own. Chris was involved in a head on motorcycle collision with a car that had pulled out and hit him. Closing speed would have been over a hundred miles an hour. No time to think and had it not been for years of riding experience Chris would have died out there on a dark, nighttime piece of highway in Northern New Brunswick. Chris had managed to avoid the worst of it and survived with a couple of missing body parts. He lost the end of his pinky finger and he awoke in the hospital having had part of his left foot amputated because of the accident.

Chris was an inspiration to me in so many ways. He had gotten his head wrapped around his accident and very quickly had become a member of the Soldier On program. Chris had just been out of the hospital a few months when he had headed off to the Marine Corps Wounded Warrior games to compete. His first time down he competed in Rifle, Pistol and in Biking. Is second trip down he had the opportunity to receive archery coaching and he loved it. Chris knew of my self-imposed "No Firearms" rule. Someone with the kind of serious anger management issues that I had should never be around firearms. I know there are some who may have issues with my position, but you can take your opinion and two bucks and go buy yourself a coffee. I know the struggles I have and the demons I face and trust me, the world is a better place if I do not have firearms. Chris knew it, acknowledged it and embraced it. But he managed to convince me to try sending a few arrows down range.

Archery became a release for me. The intense focus required to get a grouping was good. To be effective, I also needed to clear my head of the other issues and try and remain focused on the task at hand. Chris could also read my moods and my ability to focus by watching my groupings. A sloppy grouping of arrows were reflective of headspace that paralleled that position.

"You mind if I make an observation?" Chris was always very respectful and as a man of few words, if he had something to say it was most likely worth listening to.

"Shoot the puck." I was waiting intently for his observation.

"A huge part of what I had to come to terms with after the accident is a thing called my New Normal". I am never going to be the same.

"You are right about that Chris. You are not a salamander, and the chances of growing back your foot are negligible. Not happening. Not today, not tomorrow, and not anytime soon." I was not being a smart ass. The conversation was an acknowledgment of the harsh, brutal reality that he would face for the rest of his waking days.

"Exactly. So I have had to come to terms with that reality. This is my "New Normal". This is how I am. I have had to come to terms with my PTSD, my demons."

I nocked another arrow and pulled against the forty pound draw on my traditional recurve bow. I exhaled slowly, my index finger anchored on my eye tooth and let the arrow go. Thwack!

"You know Cous, I think you might be struggling with your New Normal."

"You're right Chris. You are goddamn right I am struggling with it. I struggle with it every day. I am not a fucking happy camper, not in the least. It pisses me off." The floodgates had opened and the emotion welled forth. Chris got it because he lived there at one point. But unlike me, Chris had found a way to move beyond where he was to occupy some new headspace, better mental real estate than he had been occupying. I was resentful, angry, and hurt.

I was haunted by the ghosts of "What if" and too often I second guessed myself.

"You know Chris, it bugs the hell out of me. I have days when I can't seem to get out of my own way. I get so wrapped around the axle that I cannot think straight. I am not the happiest Pooh Bear at the picnic." I draw back another arrow. I steady myself and at the right point let the arrow fly. This time the arrow drives home on the opposite side of the target. Not exactly focused.

"Sometimes I just hope I can get through the day without the anger and the rage." One more arrow heads downrange. I rest my bow on the chair we have set out and I head down to pull my arrows from the target. But Chris had nailed it. He knew it and I could respect his opinion since he had walked the walk of the talk he was giving. I had to come to terms with my New Normal, and if I do not, I will live out my remaining days an angry, bitter, and resentful man. Not much of a choice.

Surprisingly, Thai had not moved during our exchange. She was sprawled out in the sun basking in the warmth of the spring day. My "New Normal" had been taking shape for nine months now. I was coming to terms with the fact that I had blown fuses and rewired brain circuitry and I ought to get on with at making the best of my remaining days. My New Normal.

The Reaper Knocks
06 July, 2013

Today was an amazing day… I was feeling strong and powerful as the preps for the Long walk to Sanity were falling into place…. Less than seven weeks out and I was getting more confident, but I realized that the weak link would be me. I was questioning myself and on different days vacillated between feeling ready to rock and scared that my body would break down under the strain of fifty straight days, rain or shine, averaging a half marathon walk. I reviewed my training logs regularly and knew I could pull it off as long as I did not succumb to a physical injury. Kate had been helping me with the planning preps to make sure I could hold up. Where the rubber meets the road would yield the biggest potential for injury. Feet are susceptible to injury and the three biggest culprits are heat, friction and moisture. Thanks to Luke at Aerobics First and the "Boot" plan he'd devised, we were hoping friction was not going to be the issue. Waterproof, breathable Gore-Tex boots along with moisture wicking socks should help minimize the "sweat" factor. Heat? That was the big variable. Southern Ontario in late August and early September could be brutal if I had not hardened my feet by the time I got to those legs of the trip. I briefly recalled rivers of sweat pouring out of my football helmet while running the Burma Road drill during late summer football practice. I felt the cold sweat of day old shoulder pads, smelled the funk from the training camp locker room, and tried to remind myself that I could do this, I'd done something this hard. At least on the Long Walk, 250 pound offensive linemen wouldn't be trying to knock me on my ass every thirty-five seconds.

The "Bink" of a social media message snapped me out of that train of thought and brought me back into the moment. The text message was from Tracy.

"Did you hear about Pam?"

"What about Pam?" I had seen her three days previously at the Bikers Down Society Angels ride. She was sporting a cast post op from an accident very similar to mine the year previous. She had dumped her Harley Ultra on top of her ankle when she was leaving a gas station. There'd been a diesel spill that had combined with light rain to turn the asphalt into a treacherous place. Pam was one of the best Lady Riders I knew and a long time motorcycle instructor and her accident legitimately highlighted some of the inherent dangers of being a biker.

"Seadawg, you had best call Jimi." Whatever this was, it wasn't good.

"K, sweetie, will do."

My mind raced through a lot of situations wondering what had prompted the message and the need for the call.

"Hey Jimi, it is I, 'Dawg of the Sea! Tracy said to give you a call about Pam. Whaddup Bro?" Jimi was my best riding buddy and President of Bikers down Society and one of its co-founders along with Pam. Jimi and I had covered a lot of miles together. A former motorcycle cop who was hurt in a bike related crash that ended his career and left him struggling with chronic pain, Jimi was a Salt of the Earth, standup guy.

"Seadawg, she's gone." His voice was cracking and strained.

"Gone? As in where?" I was thinking road trip in a cage. I knew she could not ride with her cast, so I was thinking the travel bug endemic to all Bikers had grabbed her yet again even though she had just returned from Bike Week in Laconia, New Hampshire.

"The Angels. She is riding in the Wind. They think that a post op blood clot let go and she's gone." His voice trailed off and I sat in stunned, moribund silence. Then the assortment of images started to play through my mind's eye. Pam's infectious smile, her no nonsense attitude, her amazing skill with a camera lens, all gone. I felt guilty for my next thought about Paws Fur Thought and Pam. She is gone, never to be back, her work unfinished.

Once again the Grim Reaper had come knocking, but this time he didn't wait for permission to enter. No, this time the Grim Reaper had kicked in the Door of Life and reached through and dragged a great soul into the Darkness of Death. I was overwhelmed with conflicting feelings. In this case, the accident and injury I had survived had claimed her life. In April of 2013, on my way home I had dumped my bike in a low speed turn 500 yards from the hotel where we would be staying in Gettysburg, Pennsylvania. When more than fourteen hundred pounds of motorcycle, gear and people land on your ankle, something is going to give. In this case, I fractured the ALS bone on the outside of my right ankle. Just thinking about it was enough to cause a searing pain followed by a dull ache in my ankle, the same ankle that I was preparing to walk more than a thousand kilometers on in a few short weeks, now carrying the heavy burden of Pam's passing.

This wasn't the first time that the Reaper had come close and then claimed another life. Sgt. Al Smith, my Aesop onboard Nipigon and the man whose quick thinking had saved me on that night decades ago, he was gone too. I struggle with this. The entire crew that had been airborne that night had cheated Death and side stepped crossing over the line. Yet months after the rescue, Al was hit by a drunk driver at night when he was ashore in Montreal. I struggle with the ironic twists of fate that seem to definitely cause more questions and make figuring out the "Game of Life" even more difficult. How could I have survived everything that had happened, how I could actually be alive because of Al's quick thinking and amazing reflexes and here he was gone. He had saved me, and yet he gets claimed in a pointless, senseless car pedestrian accident. This hardly seemed to make any sense.

I feel Thai's paws upon my shoulder. I look over and am staring into her deep brown eyes. She knows I have drifted off and she wants me back.

"Easy, good girl Thai." I reach over and vigorously rub her belly. "It's ok girl, I am back with you." Once again she has brought me back from a bad headspace and trains of thought that would surely crash headlong into some mountain of desolate despair.

None of it made any sense. Not to me. Not from where I sat.

None of it.

Pam's Funeral
14 July, 2014

It was hot. Partially cloud covered but hot. There was a continuous thump and rumble of large V-Twin bikes up and down Lake Major Rd in front of Toads Cycle Works. The bikes would come and keep coming, for the next two hours the sea of chrome, black leather, and sunglasses continued to grow. Solemn was the word that best described the mood, while the faces were best described as somber. Bear hugs, chest bumps, grasped hands, and tears flowed as countless bikers convened for this sad event. Today we would pay homage to one of our angels, one of our fallen, a member of the blacktop brother and sisterhood.

Pam would be sorely missed. She was an icon in the Nova Scotia Biker community. In the Biker world respect is given but most importantly it is earned. Your actions speak volumes and from the turn out for Pam's funeral, it was becoming abundantly apparent to all the high degree of respect in which Pam was held. The sweltering heat continued to mount as the sun now peaked in and out through the clouds.

And still they came. The parking lots and driveways in and around Toad's were overflowing and bikes where now lining both sides of the road. The funeral procession, Pam's final ride, would be huge. Amongst the throng, I spied Rhonda and I started to navigate my way through the crowd so that I could go give her a big hug. When you thought of Pam, your next two immediate thoughts were her beloved Harley and her camera toting photography fanatic buddy Rhonda. They both rode, enjoyed life, and had amazing skill with the camera lens, often capturing life from genuinely unique perspectives. Pam's death had caught us all by surprise and reinforced the fragile nature of our time on this planet. No one beyond Pam's immediate family would feel the harsh cut of this knife more than Rhonda.

"Rhonda, sweetie, I am so sorry…." I tried to keep myself together but was betrayed by the salt stained tracks that were flowing down my cheek from under my sunglasses. Our big hug helped each of us stay upright since the weakness in our knees was collective.

"Seadawg, I am hurting so bad...." Her voice trailed off and her own salt stained rivers belied her exterior calm.

"Rhonda, I have no clue what to say... too young, too early, not fair, I am so angry... so pointless." My voice trailed off. My mind was starting to check out.

Thai started her bumping. She knew. The anxiety in me was starting to mount.

"Rhonda, did Pam tell you about our project? Did she happen to mention what it was that we were working on?" I was hoping to change the subject to something positive and, very selfishly, I was about to make a big ask.

"No. No she had not." Damn, this would certainly be harder than I thought and while I was trying to formulate a plan, Pam's sister joined us. The hugs and tears continued.

"Seadawg, we found a notebook at Pam's, it had your name on it, but it was in her writing." My heart leapt ten thousand miles in the scant seconds that it took for Pam's sister to utter those few words. The Gods of Fortune had smiled. All was not lost in the finality of Death.

"Ladies, do you know what that notebook represents?" I hung the sentence out there with a vast pregnant pause for effect. "Here is the skinny. On the first of August I am going to be leaving on a walk that will last fifty days and end in Ottawa on the 19th of September. This walk is to fund raise and advocate for Service dogs for disabled veterans battling PTSD. The plan was that Pam was going to use her photos and those quotes to come up with a daily motivational poster to keep me going and to help inspire others who may be struggling." The reality of the hurdle that now faced us was starting to sink in.

"Ladies, I need to ask you both a huge favour. I know that this is going to be a tough ask, and today is more than tough enough as it is, but given what we are here to celebrate, perhaps there is no better time. Linda, if you could give the notebook to Rhonda, I would be very happy. Rhonda, I know this is going to be beyond tough. Would you consider going through Pam's image library and picking up the project so that her memory and work lives on?"

I had asked, and my insides heaved a collective sigh. Ever since Jimi had told me of Pam's passing I was a mix of conflicting emotions. On one hand a dear friend and wonderful biker advocate was gone, and on the other, a huge piece of the plan the plan for the Long Walk to Sanity was blowing aimlessly in the breeze. I was sure in my heart of hearts that if we could have asked Pam personally, I knew what the answer would be.

Pam's sister spoke first. "That would be wonderful." The salt tracks were moistening again.

"All I can say is that I will try." Rhonda's usually strong confident voice was anything but.

"Thank you ladies." That the best reply I could muster on a moment's notice. Perhaps it was the very best that would ever be said under the circumstances.

"Hey Seadawg." Momma Toad, Marlene Roach, the matron of the Nova Scotia biking community called out my name. "Do you think you could give us a hand mounting the Urn on Pam's bike?" Would I? Could I? My heart leapt. I would be getting Pam ready for her final ride on her beloved bike in a funeral procession of bikes that would number in the hundreds.

A very nice, wooden, varnished box. Simple, just like Pam. No extraneous bullshit, again, just like Pam. So I carefully sat it on the luggage rack of her bike and snugged it down with bungee cords and a cargo net, two of a biker's road trip allies. Pam would be pleased. I reached over and placed my hand on the urn. "Pam sweetie, I know you are riding with the Angels. You may be gone but you will never be forgotten."

I then took one of our Paws Fur Thought Dog tags out and attached it to the hinges of her urn. Most who saw it would never appreciate the significance of what it was or why it was there. I would never forget.

Getting right with God.

I know there are a whole pile of things that are guaranteed to start an argument in no time flat, so just for grins I know I am treading on thin ice, even if this was a polite society dinner conversation. But this isn't, and if you are still with me, you are along for the ride.

You are going to take it as absolute Gospel that the last place in the world you want to have a "Come to Jesus Meeting" in which you are going to attempt to find religion or whatever else you make think may save your life is staring into the blackness of a North Atlantic storm tossing a fishing boat around like a cork on a black ass stormy night. I have been there and done that. Yes, I swore solemn oaths to anyone I thought was listening. It is a real sobering and humbling experience when you realize that what you are about to undertake is quite possibly the last thing you would attempt.

So why did we press on? Why were we going above and beyond? The strain in the voice of the captain of the Sea Hawk on the radios spurred us on. The desperation in his voice, the pleas, the fact that he was considering floating his men out to sea so we could get them. At one point it was all that could be done to convince him not to do this. What would drive a hardened sea captain to break? Whatever was waiting for me on the boat had to be bad. This was not going to be a case of "terminal hangnail".

His voice haunts me after all these years. At the time I questioned why he would even consider it. Before the night was out I would know and never forget.

By the time we finally got a guideline safely to the Sea Hawk I had plenty of time to watch. Some may find it strange what one thinks about at moments like that. I had a sickening feeling of what it felt like to be in the trenches, not that my physical hardship was anything like what those brave men endured. When the whistles blew, the trumpets sounded, many, too many young, innocents would go over the top to the slaughter that lay before them. They knew what was waiting and they did it. Plain, simple, the harsh brutal reality. I like so many before me and so many after me, generations yet unborn, do what has to be done.

Newsflash sports fans. The business of soldiers, sailors and airmen, and those that support them, exposes them to things that the average person would never quite get. Working at the back door of a Sea King is a rush. Heavy jackstays between ships in heavy seas and the awesome sight of a 105 mm howitzer at dusk are things you never forget seeing. You just don't. You do what has to be done in circumstances where you have trained your best to minimize the damage, to bring everyone home safe. We in the military pray. Sometimes we pray for things, very selfish things. We hear of a crash and we think of who we know that could be there and pray it is not them. Then we feel guilty for having prayed it. For having tried to shift that kind of pain onto someone else, instead of taking it ourselves. Not that it makes it any better that it someone else, but sometimes it is just so much easier when it isn't personal. We pray for the friends and families of our fallen and our wounded. Those names in the book of Remembrance are real. They are not numbers. They are not sound bites. They are ours. And we pray selfish things…. Never again. Please not ever.

So as you are standing there with a knot in your stomach you realize you have been praying to someone. To keep the conversation simple, I will just call the Great Divine, God. So there I am talking with God, listening to the radios, the pilots trying to keep us off the bulk carrier, the Sea Hawk, and out of the damn ocean. Right then and there I realize that I am either crazy or I have to be talking to someone. The singular entity who could have been the least little bit of help at that exact moment was God. Based on what I had witnessed for the past couple of hours, I was trying to get my affairs in order with God and swearing solemn promises if he got me out of that night in one piece.

There were several variations of the ending, I had time.

In one brief fleeting instant, the second guideline hit the deck, I unplugged from the radios and swung out the door. I had a moment to square myself and look into Ken's eyes. Everything that ever needed to be said was said in a single mutual nod and in the next seconds I was launched over the ocean upon which danced the Sea Hawk's rigging and machinery.

So I have been talking to God, but then I got the idea about how big the Universe was. For me, I came to that realization that when

I was chest deep in the North Atlantic, hooked to the hoist wire and the guideline, getting heaved about like an oversized nut on a string that you twirled and snapped as a kid. I am looking up at twenty plus feet of waves and swell, and you look out into the blackness of the swells, and you realize how big the damn ocean is.

Dust in the wind. All we are is dust in the wind. And you feel very small.

Seconds later, skipping off the wave tops, I just knew I had no way to protect myself and I was about to hit the ass end of the boat (yes, nautical aficionados, transom) and it, undoubtedly, would hurt. For all of us who grew up with Bugs Bunny and the Roadrunner this is exactly what flashed through my mind as I hit the boat: the coyote smacking off the side of the cliff and sliding to earth? Same thing, except we had a whole ocean and a small boat.

The next few seconds were spent trying to fight my way clear of the rigging. I knew as I was flying through the grasping wires that I would have to cycle the quick release when I was as close as I was going to get. My chance came about three seconds later and from about twelve feet I free fell to the deck of the boat. I had arrived onboard and was going about the business of what needed to be done. The count down to the beginning of a horrific spiral into the depths of Post-Traumatic Stress Disorder and in the next few seconds events would unfold from which I have never been able to recover. I have prayed to that same God so many times over the ensuing years that I gave up, my prayers apparently falling on deaf ears.

But maybe not. Maybe all that suffering and all that journey happened for a reason, as Joc would say. Maybe it was all to get me to a place where I could find Thai, and realize that my real reason to be here wasn't to play football, or to go out the ass end of a Sea King, or even to walk across the country. My real purpose may have been to get so screwed up that I'd have that moment when I realized there was something I could do for all the others who were suffering and had no idea of how to help themselves.

The bobbing and weaving deck of the Sea Hawk was awash in salt water and I was intently focusing on getting the two Stokes litters onto the vessel. After successfully getting the litters apart, I turned to get the first casualty to secure him in the Stokes litter and prepare him for the upcoming transfer.

Up to this point had the whole evolution ended right then I would have probably never had the problems I have had.

I STAB YOU. You bleed, you heal, and you scar. The world gets it. Why it is I stab your brain with trauma the scar is magically supposed to go away and you are going to be able to "Suck it up" and get over it? Some wounds never heal, some scars stay fresh, and sometimes no matter how far off you stare things are right there. Why God? How did he live? How? I dry heaved.

"You know Joc, I may have figured out how to describe who God is. Presumptuous I know. WHO IS GOD?"

"Keep your voice down, ok so God is?"

"God is whoever I was talking too at the back door of the aircraft that night. Unless I am completely off my rocker, and there will always be some questions as to whether this is indeed true, I was talking to God. God as I know God. "

"Does that work for you?"

"For Now."

"I am so happy for you." She had no idea. How many years since I could even get to this point in the conversation? I was going to take Thai for a walk. If I had to bet, a long walk.

"You know Thai girly, I wonder it if the world is going to get it. First Principles just like Descartes. Eh girl?" Cognito Ergo Sum. I think therefore I am. I cannot be separated from my thoughts. Now isn't that just special. So in my convoluted world of disconnects and abstractions, I was talking to someone at the backdoor of the Sea King that night. So we arrive at a very simple juncture, one where I have to believe I was talking to God or I have completely lost my mind. Faith, belief, knowledge, certainty, the lines between semantics and definitions blur. Your life flashing before your eyes makes you realize that we are actually no more than Dust in the Wind.

So what do I know.......

Houston, We Are T Minus Nine and Counting

Commence preflight checklist now... Holy old what the frig happened to the last couple of months? In two days I will have seven sleeps and a wakey left and Thai and I step off on our Long Walk to Sanity. I have to share a funny exchange. I had recently told someone of my plan to walk 1100 kms over fifty days to raise the money to buy fifty more PTSD service dogs for disabled veterans.

"Are you nuts?"

"Actually the doctors try and use gentler phraseology but you are definitely in the right area code."

"Seriously?"

"As a friggin heart attack."

"Isn't that going to hurt?"

"How about them Blue Jays?"

I have to tell you though, I am scared about the upcoming journey. The fear does not come from the physical challenge. I have done over 2,100 kilometers and 8,700 flights of stairs and hills since the 21st of January. My physio and kinesio team (thanks Kirsten, Richard and Kayla) have done a great job with my physical preparations. Beyond the walking and stairs, I have been doing training with a TRX suspension Trainer, a TRX Rip Trainer, and some other assorted bits to strengthen my core and upper body. I went from crappy planks and one of the ugliest single rep plank roll throughs to holding solid in all positions for a length of time and hitting twenty aside on the plank roll throughs. I have been doing my own version of Ironman in training for this epic walk. The days I absolutely crank it out I walk from my house to Colby village pushing Thai for a little over ten clicks, hit the TRX, RIP, and Core Hard for a solid hour, moving from exercise to exercise nonstop, return home pushing the same cart (Thai & gear about 100 lbs.) then finish with another fifty flights of stairs, bringing the day to look like 25 kms, 100 flights, and a core & upper body workout that my kinesio scores a solid eight out of ten for intensity. My post motorcycle accident right ankle will be the weak link. But I am feeling physically very good.

So where does the fear come from? The fear is the stakes. Yes the feel good side of the story is the service dog story. The dark flip side of the coin is serious mental health issues, suicide and homelessness. Throw in the Veteran adjective and it is a very unpalatable conversation. The problem is that failure to acknowledge and effectively intervene will result in more of what we currently have.

Jim Lowther from Veterans Emergency Transition services deals with the homelessness issue on a daily first hand basis. The suicides are happening. The stakes in this are human lives, Veteran's human lives. Veterans that have paid the price for our freedoms.

Pierre Poilievre, MP for Nepean has been quoted as saying "Canada was built of Freedoms, not Freebies." I agree, but might I suggest that he might want to come out on the road this summer and meet some of those who gave him his? Those freedoms he so glibly flips off in political rhetoric were bought and paid for with the blood of our fallen Veterans, paid for with the minds, bodies and souls of its injured Veterans. He wants to relish in the freedoms of being Canadian? Then he had best ensure that those that he is asking to provide them are given respect, honour, and if injured, proper care.

Social contract becomes sacred covenant the moment one side pays in blood, as is the case with our Veterans since Canada became a nation up to and including those who have fallen in the War in Afghanistan.

I am not a Combat veteran. My military career coincided with the end of the Cold War. Had I seen shots fired in anger, the face of the world today would most likely be radically different, if it existed at all. My injuries are Search and Rescue related. FILO's (First In, Last Out's) Red, White and Blue, (Fire, Paramedics, Police, RCMP) can and do sustain post-traumatic stress disorder injuries.

So in the handful of days left before the start of an epic journey that I hope and pray will make Canada a better place, I have been asked why I am doing it?

This past June, I stood at Beechwood Cemetery in Ottawa, by the National War Memorial, at the foot of a grave with a Silver Cross Mother and was struck with the very stark realization that the only way any of what lay before me made any sense is if the country he had died for was worthy of the sacrifice he had made.

When his mother asked if I thought we could get help for some of his buddies who were struggling, I was able to choke out one short sentence. "I sure hope so."

Part Four:

The Long Walk to Sanity

Invictus

Out of the night that covers me,

Black as the pit from pole to pole,

I thank whatever gods may be

For my unconquerable soul.

In the fell clutch of circumstance

I have not winced nor cried aloud.

Under the bludgeoning's of chance

My head is bloody, but unbowed.

Beyond this place of wrath and tears

Looms but the Horror of the shade,

And yet the menace of the years

Finds and shall find me unafraid.

It matters not how strait the gate,

How charged with punishments the scroll,

I am the master of my fate:

I am the captain of my soul.

- William Ernest Henley

Day One
01 August, 2013

"On the edge of destiny you must test your strengths."

Billy Bishop, VC, CB, DSO, DFC & Bar, MC, ED

The words rang in my ears and I could feel them in my heart. The problem was the anxiety in my gut, overpowering and paralyzing. I looked at the long hill ahead of us. Sunny and warm and the day was going to get warmer. All of the butterflies of getting the Long Walk to Sanity started had been released. Now I was confronted with the very real task of doing what I had pledged to do. Done right, this walk could help a hell of a lot of people.

Today was day one of fifty and I was just seven kilometers into a walk of well over a thousand. The excitement, the fanfare and the energy of the well-wishers who had been there for the kickoff had instantly been replaced by an overwhelming sense of dread as I was struck by the enormity of what I was undertaking. Things were now very real, and very live time. It was a go. Less than thirty minutes ago, Thai and I had been at the Afghanistan Memorial at CFB Shearwater with several of our Memorial Cross families. We'd released some doves to the Heavens. Angela Reid, Christopher Reid's mom, and Lindsey, my oldest daughter, sent the first two doves skyward as two baskets of the lovely birds were sprung open to let another dozen join them.

Prayers of Peace.

Prayers of Hope.

Pangs of anxiety.

But already I was alone: just Thai and I.

I checked the time. Ten forty five. I'd left the house at seven am after some initial time with the media. Jocelyn and I had walked to the Cove for the official start at eight. A solidarity victory lap of the Passage boardwalk had been organized by Becky Kent. The first hour gave Jocelyn a few moments alone to talk about the change that was about to happen. In many ways our lives would never be the same. I was struck by the similarity to the feelings that I had on a particular night decades ago. "Truth, Duty, Valour," the motto from the Royal Military College, once again drifted through my stream of consciousness, not unlike another night when it had played before.

Thai was body checking my leg. This was and is her sign that I am drifting off to a less than productive head space. I knelt and gave her ears a rub, and from that perspective the long hill looked even more daunting.

"You know what sweetie, I am thinking of that old Buddhist saying, *sometimes all that is required is to point your boots in the right direction and keep walking.*"

I wondered to myself how many times in the upcoming fifty days I would need to remind myself of that?

It would be too easy to quit, to "shitcan" the whole damn plan, and just continue on as life had been last fall. I was feeling good. Life was getting much better and the family was enjoying having me back. In fact my kids were seeing a side of me that they had never seen. They'd never seen it because both were born after my injuries. How could they know? They couldn't, and in a lot of ways it absolutely highlighted the problems posed by struggling with PTSD, the Beast, a hellacious monster that can suck you into the depths of despair in an instant.

"Woe to you oh earth and sea…" Vincent Price's words from the start of Iron Maidens Number of the beast crept into my consciousness. "Six Six Six, the Number of the Beast." And the letters P, T, S and D.

Thai's body checking became incessant. I had been lost in another flood of negative thoughts and had drifted out to sea on a wave of bad memories. I needed to stay focused if I, we, were going to pull this off. All I was attempting to do was raise a lot of money, get help for others, and get the government, namely VAC and the Military, to acknowledge the efficacy of service dogs in the treatment of PTSD. Some might have said it was an overly ambitious undertaking. I put it to you that it was absolutely necessary. I had seen the change in my life because of Thai. I would never be able to get the voices in my head to be calm if I didn't do something to help others. I know that it sounds just a bit strange that someone who has serious and documented mental health issues is talking about debates with their inner voices, but in this case it is more than justified.

I think there comes a time in everyone's life when they are challenged and kicked out of their comfort zone and are going to engage in those wrestling matches of self-will, self-survival, and actions that altruistically serve the greater good. The rub in my case comes when you have had those debates with yourself and what hangs in the balance is tomorrow or the lack thereof. What happens when you cannot deal with one more anxiety attack or one more panic attack? What happens when the darkness of the depression is so encompassing that it has swallowed your soul and your will to live?

What happens?

Again, Thai body checked me and this time I realized I was down past the Nova Scotia Psychiatric Hospital. It's a place that does not hold fond memories for me. I was sent to the Emergency Assessment Unit there back in September of 1996. The anniversary effect surrounding my release and the rescue hung over me like the sword of Damocles, threatening to skewer my sanity. I kept walking at a brisk pace. I wanted to put as much distance between this place and my boots as quickly as I could. There is nothing pleasant surrounding my experiences there. This was the place that I first heard the words Post Traumatic Stress Disorder and my name used in the same sentence. This was also the place where I had admitted to someone that I had contemplated suicide as a means of ending the nightmares that I would come to know as night terrors. It would be the place where I would come face to face with addictions beyond alcohol, some I was willing to admit, others drowning in a sea of denial.

I realized that a geographic cure would not solve the problems or eliminate the associations, but I was much happier as I walked away from the psychiatric hospital. I also had about another twenty kilometers to cover to get to Point Pleasant Park, the Naval Memorial, and back to Grand Parade. Day One was ambitious, but I wanted to put some extra kilometers in the bank. I knew I was going to run into bad weather, rain, heat, humidity, bugs, you name it. I was ready to battle the elements. I was ready to battle my body. Perhaps most daunting? I was ready to battle my mind and my desire to succeed. Failure was not an option. As Luke from Aerobics First had pointed out in our discussions about the walk, "Most people quit in their mind long before they get anywhere near the limits of their body. You on the other hand are the exact opposite. You will physically hurt yourself before you get anywhere near the word quit." I have to admit I took great pride in those words since Luke had no idea how close I had been to hurting myself on so many occasions, absolutely signifying the ultimate quit but gaining relief from the darkness.

"On the edge of destiny...You must test your strengths"- I had purposely chosen Billy Bishop's words for day one of my walk. William Avery Bishop, VC, DFC and bar, ex cadet of the Royal Military College and World War I aviator. Perhaps I could draw strength from his words. I would need physical strength in the days to come, but I had no idea of the challenges I would face from my inner demons. Six Six Six, the number of the Beast...

Opening Remarks
01 August, 2013

Ladies and Gentlemen, Brothers and Sisters (Veterans & Bikers), Family and Friends, to those who would like to be here, but can't, know you are all in my hearts. To our Silver Cross Families, I have not forgotten. We will arrive at Shearwater very soon.

When my wife and I first dreamt up this plan, we did so with the inspiration and motivation of some key people, some of whom are here with me today. Brenda Anderson, blind and she taught me to see, and taught me a lot about living with a service dog. Dennis Manuge, Veterans Advocate, who is one of the finest examples of you do the right thing. Kate MacEachern, 562 kms in nineteen days in full battle dress, toughest soldier I know with strengths most will never know. Chris Hatton, my CAV brother, who helped me to learn to start coming to terms with my new normal. Trapper Cane, President of the CAV, gave me something that had been stripped away; a sense of purpose, strength and honour, Arte et Marte. Pam Vickery, now riding with the angels, our project will live on through your eyes. Our motivational posters will be released on the Paws Fur Thought Facebook page. Today's quote comes from Billy Bishop, VC, DSO and Bar, Distinguished Flying Cross

"On the edge of Destiny, you must test your strength."

To Peter Stoffer, my MP, and, Becky Kent my MLA, thank you both for all you have done so far, but know that the heavy lifting is yet to be done. I must also thank Angela Seguin of Krazy Kritter cookies for Thai's Labrastrudels and PetValu for supporting Thai's needs. Belt Drive Betty whose cross country motorcycle tour is raising funds and awareness and is supporting our cause.

You will notice a lot of bikers here this morning and throughout my walk. I am a biker. There are a lot of Veterans who are bikers. The open road calls, the camaraderie, the respect, the freedom and most importantly, a code of behaviour, we do not leave our brothers and sisters stranded on the road. So please do not judge books by their covers. To do so, would mean that you are often judging Veterans by appearance and not actions.

To my family, the world will never know. My darling bride Jocelyn and I were married 298 days when I sailed and never returned home the same. She never bailed in the darkest of times. NEVER! There are no words. My children, Jennifer, my youngest is currently in nursing school and unable to be here. I will take one word, focus. To my other daughter Lindsey, three time cancer survivor, ARDs survivor with 57% lung function with her fibula grafted into her spine. Tough.

So how do I describe what happened? Twenty six years of hell living with PTSD, addictions, depression, panic, anxiety, and serious anger management issues, describe one of the most complex and devastating psychiatric injuries, describe what my service dog does, how she does it and why I am doing this with my families support, and do it in a manner that makes sense all before we all start celebrating birthdays.

So here goes in record time.

I was awarded the Star of Courage for an act of conspicuous courage in circumstances of great peril. Chancellery decided the first part, Hans Kleeman's citation for his Meritorious Service Cross, will clarify the latter.

When I told people I was planning to walk a half marathon average a day for fifty days, over 1100 kms, so that we could raise the money to get fifty more PTSD service dogs for fifty more disabled veterans, the two most often voiced sentiments were "Are you crazy?" and "Are you insane?" Actually the doctors use kinder words but I got enough paper with my name on it that will certainly confirm I have some admittedly serious mental health issues. So I have a team behind me that are doing pretty much everything. I walk and I talk. The support you have given my family so far is invaluable. Again, the heavy lifting is yet to come. I will do my best to stay on the page. Thank you.

I now live with a psychiatric service dog. This is my girl Thai, and in a few days we have our one year anniversary as a team. She has had a huge impact on both my physical health and my mental well-being. For me, the three most important things she does are nightmare intervention, watching my back in public, and flashback-dissociative recall.

She was made possible with the support of the NS Nunavut command of the Royal Canadian Legion. Impressed with what they saw happen with me, they are helping to act as the charitable receipting and financial controls for our project. Commands and branches in Nova Scotia, New Brunswick, Quebec, and Ontario are all involved in helping us help other Veterans.

But a funny thing happened on the way to the start line. This was to be the official launch of the Long Walk to Sanity. The Reality? We have already paired two veterans; we have four more in the mill and five on the wait list. So why service dogs for PTSD? Guys and gals like me with a dog like her do not go on to hurt themselves. Cards that were once in play are no longer in the deck.

Here comes the pitch folks. Every time we put $7,000 in the pot, we save another Veteran from the hell they are in; we give them a chance to re-establish with their family, eventually their community. In a few days, the numbers will be four paired, two in the mill, and more on the wait list. The only way we can solve this is with money. Your donations and sponsorship, each and every time we do this, know that you have helped save a life.

"Let him who hath understanding reckon the number of the Beast, for it is a human number and its number is six hundred and sixty six" and its letters are PTSD, a living hell that is unimaginable.

So what do you call something that comes onto Canadian soil, uninvited, and fells Canadians, destroys their lives, devastates their families, and harms our communities? Sadly, it is in every community in Canada. I call that thing an enemy. This enemy attacks our Veterans, it attacks our FILO's, First in Last out's (Fire, First Responders, Police and RCMP). This enemy lives amongst us. The hard part is you cannot see the enemy, but he is amongst us. I have fought this enemy for almost twenty-seven years. Most of it was a never ending hell. The enemy is PTSD. One of its most powerful weapons is stigma. The stigma of battling serious mental health issues is not to be dismissed or taken lightly. Hopefully I can help others to *Put The Stigma Down* and get the help they so desperately need. I have understanding and I shall reckon with the Beast.

So what happens when you have such an enemy? You fight, but to do that there should be a declaration of War. From this moment forward, I am at WAR. I will continue to fight my PTSD daily for the rest of my life. But now I have something that was desperately missing. I have hope, and that hope is spurring me on to get others help, and in so doing maybe quiet some of the voices inside of me. For all of us in the military, former, current, and those yet to come, on day two, we learned the fireman's carry. We do not leave our wounded on the battlefield.

I have trained very hard. I have a team that has helped me prep physically. I have walked over 2,200 kms and climbed up 9,000 plus flights of hills and stairs since January 21 in preparation. (Put on old vest)

So folks, the time is nigh for words to give way to their most useful byproducts, actions and inspiration. So the rubber is about to hit the road in New Balance 978's fitted and planned by Luke MacDonald of Aerobics First and Rudy Lauzier of New Balance, morning and afternoon boots, even and odd days. For those who wish to join me for a lap of our beloved Boardwalk please do so. We who live here have some natural beauty that also overlooks the place where so many Canadians left to do their duty. As we do so, please consider the sacrifices that our Veterans and their families make. We as a country have a sacred obligation to our fallen and our injured. Then we shall parade to Shearwater, and there we shall honour our fallen and their families. For those who are waiting, there are those here who will accept your donation or sell you dog tags that quite simply say, "Prescription for Sanity: Keep Calm and Walk the Dog, repeat as necessary." We need to raise $350,000. So if anyone would like to write a very large tax deductible cheque, or if a corporate sponsor would like to step in, I will get a better night's sleep sooner.

Beyond my undying thanks, you will have the gratitude of countless disabled Veterans. This would be a great start, but my walk continues, and I will walk and I will talk. I need to recruit an army of Canadians, Paws-itive supporters, to help combat the War on PTSD and the battles the injured face.

Paws Fur Thought Parade, by the left, on your own time, Quick March."

Bass River Fallen Warriors
05 August, 2013

The black granite monument stands stark sentinel amongst the trees and the grass still wet with the morning dew. Day five of my walk and I was walking from Bass River Veterans Memorial Park to Masstown with a very special stop along the way.

On the northern shores of the Bay of Fundy, there is a tiny village, Bass River, home to a former chair factory and center of town for a few farms and fishermen that lined the coast of the greatest tidal forces known to man. It is also home to the Veterans Memorial Park. Monuments to conflicts from the First World War onward including peacekeepers and Merchant Mariners serving as reminders of the sacrifices of those who came before us. Outside the park has trees and memorial plaques honouring those who have fallen in Afghanistan.

Tucked down in behind is another very special memorial. Noah Tremblay, when he was eleven years old, started pushing to have a monument to Canada's fallen war animals installed. He got his wish and just a little over a year before, I was honoured to be at the dedication. Beside the monument there is a statue to Sgt. Gander, the Newfoundland dog who was awarded the canine equivalent of the VC, the Dickin Medal of Bravery, for his actions in the Pacific theater with the Royal Rifles of Canada.

On the Peacekeepers Memorial, my father's name is proudly displayed. He was a man who believed in peace and was willing to fight to keep it. He was the inspiration for the crest on my biker vest that said just that: Aggressive Pacifist will fight to keep the Peace.

It was yet another gorgeous day in paradise, and after some quiet reflection on the sacrifices of all those remembered in the park, I started out on yet another day's walk. Bass River to Masstown Market, twenty four and a half kilometers and more when I add in the detour, so it was time to get hoofing it. As the expression goes, we were burning daylight and I had places to be. I had Thai in her Petgear Stroller. I think she was liking the ride as I walked and pushed. I was very cognizant of how quickly the temperatures would heat the pavement and asphalt to a blistering temperature that would burn the pads of her feet and I was not about to let anything happen to her. So, having bid Joc a farewell for a couple hours, I plugged in my MP3 player, cued up Lynryd Skynrd's Gimme Three Steps, and started picking them up and putting them down.

I was feeling strong and all the training up to the kickoff day was definitely paying off. I settled into a pace where I was pushing five and a half to six kilometers an hour. I had a good steady pace going and it would allow me to get most of my walk in before the midday heat arrived to start sucking the life out of me.

Today, though, there would be another event that would drain the energy from me. I knew it would. How could it not? About two thirds of the way into Masstown, I was meeting Angela Reid, Silver Cross Mother to Christopher Reid, and we were going to visit Christopher's graveside. Angela had been with me on the opening day and had released the dove for the families of the fallen. She understood what it meant to me and why this walk was so important. She understood the impact that tragedy could have in one's life. Illness had claimed her only daughter, the war in Afghanistan her only son. More than anyone I knew, she understood the pain of loss of a child.

Right around eleven, I met Angela and Jocelyn at the church and she guided us back to the Christopher's graveside. For the next hour I heard her share stories of Christopher's life, and sadly, his death. It was heart wrenching, moving, personal and a glimpse into the War that I was both honoured to have and wished I hadn't. I wished no mother had to deal with the pain of giving up one's son or daughter for a country.

In the midst of the stories, she stopped. She held her breath for a couple seconds. Then she asked me a question.

"Do you know what I want more than anything?" In my mind I assumed she would for her son back. That would be a natural request. I nodded to indicate that I didn't know.

"All I ever want is to ensure that no one ever forgets Christopher or any of the others. We have to make sure they are remembered. For if they are not, this is so pointless."

The lump in my throat threatened to choke me. I could not swallow. I could not speak. I could only nod.

We stood there silently, sharing a few quiet moments and then we hugged.

"You give them Hell." Her words of encouragement were powerful, and in the coming weeks, when the pain of blisters and my rheumatoid arthritis would rear its ugly head, I would think back to the pain of a mother, and I would ensure that no one forgets. How could I?

Dieppe
20 August, 2013

Yesterday Jocelyn and I toured the National Field of Honour in Pointe Claire, Quebec. I had risen very early and logged my kilometers so that we would be free to wander the fields with no pressure. Today was a very special day, marking the seventy-third anniversary of the raid on Dieppe. Dieppe remains a very contentious point of historical debate. Was it a precursor to Operation Overlord, the ultimate invasion of Normandy? Was it a giant ruse to cover the attempt to capture a copy of the German Code machine, Enigma? There are theories and speculation, but what is known is that in six hours the operation ended in chaos with many killed and captured. Lt Col Cecil Merritt, RMC Ex cadet was awarded the Victoria Cross for Gallantry on the shores of Dieppe. Even more amazingly, Captain Padre John Weir Foote was also awarded the VC for ministering to the injured as the battle raged around him.

Jocelyn, Thai, and I had a clear sunny day ahead of us to wander the grounds and visit Canadian Veteran's graves that stretched from the Fenian Raids to present day. Death, the great equalizer in the march of time claims all from private to general, and row after row of carefully arranged bronze markers stretched out over the vast acreage before us. I could not help but think that some of the men who lay before us had survived the horrors of Dieppe.

The Long Walk to Sanity had already been punctuated by some powerful moments: The Dove release, visiting Christopher Reid's grave, and touring the Bass River Veterans Memorial Park numbered amongst them. But they would pale in comparison to the afternoon of the 20th of August in St Jean Sur Richelieu.

I had spent two summers trying to improve my mastery of the French language, in 1980 at the College Militaire Royale and again in 1983 at CFB St Jean, affectionately known as the Megaplex. So it would be absolutely fitting that I would log some kilometers in and around the grounds. Upon completion we made our way to the Legion where I was genuinely about to be humbled.

While at the Legion, I was introduced to an older gentlemen, still spry, but time was taking its toll. I met Jacques Nadeau, who had been taken prisoner at Dieppe, the day before, seventy three years earlier. I was speechless. I did not know what to say to a man who had endured so much. I was lucky that he was in the mood to talk and today I was the one chosen to listen to his story. His quiet reflections were not ones of great deeds or glory. No, his story was one of having survived hell and mourning the loss of those who never made it off the beaches of Dieppe or out of the Stalag where he was held until their eventual liberation by Field Marshall Zhukov and the Russian Army. The march from the Stalag to the shores of the Black sea, the tramp steamer to Gibraltar, the eventual landing back in England were all fascinating and I listened, both enthralled and in awe. He nursed his beer, and slowly, bit by bit, a story of sacrifice and the power of will unfolded. I dared not interrupt for to do so would run the risk of opening up old wounds that may have scabbed over with the passage of time. I could see in his eyes and hear in his voice some of the same elements when I describe a certain night on the North Atlantic. The passage of time does nothing to dull certain memories.

I ordered him another beer as his mood lightened and he told of the amazing Vodka party with Zhukov's private dance troupe. He was trying to move away from the dark edge. When he paused for reflection, I respectfully asked if he would not mind answering a question. He assured me that he did not mind at this point, though I could sense that he hoped it was not one of the trite questions that veterans often get asked.

"Jacques, this may seem a bit strange. Did you come home in the same boots you landed on the shores of Dieppe in?"

Jacques stared off into space, deep in contemplation, and I could see him searching the deep recesses of memory banks not frequently accessed.

"Yes, yes I did come home in the same pair of boots." His voice was soft and muted, but still somber. "Why do you ask that?" I think he was shocked by the question.

"Jacques, in three years in a POW camp, I am sure that boot care, brushes and polish were the last things you were going to get, and if you were not getting basics, I do not imagine you were getting much else."

His eyes welled up. He nodded a faint nod. With one question I had validated his entire POW experience.

"We got a couple of Red Cross packages and letters from home that was all." His voice trailed off.

He was done talking. He eased his way out of a chair, and walked over to a bookcase in the corner of the Legion Hall. He removed a book and asked for a pen. Slowly, he wrote inside the book and handed it to me.

The book remains amongst my prized treasures. The book, "Dieppe Ma Prison, recit de guerre de Jacques Nadeau" was handed to me.

Inside the cover, his signature, and the simple inscription, "20 Aug. 2013, Dieppe plus une".

Lest we ever forget and the memory of this day I shall not.

Kapyong Beast
29 August, 2013

Peterborough, Ontario. It is the 29th of August and I am several days past the halfway point and two days out of my hometown of Marmora, Ontario. Marmora is a small farming and tourist town at the juncture of Highways Seven and Fourteen. I would continue my walks but it would be a chance to be out of the spotlight for a few days and recharge for the final push. Standing between me and some earned time off out of the public spotlight were two more walks and two more Legion presentations.

I figured I would get a real early start on the day and was walking on some of the trails in Peterborough to get as many kilometers behind me before the heat took its toll. The memories of Port Perry and the stifling humidity alongside Lake Scugog were still too fresh.

Thai and I were picking them up and putting them down, enjoying the solitude of the early morning, when around a bend in the trail another walker appeared striding confidently and with purpose. As we were about to pass he stopped me by saying "I know you from somewhere?" I was not sure but I figured I would stop and at least be pleasant.

"I am not sure. What is your name?"

"Greg Hanley."

"Holy old crap on a cracker…. Medric Cousineau." I had grown up playing hockey with Greg's brothers Mark and Justin in Marmora. I had not seen Greg in over thirty years since he'd left for the Police College and I'd left for the Military. How he recognized me was beyond me, but I was glad. We shared a few kilometers and caught up on decades of life in a few moments. It was just another of the strange twists of fate and coincidence that seemed to be occurring with ever greater frequency as the Long Walk to Sanity gathered steam and Ottawa drew ever closer.

I wish I could say that was the biggest twist of fate on the emotional roller coaster for the day, but it would barely register compared to the events that would unfold later.

After returning to the hotel and a quick bite of breakfast, Jocelyn and I headed out to do a few kilometers on the Trans Canada Trail alongside the Trent Canal system. Huge shade trees and well groomed trails and paths made for easy walking before we were due at the Legion for lunch, my presentation, and a relaxing afternoon. My days were actually starting to settle into a groove. Walk, talk, presentation, media, reload, and prep for the next day.

The lunch at the Legion was good home cooked fare and after lunch I gave my presentation touching on PTSD and how Thai had changed my life closing with my thanking them for their support of the cause and other disabled Veterans. I had an hour to kill before my next media interview so I was looking forward to a few moments of quiet reflection to get my head back together.

Jocelyn approached me with an older lady in tow. "Hon, this Lady was wondering if she could have a chat in private."

"Sure, can you grab me a coffee and we will be over in the corner?" Due to what comes next I will guard her anonymity and respect her family's right to privacy. She had a large Manila envelope that was worn and showed its age. We pulled a couple chairs to the corner where I could keep an eye on the room and Thai curled up at my feet, content that I was not moving for now. I think we were both starting to get road weary.

She gently removed a large photo with a smartly turned out soldier in his battle dress. Good looking soldier and I noted the PPCLI shoulder flash on his shoulder. Infanteer. Seek out, close with, and destroy the enemy. Next she showed me a picture of some troops humping gear up a mountain. There was a pencil drawn arrow pointing to one of the soldiers with the inscription "This is me in Korea." Oh No! This was not just an infanteer. I was talking to the wife of someone very special.

The tears started down her cheeks and her voice cracked. "I am so glad I came to hear you talk today. Now I know. And for the first time in thirty years, I have an answer, an answer that I can share with my boys."

"Thank you." I did not know what to say.

"For all those years we thought it was us." She was trying to reconcile actions, thoughts and outcomes.

"It wasn't you. It wasn't the boys. It was the injury."

"When he killed himself in 1982…" Her voice trailed off.

I sat in stunned respectful silence. What the hell was I going to say?

"Nights were always the worst… he would scream…." Her voice was breaking and it was getting harder for her to finish sentences. "We thought it was us."

"Do you know what the Battle of Kapyong is?" I was hoping to give her something to hold onto, something that would validate her emotions and give her sons something to look back at fondly and remember their father for his actions of heroism and not for the final act that claimed a tortured soul.

"For three days and nights in late April of 1951, the 2nd Battalion of the Princess Patricia's Canadian Light infantry not only held hill 677 against immeasurable odds, but were instrumental in shaping the outcome of the Korean War. For those who were there, what they faced was hard to comprehend. Eventually, the unit was awarded the Presidential Citation for their actions. They were heroes. One and all, including your husband. Very few knew what really happened out there. It would not be easy to find inner peace after what they had been through."

"After all these years… Now I know. Thank you."

PTSD had claimed a victim thirty years after the conflict and thirty years ago… the Beast never sleeps. Bastard!

Trenton
03 September, 2013

Today's walk would be a tough one. Not the physical challenge. Nope, today was going to be a tough one because we were starting the day with a parade into the Afghanistan Repatriation Memorial in Trenton, Ontario, which is the start of the Highway of Heroes. I had visited the Memorial with Thai back at the start of June when we were up for the Highway of Heroes Ride.

The Highway of Heroes runs from Trenton down the 401 to Toronto to the Coroner's office, the stretch of road that all of our Afghanistan fallen have travelled before making the final journey to their ultimate resting place, be it Beechwood or elsewhere. The Highway was renamed in 2007 to commemorate the ultimate sacrifice of those that journeyed down that stretch of road one final time with the overpasses being lined with Canadians waving flags and showing respect.

On November 10th, 2012 a stunning granite monument was unveiled and dedicated to the fallen. A soldier saluting two granite maple leaves, one red representing our country, the other black, with a soldier fractured from the rest of his family, and the names of each of our fallen adorning the back makes a stunning statement ensuring that we as a nation will not forget. Angela Reid's wish would be honoured.

So it was that we gathered in the early morning with the Legion Colour Party and a piper to parade us into the Memorial to have a short service of remembrance before I started yet another day's sojourn in the Long Walk to Sanity. Perhaps most telling were the moments following the memorial service.

I gathered those in attendance and was sharing brief bits and anecdotes about those that I had come to know through their buddies or the families of the fallen. My way of paying tribute and ensuring that I would ensure that Angela's wish was upheld. Having shared brief bits about several of the soldiers I arrived at the name Braun Scott Woodfield, or "Woody" to his buddies. I had come to know "Woody" through Shane Jones, who sustained horrific injuries in the accident that had claimed his buddy "Woody." Shane bears both the physical and mental scars of a sequence of events that will likely never leave him. As I read out his name the piper asked if he could speak.

"Most certainly." How could I not let someone share who wished to honour our fallen?

"Braun was my nephew and I piped him home." Yet once again the lump in my throat was instantaneously large. I nodded knowingly and the teardrops fell. Once again, the connection to our fallen was highlighted and the impact made crystal clear, hitting like a freight train and sucking the breath out of those in attendance. They were not names. They were people, brothers, sisters, sons, daughters, ours and gone.

It was against this very somber backdrop that I began the day's march. I had a lot to think about. The stark realities of the losses in the war in Afghanistan could not have been more in the forefront as Thai and I headed out to continue our quest to help those that struggle with PTSD. Many of those who served with those whose names we had read this morning struggle and need help. I know it. Darlene Cushman, Darryl Caswell's Memorial Cross Mother knows it. Angela Reid knows it. Countless others who were all stepping up to help those who struggle before they too become victims of an injury that started elsewhere but would claim lives here at home if serious help was not forthcoming immediately. How do I know? I have been to the edge more times than I care to admit. I was thousands of miles from the North Atlantic and decades removed, yet the demons threaten to steal my soul and my life if I am not ever vigilant.

Later that morning, Jocelyn, Thai and I would visit the Aviation museum in Trenton and I would come face to face with the Reaper yet again. We had been enjoying the pieces of aviation history and I particularly enjoyed the display marking Flying officer Bagg's acceptance of the surrender of the German Cruiser Nurnberg. Then I walked around the corner and there was a Search and Rescue display and the mannequin was wearing a double lift harness. The identical piece of kit I had worn that night so many years ago and last night in my dreams, no nightmares.

Instantly Thai was on me and I was bolting for the door and the building threatened to crash in on us. My anxiety level had a near vertical trajectory. Not good. Triggers. Sights, sounds, and smells all capable of unleashing an uncontrolled avalanche of intrusive thoughts that take you back to places you do not want to be having sensory overload that you pray would have diminished with time. Sadly, it hasn't.

Thai is on me, alerting and persistent. She knows that I am not doing well. Today I wish that somehow she could know what my triggers are and somehow keep me away from them. I know that this is completely unrealistic but having had an emotional morning I was running on fumes and did not have the energy to put up much of a fight against the relentless onslaught of the visions and the smells.

Decades removed and as clear and sharp as yesterday. The mind is a powerful weapon and an inescapable prison at the same time. I wonder if those whose business it is to treat those of us who suffer have any idea how bad these episodes are, sucking the very life out of you and with it the will to carry on. Thankfully, now I have Thai who has helped drag me back from the abyss and given me a reason to live. "You know sweetie, I wonder how many more like you we can get for others like me, victims of unseen injuries, carrying deep wounds and scars that most will never understand."

I look deep into Thai's big brown eyes and I see a singular unconditional love with no judgment. I wonder if those who take care of us know the power of that love and lack of judgment.

I think back to the Repat memorial, the 158 names and wonder how many carry scars from those incidents that claimed our heroes? Today, it is very raw. Ground Zero of pain for the Afghanistan War and because of my incident at the museum where my heart rate exploded and the taste was in my mouth, all too real.

"Thai girly, have I ever told you how much PTSD sucks? I am sure I have." I reach down and rub her ears. The furry four legged therapist seems to know just what I need.

202 | P a g e

SOS
15 September, 2013

The days have begun to blur and I am lucky if I know where I am and where I am going next. The road has become a blur of media, presentations, walks, and the emotional roller coaster has begun to careen hopelessly out of control. I feel like I am just a passenger hanging on. Focusing on getting through the next few days will be critical, but I can see the end zone and feel somewhat energized by that fact. I am starting to wonder what it will feel like not to get up, pound the pavement for twenty plus klicks, and then try and explain the mission that I am on to those who don't understand PTSD. A few more days and I get there. First we have today.

I am starting the day in Smiths Falls Ontario, the small town where my father was born and is buried alongside my mother. My grandparents are buried in the same cemetery. This will mark the end of today's walk. The chance to spend some time with my parents and ancestors will be a moving time before the main event of the day. As soon as I am done at the cemetery, we are off to Beechwood for what will be a powerful experience fraught with emotional land mines.

Today, at Beechwood, a plaque and tree are going to be dedicated to the SOS project. SOS: Soldiers of Suicide and military shorthand for Struck Off Strength. Several of the SOS families will be there and I feel guilty. Survivor's Guilt. I'm crawling up out of the dark chasm that claimed their sons and daughters.

I've spent the last forty-five days championing the cause of PTSD: Put The Stigma Down. Today I have to honor to meet several families whose children fell to the hand of an unseen enemy in a war that most Canadians have no idea is being fought right here on Canadian soil. It's being fought by hundreds, if not thousands, who are casualties of military operations stretching back to the beginnings of our country. Alexander Cameron in the War of 1812, Thane MacDowell, VC, First World War hero, and many of the Second World War and Korean Veterans I've met on the road. They knew. They know. They have the look, the stare, and the unfinished sentences that trail off into a sea of emotional turmoil.

It will be my first trip back to Beechwood since I'd spent time with Darlene Cushman at Darryl's graveside. I was hoping that this small effort would provide a degree of closure and validation for those who had lost their loved ones to their own hand. I wrestled with the demons and the anguish. Would I be able to face those families knowing that the Reaper had swung his scythe for me and I had narrowly escaped several times? I was championing an effort to ensure that our injured would not become our fallen, yet I was too late for some. Hopefully in the pain, the tears, and the anguish, there would be born a light of hope. Hope that for those who struggle with the demons that erase all tomorrows that there would be answers.

First I had to finish today's kilometers with Jocelyn and Vaughn Cosman, my OPI who had done a yeoman's job handling all the behind the scenes administrative work so that I could continue to stay focused on the mission. Walk and Talk. The talk was getting more powerful with each telling as my list of experiences grew. Dieppe, Kapyong, Bass River, Doves, Memorial Cross mothers, and soon the families of the Soldiers of Suicide, all of whom were leaving marks on my soul in ways that I had not expected.

I do not think that any of us involved with the Long Walk To Sanity could have envisioned where this was heading and how it would end. In a couple more days I would meet the Minister of Veterans Affairs and then two days after that would have the final walk. The funds were starting to come in and the story was starting to precede me, but I was still wracked with doubts. I know it seems mildly ironic that after forty five days and nearly a thousand kilometers in towns and cities in four provinces I was still second guessing myself.

Perhaps one will always be second guessing oneself after staring into the abyss and deciding to end it all. I had survived the car wreck. I can never wear a neck tie. Between the neck seal on a poopy suit and the feel of rope, let us just say that I have developed a serious allergy to the sensation of anything around my neck. It is why I fear I am going to struggle with meeting the families of the fallen this afternoon. There but for the grace of God go I. Maybe I was spared to do this.

Manotick Summit
17 September, 2013

Forty eight days on the road having covered more than a thousand kilometers through sublime blue-skied summer days, rain, hail, cloud, winds, and unrelenting heat, and Thai and I had strode on. Yet here we were, about to walk into the most important meeting of the past seven weeks, the meeting that could define this entire trip. The entire Long Walk to Sanity was about to come completely into focus.

One chance to get it right.

I have to admit I am nervous. I am at the Manotick Legion waiting, keyed up like before a big football game, knowing this meeting could make or break this entire walk.

Minister Fantino strode up to me and we shook hands.

"Glad to meet you Captain Cousineau and let me say you do not have to walk any more. You have made your point."

"Thank you Minister Fantino. But I have some unfinished business, so I've got a few more kilometers left in this old war horse. I do have to admit it has taken its toll." My knees and ankles were shot. My Rheumatoid Arthritis was screaming and I had pounded my body every single day for the previous seven weeks. This was worse than two a day football practices in the unrelenting August heat in Kingston.

In reality though, the past seven weeks were just an extension of the months before. The countless stairs I'd climbed and kilometers I'd walked to prepare to accomplish what I was doing were the entrance fee to the dance, and failure to have paid the piper his due would have been cause for failure.

"I can imagine it has. So why don't you tell me what you have been up to? I have gotten some of the notes from my staff but would like to hear it from you."

I was gripped with panic and anxiety. The lump in my throat swelled and Thai was up from under my chair, paws in my lap staring at me. She knew, I knew, Jocelyn knew, and my buddy

Vaughn Cosman who had organized all the administrative stuff certainly knew and those who did not were the Minister and his staffers.

"Easy girl, I am with you." I tried to sound calm and confidant but Thai knew my insides were a mess. After thousands of kilometers on the walk and in training, I had gotten what I had come for. A meeting with the Minister of Veterans Affairs to explain why PTSD service dogs needed to make it on to Veterans Affairs Canada's Radar.

"Well sir." I started reluctantly. My mind flashed back to hours walking on the beach at the Sandbanks Provincial Park with a former RMC buddy, another member of the Stone Frigate English Fellowship who also suffers from PTSD from some times and places he still can't discuss. One day he'll open up to me, or maybe he won't, but, like me, he's found some comfort in the mission to help people through service dogs. He works in the background, while I'm out on the front lines. Maybe one day I'll see him with a dog, and with a smile, instead of the chronic tense expression and sleep-deprived eyes from the night terrors. We'd rehearsed the conversation, tried out what might work and what wouldn't. Planned for point and counter point.

"Call me Julian please."

"Well Julian, you can call me Cous, and here we go. I started this walk because very few people understand what service dogs can do for those who suffer from PTSD."

"You know we are studying the use of Therapy dogs?" Julian said. The tone in his voice made me suspect that, like his staffers up until a few days before, he didn't know the difference between a service dog and a therapy dog.

"I realize that, and I applaud you for that, but that is not what I am talking about. A Therapy dog is not a Service Dog. Yes, they are both furry, four legged, well behaved and have great skill sets but they are not the same thing. Not even close. Let me explain."

I could see from his look and from his body language that we were heading where I needed the conversation to go.

"A Therapy Dog is a dog trained to work with one handler in an institutional setting, primarily providing emotive support in five to ten minute blocks to a variety of clients or patients. A Service Dog is task specific trained to work with one handler for their unique issues. One handler, one dog, one job, always one. So Thai has been trained to work with my PTSD. She is mine, I am hers, and we are a team. What you saw a few minutes ago was part of what she had been trained to do."

I could see the Minister glancing over at Thai who was curled up quietly watching my back as the meeting rolled on.

"When she got up and put her paws on me, what you saw was one of those specific tasks. She could sense my rising anxiety and she needed me to stop where I was going mentally."

"I apologize if I caused it," Julian said. His voice was sincere and concerned.

"Thank you but it had nothing to do with you and everything to do with me. Sadly, as a result of my injuries, my emotional and mental thought trains can derail and there's nothing I can do about it. Most days I have no idea that the train wreck is underway and by the time I do we have most likely crossed over a line from which I do not easily recover."

"Fascinating," Julian said.

I could see the gears working and the Minister was trying to assess where to go next. "I understand that there has been very little research done into the use of service dogs and what has been done is mostly based in the United States."

"Exactly. Therein lies the rub. There needs to be more research done, and specifically we need to study the Canadian cohort, the Canadian experience. Our social networks are different, and our health care system is very different and we need to study that uniquely Canadian experience."

"You up for a walk in the fresh air? I think it might be time to discuss some of this in a less formal setting. I would like to get to hear more of your experiences on the road."

The Minister of Veterans Affairs wanted to go on a walk. The Long Walk to Sanity had just picked up another passenger. We adjourned the formal part of the meeting and headed off to tour the Historic Watson's Mill, a flour mill that predates Confederation. We had an opportunity to talk about the challenges of living with PTSD and the complexity of the injury, which in many ways stood in sharp contrast to the historic mill we were touring. Using water to drive a turbine to turn the mill stone had been known for hundreds of years, the principles used for centuries, the elements harnessed. The mill stands in sharp contrast to the uncharted complexity of the mind and injuries we do not fully understand or appreciate.

By the time the tour and the afternoon had finished, the Minister had arrived at one decision. A research assessment into the existing body of knowledge would be announced so the government could start the complex process of developing a veteran's PTSD service dog initiative.

The announcement would be made on the 18th of September, one day before the formal finish of the Long Walk to Sanity. The advocacy work was paying off. Even though the Minister said I didn't need to walk any farther, that I'd made my point, the Walk would continue, and the fund raising would continue.

Because in my heart I knew that so many needed help to combat the beast, PTSD. And, on my personal level, in my personal battle, putting one foot in front of the other, with Thai at my side, keeps the beast at bay.

Research Assessment Announcement

http://www.veterans.gc.ca/eng/news/viewrelease/1939

September 18, 2013

Department of Veterans Affairs

Ottawa, ON — The Honourable Julian Fantino, Minister of Veterans Affairs, today announced that he has directed his officials to proceed with a research assessment on whether psychiatric service dogs can be effective in treating post-traumatic stress disorder (PTSD). This first step will serve to fully review the existing international research on the topic, identify areas where data may be missing and determine what knowledge would be necessary to inform a Canadian approach to the use of service dogs.

"The health and well-being of Veterans and their families is a matter of paramount importance to our Government," said Minister Fantino. "The use of psychiatric service dogs to treat Veterans with post-traumatic stress disorder has generated a great deal of interest and attention. We seek to partner with academics who have expertise in the field to gather scientific evidence to see whether this approach can enhance the care we provide to Veterans and their families."

Earlier today, Minister Fantino met with Captain (retired) Medric Cousineau, a Veteran who has been leading the Long Walk to Sanity project, a PTSD awareness and fund raising walking expedition. Captain Cousineau started walking on August 1 in Nova Scotia to help raise awareness about the potential benefits of service dogs for Veterans who are coping with mental health issues. The walk will conclude tomorrow in Ottawa.

"By forging ahead on his walking expedition and working to spread the word amongst Canadians, Captain Cousineau has demonstrated incredible persistence, grit and strength of character. It was a true pleasure to meet with him today," said Minister Fantino.

Further details on Veterans Affairs Canada's project partner and the scope of work will be available in the coming days.

The first Canadian Military Assistance Dog Summit will take place on Saturday, September 21, at the Canadian War Museum in Ottawa.

Veterans Affairs Canada's support and services offer the right care at the right time to get the best result for the new generation of Veterans and their families. Find out more at veterans.gc.ca.

DAY 50, Part One
19 September, 2013

I was awake. The Butterflies were plentiful and I had more than a twinge of nausea. I could feel Thai at my side and Jocelyn was still sleeping. We had been staging out of my buddy Vaughn's for the past week and finally, after forty nine long days and more than a thousand and fifty kilometers I stood on the very brink of completion. The Long Walk to Sanity in support of Paws Fur Thought would be in the books in the next seven hours.

The miles walked, the hills climbed, the people I had met and the stories that they had shared had helped spur me on to the finish and it was but a short walk away.

Major Francine Harding, a friend of Dee Brasseur, had worked with Vaughn on the preparations for the final day. We would start at Beechwood and finish in Memorial Hall in the National War Museum, having stopped at the Tomb of the Unknown Soldier and the Terry Fox Monument enroute. Physically it was going to be a very short walk, but mentally I would be dealing with the sea of emotions that at many times throughout the walk threatened to capsize the leaky boat of my sanity.

From the Memorial Cross Mothers to the Kapyong Widow, the SOS Dedication and Jacques Nadeau, Dieppe POW survivor, the juxtaposition of life and death, the transient nature of life, weighed heavy on my shoulders. I was both elated to be finished and strangely, I was going to miss the routine of rise, prep, walk and talk. It had been a very long walk, a Long Walk to Sanity, for if nothing else happened, we, all of us, the team and the supporters, all of us would be able to look back on what we had done and know that we had changed lives for the better. We had an impact. We made a difference.

My Buddy Kate MacEachern was somewhere out on the road in Quebec working on finishing her Long Way Home, helping raise funds for Military Minds, a huge Facebook community for PTSD survivors and sufferers. Kate had inspired me with her first walk. Dennis Manuge, "Cpl Justice" of the SISIP class action fame, would be in Ottawa today, another hugely inspirational source of motivation. You have to do the right thing, even when everyone else doubts what you are doing.

Kate and Dennis were such huge inspirations. So too would be the Soldiers of Suicide and the Soldier buried in the Tomb of the Unknown Soldier. They all embodied the face of sacrifice. The living and the dead. I could only hope that our efforts would pay off. I knew that they had. George and Vardo, Dan and Kenya, were living proof that what we're striving for was so necessary. Disabled Veterans battling PTSD with a new "leash" on life.

Karen McCrimmon former squadron commander, Jeff Page, ex RCEME Soldier, Harold Wright, and countless others flood through my mind. Day after day out on the road, there was something in each community that provided fire or re-enforced my decisions. Simple headstones in Beechwood, brass plaques in the National Field of Honour, and monuments like those at Bass River Veterans Memorial Park stood sentinels to sacrifice. The Arch at RMC, huge and imposing, and some of the names were names I knew. Thane McDowell, VC winner and PTSD sufferer from the First World War was often in my thoughts.

"On the Edge of Destiny, you must test your strengths." Pam, Rhonda, and Brenda all had a hand to play in the story. From training and preparation to the daily motivational posters. In Pam's case, another permanent reminder of the tenuous grasp we all have on life. How quickly the sands can slip through the hour glass of life and once gone, the change is permanent and irreversible. My new found "joie de vivre" was a direct result of witnessing the carnage that war can inflict. Some of the enemies are clearly identifiable and visible and my mind conjures up a picture of the grey German Second World War uniforms while others are unseen, relentless and claiming victims in an individual's battle to win the war for their sanity. I get it, having fought the battle too many times. Over the past fifty days, I had many hours and opportunities to reflect upon some of the high risk behaviours I had employed in my desperate fight to feel emotion, to feel anything.

"Maybe if I could feel, I could convince myself I was alive." There were times when I would inflict pain upon myself to see if anything would register. There had been times when I had been so heavily medicated that nothing registered.

Emotional flat line.

There are also huge gaps in my memory that have been eradicated by massive pharmacological intervention. The good news, if there is any, is that I survived to share my story with others. I had stood at the brink, I had trudged down the road of despair, I had contemplated the end too often.

Thai's wet nose is bumping my hand. I snap back to the reality of the moment. She wants me in the here and now and not drifting off to some dangerous head space of disassociation.

The gentle rap on the door.

"Hey Cous. Buddy it is time to start moving, we have got to get ready to get to Beechwood. Traffic can be a pain."

Vaughn was right. We needed to get from Carleton Place to Beechwood. The final pages of the story of the Long Walk to Sanity were about to be written, including a benediction by BGen John Fletcher, the Chaplain General of the Canadian Forces, and member of the class of 84 from RMC.

After some easy stretching, I laced up my boots for what would be the final walk in the Long Walk to Sanity, but just another day in the continuing struggle with my PTSD.

Today, I hope to make peace with a demon that has haunted me for 22 years. My walk was not started on the First of August and scheduled to end Fifty Days later. I have carried a secret. The Long Walk to Sanity was scheduled so that it ended today, hopefully in triumph with a legacy I could be proud of. Twenty two years ago, today, I left the Canadian Armed Forces, broken, hurt and ashamed battling unspeakable demons that no one, including myself, understood. It was not a legacy that I envisioned or aspired to. I cannot go back and write a new beginning, but I can start today and write a new ending. Write I will.

Day 50, Part Two
19 September, 2013

The trip from Carleton Place to Beechwood had been pretty much what we had expected. Early morning traffic in the Nation's Capital was always a bit of a log jam as it was in any large metropolitan center. Thankfully, we pulled into Beechwood National Cemetery with time to spare. The last thing I wanted to be was adrift for my final stage.

Several people were already gathered. Karen McCrimmon, Dee Brasseur and Francine Harding who had arranged all the logistics for today. The Chaplain General, John Fletcher, and his partner would be coming. We would start with a Benediction and Blessing by the SOS monument that had been dedicated just four short days before. The very thought still caused me twinges of guilt. I had survived, and we were going to the spot honouring those who fell to the unseen, relentless enemy. In going toe to toe with the Beast, I wanted to claim victory.

"For it is a human number, and its number is Six Hundred and Sixty Six." And its letters P, T, S and D. The Devil's spawn. Pure evil.

Dee was there with her latest puppy, Sabre, an Afghan hound and housemate to her other two Afghans.

"Dee, we sure have come a long way from Halifax." Most would think I was referring to our Long Walk, but Dee nodded knowingly thinking back to our meeting at the Legion Dominion Conference in Halifax a few months before I got Thai. It was not that long ago, but the journey had taken us miles from where I had been. Not geographically, as much as it was in reality. I no longer stood on the edge of the abyss daily contemplating suicide as a viable option.

"I am so proud of you, you have come a long way." Dee's words, heartfelt and sincere. She knew how desperate I had been and how close I had come.

"Dee, do you have my number set aside? It is mine, I own this MOFO!" I was referring to her One in a Million Challenge Coins that she was using to fund PTSD related projects. Dee was one of

Canada's first two Lady F18 Combat Pilots, member of the Order of Canada, and fellow PTSD Sufferer. I wanted a very specific coin. The number? 666... the number of the Beast and I was now willing to state openly and publicly that I had kicked the Beast's ass. The previous forty nine days had been a quest to raise funds and advocate. It had also provided me with the time for introspection and healing. The experiences on the road with the people I had met were going to be unforgettable. I met those who suffered for decades, those who had their lives permanently altered by the Beast and those who were unaware but were fast becoming staunch advocates of Paws Fur Thought and what we were attempting to do.

"Don't worry Medric, I have it set aside." Validation and acknowledgment. Both added a little bounce to my step, which I must admit had lost a little spring since day one in Eastern Passage. We had come so far. Four provinces, a thousand plus kilometers, and dozens of communities who had all helped us arrive at exactly where we were. Minister Fantino had announced the Research Assessment in conjunction with Alice Aiken of CIMVHR. We had placed dogs. We had others in the wings, completely transparent money at the NS Nunavut Command of the Royal Canadian Legion, and had done countless media interviews. Fundraise and advocate: The objectives had been met in spades because of the hard work of Vaughn Cosman, Hugh Ellis, Francine Harding, Jeff Page, Gary Pond, Maggie Van Tassel, Kevin McLean, Becky Kent, Peter Stoffer, Doug Cosman, Harold Wright, Lise Charron, Trapper Cane, Bryan Bailey and "Uncle" Frank Norman. The list could go on and I am sure that I would forget someone. Their efforts not forgotten, my mind just a blur.

After John Fletcher's service we would gather and start our walk towards the final destination, Memorial Hall at the National War Museum. Many had thought I would finish my walk on Parliament Hill. I had long since decided that I did not want to do that. There were a couple of reasons. I did not want to show up on Day Fifty of the Walk and have Mother Nature rain all over our parade and, more importantly, did not want to finish this effort on "The Hill" beside a group that could potentially show up and demonstrate for a cause that was incompatible with what I was up to, or worse, in absolute opposition to it. I had thought it through months before and made the decision that Memorial Hall was the place. Fitting and honestly a way for me to honour sacrifice, the ultimate sacrifices of those who had fought for our freedoms. Beechwood National Cemetery to the Tomb of the Unknown Soldier to Memorial Hall.

The media was coming along for the journey and several key players would be at the finish at the War Museum. Just a few emotional kilometers to go and the Long Walk to Sanity would be in the books. I was absolutely a maelstrom of emotions at this point. The pain of the arthritis in my feet had long since turned my feet into nagging reminders of every step. "Suck it up buttercup" kept playing through my head. Yes, I hurt and yes it had been one awfully long journey but the sacrifice paled in comparison to those whose headstones stood sentinel at Beechwood, those whose sacrifices were remembered at the National War Memorial, and the sacrifice that Memorial Hall signifies.

The weather was agreeable, and after the service we set off, trying to be cognizant of Francine's timings yet also trying to give to those who wanted some of our time today. It was a very special day. Jocelyn, Vaughn and so many others who had believed in me were present to see us over the "finish line." In the back of my mind, I had a nagging suspicion that *finish* would be a relative term, and that there was a lot of work yet to be done. A writer once told me that there's a lot of power in typing "The End." That The End often starts more projects than it finishes. I suspected those words were about to come true.

All I knew is that Minister Fantino's words were ringing in my ears. "You have made your point. You do not need to walk anymore."

I hoped it to be the case but I think he knew that I would do whatever it was what was required to push the advocacy further. Failure was not an option. "Focus: Obstacles are those things you see when you take your eye off the goal."

Part Five:

The Aftermath

RMC Address Delivered
25 September, 2013

The ride on the emotional roller coaster that had become my life with Thai is about to turn the page on yet another chapter. It is a clear, sunny and crisp fall day and Jocelyn, Thai and I make our way across the Parade square at RMC. I have a small moment of panic and look around for fourth years about to scream at me to "Double Rook."

At this hour, cadets of all years are scurrying to and fro, intent on the business of the day. The first years are clearly identifiable in their combats, Land Distinctive Uniforms, as they have not yet earned the right to wear the college uniforms. The rite of passage, the Obstacle Course will be run on Friday, and then Saturday morning they will receive their RMC cap badge and start the next phase of a four year journey that will see them complete their degrees and earn their Queen's commission as officers.

Today, I was here to address the fourth year class, with a smattering of other years, staff and other distinguished guests present. We would be joined by MGen Retd Frank Norman who was Commandant in my fourth year and by one of my classmates, LCol Bryan "Beetle" Bailey, who would provide my introduction to the assembly who was gathering for a professional development lecture.

I would be doing the address to a packed Currie Hall in Mackenzie building. After the class had assembled, "Uncle Frank" leading, we made our way to the front of the room. The lump in my throat was there, not like other times, this one predicated on the nervousness of hoping I nail the address. I was here to talk to our soon to be newly minted junior officers about PTSD, Mental Health and a few other bits that I would throw in for good measure.

"Ladies and Gentlemen, Distinguished guests. It is my distinct honour and privilege to introduce one of my classmates…" Bryan was confident and his intro started to flow. He touched on my track record as a Frigateer, a member of the class of '83 and my role on the RMC Redmen Football team.

"Cous, as he is known to most of us, was also the first graduate of the College to be awarded the Star of Courage." I wince, Uncle Frank had uncovered that piece of trivia, and although a matter of historical record, it is a fact that I struggle with. So many brave men had preceded me out of the College, to assume their roles amongst our troops in Her Majesties Service.

"Ladies and Gentlemen, Cous." Thai and I make our way from the seats in the front up onto the stage where I place Thai in a down and wait, and instinctively she is already scanning the room and trying to sense my mood.

"Distinguished guests, Staff, and most importantly, you the Ladies and Gentlemen of the Cadet Wing, thank you for having me here as part of your professional development curriculum. I realize that this is an honour usually reserved for those who have served at the very pinnacles of power within their respective classifications. Yet here I am, a smashed up old captain who retired in 1991, who looks more like a biker and has a dog with him. So what do I know about anything that should be of great concern to you? The short answer is lots."

"In the next few days you are going to see many of our ex-cadets here for Reunion Weekend, and inevitably you are going to hear stories from the gray beards about how things were more difficult when they were a recruit. You will hear about the "horse shit" that shaped them, but there are classes who previously had real horses and real horse shit." The giggles and laughs help ease the tension. I feel the room starting to be drawn in.

"But ladies and Gentlemen, I am here to tell you that when my contemporaries and I marched off this square in 1983, we had it easy compared to what you are going to face." You could hear a pin drop.

"When we graduated, the Cold war was in full swing and we sent a few troops off to Cyprus and a couple other mildly hot spots. It was simple. But we had it easy compared to what you are about to face. In a few months you are going to graduate, and upon completion of your phase training will assume your spots amongst Squadrons, Ship's Companies, and Regiments, and you will have troops who have served in the Gulf War, Somalia, Bosnia, Kosovo, and Afghanistan. They will have been in Rwanda, Haiti, and will have been exposed to Swiss Air. And you? You know nothing. No, I would not want to be you. But if I was you, I would do two very important things. The first is I would turn the troops you are responsible for out in their Class A dress uniforms, medals on. You do not look at their boots. You look at their chests. You try and imagine what they have been through, where they have been. Then you pull each and every Personnel file and UER (Unit Employment Record) and try and reconcile what you have seen with what is in those files."

"If you thought it was quiet before, the silence became deafening. I went from the "crazy man with PTSD and a dog" to somebody who could identify with exactly what they were about to face."

"You? You know nothing. You have textbooks and lectures, but you will be dealing with battle hardened, scarred troops who have watched ramp ceremonies that have brought their messmates home on their final journey to their resting places in this great country. If I was you, I would find those Senior NCO's who have been there and done that and start asking questions. Learn as much as you can, as fast as you can, and know this to be true: It will not be fast enough."

A few shifted nervously in their seats and a few nodded. Now I had them. Whatever I was about to disclose was very relevant and pertinent in their lives.

"So how do I know so much about this?" I point to the ribbon on my chest and then to Thai who is watching my back intently. "Folks, these two things are inseparable. One is a consequence of the other. You have heard my intro and I am sure that you all can google my name and the Governor General's website and read the account of what I was decorated for. The Star of Courage is awarded for an act of conspicuous courage in circumstances of great peril. The former part is decided by those in the Chancellery and I can certainly attest to the latter."

"Do you know how you determine how small you are in the big picture of the universe? Might I put it to you that having been flung thirty five feet through the air to arrive at the base of a wave and swell that is as high as this room, and you are hanging on for dear life in the middle of a raging North Atlantic gale, you get a real good definition foisted upon you?"

Thai was up out of her resting place and her paws were resting on my side. I knew what was going on and I had to take a few moments to regroup and then to settle Thai.

"The events of that evening, decades ago, led to my struggles with PTSD and I can tell you that bad mental health is not good. Sooner or later, one or more of your troops will pitch up in your office struggling badly from things you do not understand from places you have not been. So it would behoove you to learn as much as you can."

I continued my speech talking about my struggles with the plethora of mental health challenges that I had faced and touched briefly on Thai, and her prominent role in my recovery.

"A few minutes ago you saw Thai interacting with me?" I go on to explain the intelligent disobedience interruptive behaviour and what they had just witnessed. I walk them through the struggles that many of our injured face. Their versions of the same crap I had struggled with for years. It's time to start my wrap up so there will be time for questions.

"Ladies and Gentlemen, you make me proud and you will make me even prouder in the days, weeks and years to come. You have spent time here, learning about our motto: Truth, Duty and Valour. Sometime in the future, many of you will face challenges, great challenges in moments of paralyzing fear. I also know that you will act. You will use these guiding principles to act. You will act. I know this. I have heard it said that "Courage is not the absence of fear, but action if the face of it. Know this to be true. If someone says they have never been afraid they fall into one of two categories: they are either a bold face liar, or they have yet to do anything of consequence in their lives. Your time will come and I will be proud of what I know you will do. Thank you for having me here today."

The audience goes from muted silence to a standing, clapping mass. My head swims and my insides churn but I have done it. Hopefully I've opened the door so that many could make decisions, better than those that I had made, and get help for either themselves or their troops.

"Folks a five minute stretch in place, and then we will field questions" Bryan is confident, I am spent.

When the cadets had resumed their places, the questions started and I fielded questions about suicide, peer support, and other far reaching topics. Out of the upper deck of Currie Hall, a lady who identified herself as a professor in the Military Leadership and Management Department, having heard part of my story, figured she would open the door and pave the way for what she thought would be a scathing indictment of the Military Mental Health system.

"Do you think that there is anything that the Military can be doing to prevent PTSD?" Short, open ended and the door was undoubtedly wide open. She barely had a chance to resume her seat when I rocketed out my direct, straightforward answer.

"No!" Short emphatic and a pregnant pause hung in the air like a bomb over Fortress Europe during the Second World War. It was assuredly going to drop and, most likely, explode.

"Actually I will expand upon this. Yes and No. No from the military's perspective. Yes from the Government's perspective. As long as the governments of the day choose to send our troops off to do whatever it is they are tasked to do, then there will inevitably be those who suffer from PTSD. The military is not sent to play "Tidily Winks" and winning hearts and minds is often difficult to do when the country you are in has no time for lofty ideals such as peace. Think of Rwanda: Genocide. Bosnia: ethnic cleansing. Afghanistan: terrorism and exploitation. These things lead to PTSD in those who are trying to prevent those actions. So if the government does not put our troops in harm's way, we can mitigate PTSD. But know this to be true. If we do not go wherever it is and deal with those problems over there, sooner or later they will arrive at our borders in a bigger form than they once were. So I am back to my original answer. No."

With that our time was up, and the cadets had to return to their routine of classes and the myriad of other things that drove life within the Cadet Wing. My hope was that they would now be eyes wide open about the challenges of mental health and some of the problems they were going to inevitably face. God help them if they weren't prepared.

Veterans Affairs Committee Testimony
04 March, 2014

Mr. Medric Cousineau: Ladies and gentlemen of the Committee, thank you for giving me the opportunity to address the Committee and hopefully address an issue that you may have no experience with and that, I, sadly, have decades dealing with.

I'm going to discuss a form of trauma that is devastating on its impact on veterans: institutional betrayal, and how the New Veterans Charter and VRAB are leading to a situation where suicide has a forty five percent greater prevalence in the Veteran's community than it does in the general population. That number comes from a document that you have in the Library of Parliament.

I am Captain (retired) Medric Cousineau and I wear Canada's second highest award for bravery, the Star of Courage, which is awarded for an act of conspicuous courage in circumstances of great peril. It is what ended my military career and led me to being here today. Let me put this into context for you.

I joined the military in 1979 and by 1983 had graduated from the Royal Military College of Canada and went on to receive my air navigator's wings and joined HS 443 Squadron. In October of 1986 while a member of HMCS Nipigon's helairdet, I was involved in a dramatic air sea rescue that resulted in my being awarded the Star of Courage. Sadly, those events changed my life forever. Within weeks the words post traumatic neurosis, and ultimately, post-traumatic stress disorder would appear in my medical documents.

What I want to talk about is the institutional betrayal. The single largest wound that I received happened as a result of the actions of a department of a government for a country that I would have clearly and, demonstrably, died for. Institutional betrayal can be defined as the wrongdoings perpetuated by an institution upon individuals dependent upon that institution, including failure to prevent or respond supportively to instances such as traumatic exposures committed within the context of the institution. Please keep this in mind as my story unfolds.

In 1991 I left the forces as a voluntary release struggling with issues and addictions knowing I had problems but unaware of what they were. In 1996 I found myself in the emergency assessment unit of the Nova Scotia psychiatric hospital. Clearly, you do not wind up there because you're having a banner mental health day. Subsequent to my release, I was taken by an "old salt" to visit the Department of Veterans Affairs. Subsequently I applied and received my medical documents. Perhaps the single most devastating day was to read that my diagnosis from the Nova Scotia psychiatric hospital had been in my out routine medical documents and never actioned or disclosed to me. The institutional betrayal shattered me. I would have died for Canada and I had been betrayed. The "we will take care of you" ethos, that we in the military believed, was clearly not there. But I wish it ended there. Sadly, it gets worse, much worse.

Eventually VAC ruled that I was pensionable at a five-fifths entitlement since my injuries were clearly connected to my rescue. But the issue of assessment, that is a whole different story. The VAC doctors assessed me at 70% and I was awarded 30%. I appealed and went through another entire poke and prod process. This process alone is nothing but an exacerbation of the trauma. This set of doctors stated a minimum of 50%. The board noted the 70% and I was awarded 40%. How does this happen? The numbers and the facts do not lie. I was nothing more than a file, and every award of less than my entitlement and assessment just a cost-saving measure.

In 1999 I applied to the military and had my release item reviewed and it was determined that I should have been a 3b medical release. When I applied to VAC to have my benefits reinstated to my release date I was told, basically, "Too bad, so sad, you never contacted us until 1996." But had my release been handled properly, I would have been treated in 1991 and seen VAC. I was damaged by the errors of others.

It was not until 2006, after I had had a full psychotic break down, that my assessment was finally moved to 70%. Ten years of fights, denials, appeals and abuse by a system put in place by a government department of a country I would have died for. By then my doctors had pegged me at 90% to 100% disabled and were documenting major depressive disorders. I was done, shattered, ruined and I no longer trusted anyone or anything. Why would I? I was withdrawn and I lived in isolation from my family because the anger management problems were so severe I was afraid I was going to hurt them in a fit of rage. I battled depression, anxiety, panic, suicidal ideation, addictions and suffered from dissociative episodes, cut off from family, friends and society.

In 2007, while heavily medicated, I had a visit from somebody from VAC. I don't remember what happened or even who I met with, and it was my last contact with the department until September of 2012. By then a friend had made me aware there were things called case managers and benefits and programs I should have been entitled to and involved with. By late October of 2012 I finally had a case manager who, I must state, is the best thing to happen in my recovery as far as my dealings with VAC.

I went from some time in 2007 until I contacted the department five years later with no follow-up and no help. I was not entered into the rehab program at that time but it took my case manager very little time to enroll me in the program. It was very clear where I should have been. The five-year hiatus and no contact is documented by my case file and was discussed with me by my case manager.

But even this would not have happened without my service dog who then helped train me with my PTSD and improve my social functioning. Sadly, my service dog is yet one more example of institutional betrayal that permeates my case file. If I was blind and Thai was a guide dog, I would receive an allowance for her care and upkeep and even though she was acquired with resources outside VAC, she is to assist me in my daily living and my medical care team is thrilled with the impact she has had on my life. So I applied for that same care and upkeep allowance since she is for my pension condition. I was denied and it was stated there was no evidence supporting her efficacy in rehabilitation outcomes. I was going to appeal and I requested a definition of rehabilitation outcomes. I was subsequently told there is no definition and that rehab program outcomes are handled on a case-by-case basis.

So I was denied a benefit for standards she supposedly cannot meet for something that VAC cannot define for me. I truly think that the department was going to say no just one more time.

I will carry the scars of what happened that night in the middle of the North Atlantic to my grave. There are things you do not unsee, unsmell, unhear, and untaste. There are things that can be so deeply imprinted on your psyche that no amount of treatment will ever completely deal with them. However, I have several specialists who have noted two very important points.

One, my long-term recovery was put in jeopardy by lack of early intervention and adequate treatment. The period of abandonment from 1991 to 1996 is evidence of this.

Two, the injuries that resulted from my institutional betrayal are going to be a huge obstacle if not insurmountable in my long-term recovery. VRAB has ensured that I will never ever trust the government of a country I would have died for. VRAB, political appointees making decisions based on legal, medical, and military service who clearly do not have the adequate qualifications to deal fairly with Veterans who appear before them. Look at the woeful record that the OVO points out at Federal Court Of Appeals have been exhausted at VRAB.

My wife is very quick to point out that had I not been pensionable under the Pension Act, my family would have been destroyed. The lump sum award under the New Veterans Charter would have been gone in the war I fought battling addictions as I tried to deal with the much damaged reality that I perceive.

So ladies and gentlemen, if I was going to change just three things, what would they be?

One, the lump sum award would be abolished and replaced with a lifetime income that the ill and injured could not outlive. Their injuries last their lifetimes as a result of their service to their country. So too should the government's obligation to care for them.

Secondly, VRAB in its current form would be dismantled in its current form to be replaced with a system that is geared to deal with section thirty nine of the Act, that being, barring evidence to the contrary, the Board is to rule in favour of the Veterans. Clearly, given the number of appeals, this is not happening.

Thirdly, in the war on PTSD, suicide and homelessness are two outcomes, along with destroyed families, that impact on society in a financial way and most importantly, morally. We cannot let this happen. These need to be dealt with immediately. Given what has happened to me personally, I would say that it's not out of the question to ask for a full Ministerial Inquiry into my file at VAC. There are so many issues that have impacted not just me, sadly. My wife and children have borne the brunt of that institutional betrayal. If it is not owed to me, then it certainly is to them, for they never signed up and they deserve better from this country.

Sadly, I am one of many heroes and veterans who have been institutionally betrayed by the departments of the government for which veterans would have died for. These wrongs must be righted; for if they're not, we will not know peace, and if they cannot find peace, many may make terminally irreversible decisions.

The institutional betrayal is a national disgrace.

Thank you.

The Chair: Thank you, Capt. Cousineau.

I was spent. Now my story is a matter of public record. No one in government can ever say they did not know. Plausible deniability disappeared at the conclusion of my testimony that will become a matter of permanent record for the Standing Committee on Veterans Affairs for the Government of Canada.

The Big Disconnect
NDHQ: National Defence Headquarters, Ottawa.

Apr 2014

The large building in Ottawa houses the top end command structure for the military and is home to most of the upper level administration and policy making departments. NDHQ is also home the department headed up by the Chief of Military Personnel (CMP for short) and the department best described as the Human Resources department for all those unfamiliar with the Military command structure. The department is headed up by a two star general, in this case, Major General David Millar. The meeting was taking place in his office and Thai was curled up under the flags in the corner, keeping a watchful eye on me, her nose continually sniffing for any signs of stress in me. I felt good and the meeting was proceeding well.

Also in attendance were Colonel Scott McLeod and Chief Warrant Officer Pete Marchant, the CMP's most senior of Senior Non Commissioned officers (NCO's) while Jocelyn served as my extra set of eyes and ears. Today's meeting was focused on the use of service dogs and their use in aiding those who struggle with serious complex PTSD.

"In my world, service dogs are an adjunct therapy." I was quick to point this out. "Anyone who is seriously enough injured that they need a service dog is still going to need a lot of work in other areas. But the rule of 168 is going to apply. Scott, if we are lucky these days someone gets an hour of chair time in a traditional therapy setting each week. They would be honestly lucky if that was the case." I was not being disparaging but confronting the challenging reality that faced not only the injured but the system trying to help them.

His answer confirmed my viewpoint and gave us a great place from which to move the discussion forward.

"Scott as you know, the complexities of PTSD are a 24-7-365 challenge that can rear their ugly head at any point in time. Emotions, situations, external stimuli, can all be the basis of the triggers that can bring on a whole host of reactions from Panic,

Anxiety, Anger, Rage, and other dysfunctional behaviors. The problem that those who suffer face is the uncertainty, the lack of predictability of when and where. Would that be a fair assumption?"

"Certainly those are some of the challenges faced by both sides in this battle." His forward lean in the chair signaled an engagement in the conversation. Rather than being attacked, I got the sense that he felt he was being engaged in the conversation. I think this provided a level of comfort to him.

"So Dave and Scott, here is the big disconnect." I was about to lay the groundwork for the whole argument that was about to follow. "We could easily paper this office in studies that prove that therapy dogs have proven their worth in dealing with a myriad of conditions, including depression. Doing one more study on the efficacy of therapy dogs would certainly be gilding the lily since we have the answers to those questions many times over. They work. Scott, do you know where professional therapy dogs come from?"

"I have a clue, but why don't you inform me." He was being open to the dialogue and not presupposing anything. I was encouraged.

"Professional therapy dogs are most often washouts from Service Dog Schools. Not that they are bad dogs, it just means that they are missing something that keeps them from working in the top tier. It is like this: not every hockey player makes it to the NHL, the true elite of our national game. There are some great tier two hockey players that are missing something that keeps them from that level: a half a step slow, not strong enough in the corners, shot not hard enough or accurate enough, something. So they go onto to be great tier two hockey players. No dishonor, just the reality."

"Okay, I am with you so far." The CMP was nodding knowingly, absorbing all that was being said.

"Therapy dogs are trained in an emotive support role to work in 5 to 10 minute blocks of time and their efficacy has been proven. So here comes the big disconnect. You take a dog with a better skill set and assign it 24-7 to one handler and some would have you believe there is no proof of their efficacy. Unfortunately, it is impossible to draw the Venn diagram to logically arrive at that conclusion."

I was calmly and coolly leading the conversation in the direction that I wanted it to go. I could see that I was scoring points and I was on a roll.

"Dave, you are probably looking at Thai curled up and thinking what a great service dog. How well behaved. But the reality is those behaviors are what ensure public access. A service dog is defined by the work that it does for its handler, those specific tasks that the dog does for the handler that the handler cannot do unaided."

"This is something I was unaware of." In his defense, why would it be something that was in his lexicon and threshold knowledge level? He was learning fast. "So if I may, what tasks does Thai do for you?"

"Not a problem Dave. The big four for me that Thai executes for me are Night Terror Intervention, watching my back in public, recalls from panic or anxiety attacks, and dissociative recall. Most of her work is based on sensing the changes in my bio-chemistry. Scott as you know as a medical practitioner, as soon as the stress response starts a complex series of neuro-biological events transpire within your body, resulting in the release of a pheromone in your skin. It happens instantaneously."

I pause to give my fingers a quick snap for emphasis. "If a dog can discriminate a teaspoon of sugar in an Olympic size swimming pool, it can sense the changes in your chemistry when they are right beside you. That is why the service dog is with their handler 24-7-365. The dog can sense the issues long before the handler can even be aware of the onset." Little did I know that less than twenty-four hours later Scott would have a front row seat to watching Thai work with one of my anxiety attacks at the unveiling of the Chief of Defence Staff's new mental health initiatives and the "You're not alone program." If seeing is believing then watching Thai in action certainly opened up a whole new thought process.

The meeting continued as we discussed many of the complex issues facing not only the injured but the systematic challenges faced by the Military. Service Dogs were new. The system was struggling to come to terms with the reality of their use and implementation.

"One of the challenges we are facing is that there are individuals who are showing up saying I have a diagnosis of PTSD, where is my service dog?" The concern clearly showing in the tone of voice and the facial expressions around the table.

"I hear you, and I can see how that would be problematic. In my world though, that needs to be re-framed. It should go something like this. "I have a diagnosis of PTSD, I need a service dog and I know my career is going to be over in time." I let the reality of my statement sink in. "There are those outside this room who will probably throw rocks at me for saying so, but the reality is such that if you require a service dog, then your career is over. We are not talking about small injuries here. Remember I have been you. I know how badly I am messed up. I would be a detriment to the Mission, to the Team and to myself. Nobody wins and everybody loses. Getting to this point means you are well and truly done. It is over. It has taken me a while to come to terms with that. Perhaps far longer than I would ever care to admit. My buddy, MCpl Hatton has been so instrumental in my recovery. What he saw was my struggles with not accepting my new normal. Unfortunately, I think far too many of the injured struggle with that process. I think I have a real good idea why."

I glanced up at the clock on the wall and realized we had been kicking around ideas and issues for quite a while. I knew the meeting was drawing to a close.

"Cous, we are going to be striking a working group on Service Dogs, headed up by Scott. I was wondering if I could call on you to help with that committee."

I had a lump in my throat. I was having a hard time believing what I had just heard. The very thought of the military looking at service dogs was clearly a huge shift in position over the last two years.

"Dave I would be honored. It is a complex subject fraught with pitfalls and dangers. I also understand that there are those who would like to dictate policy to the military. So, yes, I will give you a hand." With that, validation. The Long Walk to Sanity and Paws

Fur Thought were making a difference. Slowly, but dealing with large bureaucracies is never easy – one as complex and unique as the military, doubly so.

Depression

Today, Thai pads along beside me, out of vest, and enjoying the world of scents in the long grass. I can't see what she smells, but she enjoys rubbing her nose in the smorgasbord of tantalizing telltales of what has gone over this ground before us. She has a wide eyed doggie smile and her big brown eyes sparkle. She loves this time. Her time to unwind and "be a dog", off duty but ever vigilant. These long walks in the solitude of Nature are great for both of us.

For me, the sounds of the birds and the bugs, and the rustle of the tree leaves and the long grasses drown out the chaos of the turmoil in my head. There are days when the simplest of decisions seem overwhelming and insurmountable. It is times like these, that the calm and the quiet of nature help me to focus on the simplest of things. The warmth of the sun, the wag of Thai's tail, and the call of the osprey are such simple things that previously vanished into the abyss of darkness that is Depression.

Depression!

You hear the word tossed around in society as some sort of casual passing condition. "Oh, so and so is just a little depressed. They will get over it." Platitudes that gloss over the harsh realities that depression, if untreated, can and will kill. Depression related suicide is the leading cause of death in North America. It outstrips homicides and war related deaths combined. Scary that half of the people who suffer do not seek professional help. Stigma? I could not be more sarcastic when I say "hardly." The harsh brutal reality is that the stigma in society is so overwhelming that people who desperately need help will not seek it out.

I know how bad the stigma is. For many years I tried to do whatever I could to avoid coming to terms with my injury and the issues that are related to it. Sometimes I get so angry that society does not get that the number one co-morbidity to PTSD is Major

Depressive Disorder and that in and of itself is a huge problem. The laundry list as I like to refer to it of serious mental health issues that accompany PTSD is not pretty. Not even close! Depression, Anxiety, Panic, Addictions, Suicidal Ideology, Night Terrors, Dissociative Episodes, Anger and Rage are some of the more common co-morbidities. Sixty per cent of those who have serious complex PTSD will suffer from three of these.

Thai's wet nose bumps up against my hand. We are a couple of kilometers down the trail from where I last remember being. I guess I have wandered off, deep in thought, and Thai is reminding me that I am heading for some bad head space. I feel pangs of guilt. I have survived and even though I still struggle with the "Black Dog of Depression" I no longer have the suicidal thoughts that were once so prevalent. When you are standing on the brink of despair, it does not take much to push one over the razor fine line that defines life and death. I can remember thinking on more than one occasion when someone had pissed me off that "If I do not care if I live or die, what makes you think I give a rat's ass about whether you do?" Harsh, brutal reality that had permeated my thought process for too long to remember.

The gratitude that I feel for having stepped away is mixed with survivor's guilt. I know that there are those who have claimed their own lives because the strain of dealing with the enormous effort to get to tomorrow, a tomorrow that looks every bit as bleak as the today they are struggling with finally becomes too much. When they cross that line, the terminally irreversible line, they become a statistic lost in the war of attrition that mental health claims. But the reality is that the person is not a statistic: they are brother, father, son, sister, mother, daughter and a part of others' lives and their loss will shape and affect countless others for years to come, perhaps permanently.

So how do we get these people help? How do we make it OK not to be OK? How do we make it acceptable to reach out for help when one is struggling in the isolation brought on by the societal stigma that surrounds serious mental health issues? I know I struggled for so many years, and now because of the advocacy work that Thai & I have done, hiding is no longer an option. The old saying that *the truth will set you free* is both liberating yet defining.

Even though I have stepped up and openly acknowledged my Mental Health Issues, taken ownership of my PTSD and all the other issues that accompany it, I still feel the pain of the stigma of the ignorant who either move away or act dismissively. The stigma is very real. It is prevalent. Stigma will only ever be shattered for those of us who suffer when we can take a stand and make sure that the world knows that it is absolutely, one hundred per cent unacceptable to discriminate and stigmatize those who are struggling with mental health issues. In fact, for the uninformed, the ignorant, if they only knew that their actions further traumatized those who suffer, I wonder if they would act the way that they do? What they fail to realize is the prevalence of mental health issues and the likelihood that they or one of their loved ones will one day struggle. I wonder if they have asked themselves the question: Would I like to be treated the way I am treating those who suffer? What if someone finally reaches out, tries to wrestle the oppressive beast of stigma to the ground, and my attitudes are the very first that they encounter? Would they be likely to continue their journey towards help or would they be more likely to have the stigma validated and retreat into the world of isolation that surrounds Mental Health Issues?

Once again I feel Thai body checking my knee as I walk on. My anxiety, the anger and stress are starting to escalate. How quick are people to judge that which they do not understand? I can guarantee you for a fact that they do not understand serious mental health issues. Only in the past few years has it become acceptable to "Talk about it!" The Canadian Mental Health Association is championing stripping down the walls of stigma. The Bell "Let's Talk About It" campaign is bringing the issues to the forefront. But the struggles continue.

Capacity and Capability are two concepts that need to be divorced from each other. If someone has a Mensa IQ they are very capable. If they can only access that functionality for a few fleeting moments each day, then they have no capacity. I know. I have dealt with the flashes of brilliance juxtaposed with the quagmire of paralyzing confusion that can accompany serious mental health issues. I have walked that walk and now I am talking that talk so that others can feel free to step into the light and out of the darkness of depression and despair.

Life Preservers and Kisbee Rings

The tunes belt out of the sound system. I am lost deep in reflection today, a serious gaze into the retrospectoscope. I am awash in the sea of "Woulda, Coulda, Shoulda's" but I am not there of my own accord or even my own PTSD. I am struggling to focus and keep a clear head, a luxury that often alludes me, and today I am finding it particularly problematic.

The "Mental Health Minute" on CTV had aired earlier this week, and there have been several inquiries for helping obtain a Service Dog for various individuals. The stories and the backgrounds are as diverse as the snowflakes in a winter's blizzard, all snow, yet each unique in their own way. So too, those that struggle with PTSD.

This morning's call hit harder than a locomotive charging down the tracks.

"I need you to describe in as few as words as possible what happened to cause your PTSD." The phraseology very deliberate on my part. I need to understand the mechanism of injury so that I do not accidently trigger an episode by using an example that is too close to home for the voice on the other end of the phone. But more importantly, it is becoming a serious self-defense mechanism for myself.

My mind drifts back to my last session with my Psychologist.

"You know Kevin, I just cannot do it anymore. The stories, the pain, they are starting to become vicarious triggers. My buddy Chris using the expression, "Getting slimed" and I can tell you I know exactly what he means. I am trying not to be a hard hearted son of a bitch, but I can only carry so much. I am struggling with my own shit, and I certainly do not need to go looking for more!"

"You are absolutely right. You have been going through peaks and valleys since the walk ended." His observation just a clear summation of the wild emotional swings that I had been on since returning home early last October. He had warned me, and tried to prep me for the inevitable let down when the emotional high of accomplishment waned. He had called it and we had worked through the issues that were bothering me.

"Kevin, this is different. I feel these dark hands reach out from the abyss trying to pull me over the edge. I am losing my ability to focus, to concentrate. I have ADOLAS real bad!" He cocks his head quizzically encouraging me to expand upon the acronym.

"Attention Deficit, Oh Look, A Squirrel". He can't repress the smile and the chuckle.

"I am all over the frigging map. The problem is that there stories, their mechanisms of injury are theirs, unique and individual. But what happens afterwards is eerily the same. SSDD. Same Shit, Different Day. Each one of them is struggling with variants of the crap I have waded through. And it hurts."

"Bingo. Is it because it is too close to home?" Honest, sincere, probing.

"That is exactly it. I have stood there so many times, on the line, the edge, the live or die, the fuck it all and never have to deal with the pain again, it is all too real." I slump back into my chair, and Thai gets up out of her curled position beside my chair. She starts bumping my hand with her nose. Thai knows, Kevin knows, and I know, but I am reluctant to admit it.

"Kevin, I am so lucky. I have a second chance. I have been there and I can tell you it is absolutely no fun on the very edge of despair. I just want to get a great big place, somewhere safe, and put them there. I know that this Utopian fantasy is not going to cut it, but damn it all Kevin, every time I hear of another PTSD sufferer committing suicide, it hits way to close to home. Many of those that I talk to are there. So how do I balance between trying to help and self-care?" The question hangs heavy in the room. The sword of Damocles. It hangs over my head by a thread, for some the most tenuous grasp on reality. I wonder what happens if they open their hands and let go? I know the answer, but do not want to confront that harsh reality.

"I feel like I am firing out life preservers and Kisbee Rings. How do we get people to hang on when they have arrived at the point of such complete, utter and total despair? The sad resignation that life is not worth living has to be counteracted. There is only one thing that I know of… Somehow, someway we have to be able to give them a sense of hope!"

"You have nailed it." Kevin nods affirmatively.

"So the question remains, how do I get that message out on a huge scale?"

"You realize that it is not your fault if someone makes that choice to…" I could see him struggling to find the words to couch what is coming next.

"Hurt themselves?" I make it easy on him. No need to watch him struggle.

"Exactly, you cannot wear that." Pragmatic? Realist?

"Nope, I get that, but I can sure try and save a few more starfish! Made a difference to that one." Forever the optimist.

"Kevin, I can absolutely say that I know what it feels like to save someone's life. I have been there and done that." Not boastful, factual.

"I can tell you that pairing these dogs up with people on the edge, watching them get their lives back, gives me exactly the same feelings. I know what it is I am doing." My gaze locks with his with a ferocious intensity.

"Kevin, I am tossing out furry four legged life preservers." I reach down and rub Thai's ears, and she snuggles over closer to the chair. I have been given a second chance and plan on not wasting it!

Introspective Question
May, 2014

Like I did so many nights ago, I caught and held the glance of Duncan. Tonight we weren't in the back of a Sea King, not really, but in my mind I'm never far from that helicopter. And in an instant, I was all the way back there. While I sat and watched, Duncan approached the podium, cleared his voice, and started speaking.

"Ladies and Gentlemen, tonight have the distinct pleasure of introducing Captain retired Medric "Cous" Cousineau. Medric was a young aviator when I was the Captain of HMCS Nipigon back in 1986. One night, while cruising 200 miles off the coast of Newfoundland, we responded to a distress call. We were on the edge of Helicopter operations, with fifty knot winds pushing us near the edge of deck evolution limits...."

In a moment I was no longer sitting on the stage. Rear Admiral Ret'd Duncan Miller was no longer speaking calmly to the assembled crowd. The flashback was instant. I was there again, back on the Sea King, back in the storm, locking eyes with Ken in the moment before descending into Hell, the same as thousands of times before. The sights, the sounds, the smells as visceral today as they were that night. I'm still in a fight for my life, a fight that's been going on since the moments after being recovered from the Atlantic. But this time the enemy is not the environment or the elements. Today, I struggle with my PTSD as a result of that night. It's an ongoing battle that I fight daily, knowing that I can never win, that I can survive. There is an old saw that goes "it must be a good day since I just set a new personal record for consecutive days lived." I know tomorrow that I will set a new personal best and I feel empowered. It was not always so. Too many times I stood on the brink, drink in one hand, rope in the other, staring into the darkest abyss of depression and despair and planning and hoping for it to end. Not today. That is not how this story ends. This story is still going, and I'm still going, one step at a time, one day at a time, one shrieking nightmare and dissociative episode at a time. With the dedication of my family and the selfless devotion and skill of Thai, I have taken my life back. Though I struggle and fight the enemy that I call the beast, PTSD, I will not let it win, not today.

I saw Duncan looking at me, saw him glance at Thai who had alerted and helped bring me back into this moment. Duncan turned back to the crowd.

"Medric reached out to me a couple years back when he was still struggling and I told him that the best thing he could do was focus on the positives and keep moving forward. Here to tell you a little more about his life with a Service Dog is Medric."

The introduction was being done by Rear Admiral (Retd) Duncan Miller, a man who outside those that were on the helicopter that night knows more about what happened than anyone else on the face of the planet. It was unbelievably cathartic after all these years.

I stood up. Thai stood up. I approached the podium, Thai taking up position to protect my six. I looked out into the crowd, turned and nodded to Duncan, then turned back to the crowd.

"Thank you so much. Ladies and Gentleman, the last thing one wishes to do is argue with an admiral, so as a point of clarification, it was the Star of Courage that I was awarded…"

"Have you ever woken up and asked yourself what have you done to your life? What were you thinking? I can honestly say I have three very clear instances and in some ways they are all connected. In 1985, our Tacco Course was participating in Exercise Salty Dip to get us used to shipborne operations and life. Midweek I landed on HMCS Ottawa thirty plus miles of the coast in a sea state four or five. Within an hour, if I could have gotten in the small arms locker, it was over. I was so horribly sea sick. My angel of mercy appeared in the form of a crusty old bearded Petty Officer with a fistful of crackers. All I could think was I was not going to last another five minutes let alone four years! And I had volunteered for this. Be careful of what you wish for.

The second was the night of the 6th of October, 1986. I think that is self-explanatory. A single night, a sequence of events that alters the course of your life forever, would certainly qualify in my mind.

And finally for the third? I can once again give you the exact day, approximate time and place. Last August first, 8/1/13, I had just stepped off on the Long Walk to Sanity. I was six klicks into a journey that was going to take fifty days and cover more than a thousand kilometers. I'd trained over two thousand klicks and climbed thousands of flights of stairs in the past seven months to get ready. And here I was, just 6k into the walk, and I'm standing on the big hill heading from Shearwater to the Woodside Oil refinery, thinking to myself, what have you got yourself into? I looked down at Thai's big brown eyes and her wagging tail. She was living in the moment while I was worried about the future. Then that inner voice that lives deep within us all escaped and whispered two things. Thank God I was listening. I heard that old Buddhist saying "Sometimes all that is required is to point your boots in the right direction and keep walking." So I did. For fifty days that covered one thousand and sixty five kilometers, during which time I met with many Silver Cross mothers and visited countless graves of our brave fallen. But in that moment, on the hill, just 6k into the Long Walk to Sanity, I heard my training mantra. How far did you go? Further than Yesterday, and that is all that counts."

NS Inspiring Lives Award
May 2014

Today, Jocelyn and I are attending the Mental Health Foundation of Nova Scotia Luncheon in honour of the Inspiring Lives Recipients. I am one of those being honoured for my work with Paws Fur Thought and the Long Walk to Sanity. But most important to me is the recognition that the stigma of Mental illness and injury had to be addressed, stomped out and eliminated. I have worked hard at re-branding PTSD into Put The Stigma Down. Thai had her "A" game going as I was called to the stage and the following citation was read out:

"Medric is a retired Captain with the Canadian Forces. Following a dramatic rescue mission off the coast of Newfoundland in 1986, he was awarded the Star of Courage. Medric helped two injured fishermen off a long liner and into the safety of a Sea King helicopter while faced with darkness, heavy winds and six-meter seas.

As a result of this mission, Medric developed PTSD. For many years he lived with nightmares, depression, anxiety, and anger issues. For two decades he was unable to fully participate in raising his children. Instead, he chose to spend countless hours in isolation. At the time, PTSD was not well known and there were no protocols in place to help with recovery.

On the advice of a friend, Medric applied to get a Service Dog in 2012. He was successful. Within a few days of receiving Thai, Medric noticed a change.

Thai is trained to sense the onset of PTSD symptoms and triggers such as irritation, bad dreams, and anxiety. She intervenes before the symptoms manifest to extremes. Before Medric had Thai, these symptoms and triggers would shut him down. Now, he sleeps better, and has re-established his confidence for going new places and dealing with contentious issues that would otherwise overwhelm him.

With the assistance of Thai, Medric now works to raise awareness about PTSD. He is actively rephrasing the acronym to mean "Put The Stigma Down." He has met with local politicians, community members, the Veterans Affairs Minister, and the Minister of National Defence. He has also developed and maintains a Facebook page called Paws Fur Thought. He and his wife Jocelyn work tirelessly. To date, they have helped thirty Veterans acquire Service Dogs or commence the training to be certified!

He also recently went for a rather lengthy walk… all the way from Eastern Passage to Ottawa! The "Long Walk to Sanity" was designed to raise public awareness and funds to help other Veterans.

Medric is a person who truly fights stigma, breaks barriers and inspires hope."

Starr Dobson's words resonated deeply inside me.

Pilot Project
27 May, 2014

"Hey Joc… How are you feeling today?" I am tense, nervous, anxious, and a bag of conflicting emotions. I suspect that Jocelyn may very well be in the same state.

Before she can answer, I continue, while stroking Thai's ears.

"I am so anxious, so nervous. Today is going to be a huge validation for everything we have worked so hard for. The Long Walk will have made a difference. I mean it already has in the lives of those that we have paired up. But you know what I mean. It has only been eight months since Manotick."

The reference was not lost on Joc. Barely eight months ago we had met with Veteran's Affairs Minister Julian Fantino on the third last day of my walk. Today, we are in Ottawa, preparing to head over to the Museum of Civilization in Gatineau for the announcement that Veterans Affairs would be funding a pilot project to analyze the use of Service Dogs in treating veterans with PTSD.

I drift off in thought. The miles that Thai and I had covered to get to this point were all worth it. Veterans Affairs had gone from using therapy dogs and service dogs as interchangeable words to funding a research assessment to now funding the research that is so desperately required.

In the past year I had heard the same chorus several times from the traditional medical community.

"There is no evidenced based research to support the efficacy of service dogs in treating PTSD."

To which I had developed a stock reply.

"Yes you are right, because the research has not been done. Period. We need to do the studies so that we can get the answers. I realize that the plural of anecdote is not data, but I have a lot of people who have changed their lives with their service dogs. All you have is conjecture, and you are planting your flag on the lack of study proving efficacy ground." This was about to change.

I had known for a few weeks that the announcement was coming following the delivery of the Research Assessment that was done under the auspicious of CIMVHR and Dr. Alice Aiken's watchful eye. I did not know what the announcement details were, but I had been involved in discussions with Jacques Fauteux, the Minister's Chief of Staff, and Dr. David Pedlar, Researcher for the Department.

Science, research, data, and a study into the efficacy of Service Dogs were all about to become a reality that would provide the necessary data for the medical community to arrive at a point that is not based on denial or conjecture.

I think of all those whose lives had changed because of their dogs. Yvette, George, Dan, Kim, Lynne, Brian, Bill and the list rolled past my minds backboard. Each one, the same and simultaneously different. Men and women, each with their own unique stories of how they arrived at the gates of Hell that is PTSD. Each of them was very similar in that their Service Dogs had already made huge changes in their lives. I was able to bear witness to this from my own firsthand experience and by proxy, watching the dramatic changes in the lives of these disabled Veterans.

The struggle that I have is that the decision makers are not the affected, and in most cases, anything that they do know about the injury and all of its drag along consequences came from either a book or by second hand observation. If they do not know the first hand horror of PTSD and its comorbidities, then in my mind it would be impossible for them to gauge the magnitude of the impact that a Service Dog can have on the affected.

I wonder if they know the comfort of being awoken from a night terror, or better still, to awaken before the unquestionably horrific part of a combination of images destroys your sleep, which is broken at best. I wonder if those making the decisions have any idea what it feels like to be so on edge in a public place, constantly scanning, ever vigilant to your surroundings, unable to let your guard down for a moment? I wonder if the doctors who stand in judgment of a furry, four legged therapist have any idea how quickly a dissociative episode can take hold of you? I wonder if the naysayers have any idea of how draining the episodes of anger and rage are and the shame and guilt that accompanies their aftermath? I wonder if those whose solution is to pound you full of pharmaceuticals know what it feels like to try and inflict pain upon yourself so that you can confirm you are still alive.

Today, the government is going to start and actually do the study required to get to an answer. I have more than my suspicions as to what will be determined at the conclusion of the trial period. If I was a case study of one, then the outcomes would prove beyond a shadow of a doubt the huge changes and positive impact Thai has had in my life and most importantly the life of my family.

"Are we ready to go?" I'm not sure how long I have been lost in thought, all I know is that I am feeling tense. Within the next hour the session at the museum will start and the announcement will be formalized.

"Ladies and Gentlemen, Today Veterans Affairs Canada is proud to announce the launch of a pilot project into the use of Service Dogs for those suffering from PTSD..." Minister Fantino's announcement continues and I drift back out on to the highway, reliving parts of the Long Walk to Sanity. Fund raising and Advocacy. I guess today can only be deemed an unqualified success. We have turned the ocean liner around and it is steering in a new direction.

FTY: Pilot Project Announcement

http://www.newswire.ca/en/story/1361963/minister-fantino-announces-service-dogs-pilot-project-to-support-veterans-with-ptsd

GATINEAU, QC, May 27, 2014 /CNW/ - Today, the Honourable Julian Fantino, Minister of Veterans Affairs, shared with stakeholders Veterans Affairs Canada's (VAC) plan to support a pilot project to assess the benefits and risks of using psychiatric service dogs to assist in the treatment of post-traumatic stress disorder (PTSD) in Veterans.

The two-and-a-half-year pilot project has a goal of having up to 50 Veterans who are in receipt of a disability benefit for PTSD and have approval from their treating mental health professional, participating in the project. VAC will provide up to $500,000 to cover expenses and new research for the pilot project.

Quick Facts

In May 2013, VAC announced a partnership with St. John Ambulance Canada and Can Praxis to research the benefits of using therapy dogs and horses to assist Veterans dealing with mental health issues.

In September 2013, VAC announced a partnership with the Canadian Institute for Military and Veteran Health Research (CIMVHR) to conduct a research assessment on whether Psychiatric Service Dogs can assist individuals with PTSD. The research indicated that a pilot project was the appropriate step forward.

On May 12, 2014, Prime Minister Stephen Harper announced the introduction of the Justice for Animals in Service Act (Quanto's Law), legislation that would ensure that those who harm law enforcement, service and Canadian Armed Forces animals face serious consequences.

VAC has a well-established national network of more than 4,800 mental health professionals, including psychologists, social workers, and mental health nurses, who deliver mental health services to Veterans with PTSD and other operational stress injuries (OSIs).

VAC and the Department of National Defence have a joint network of seventeen operational stress injury clinics, including ten specialized clinics established by VAC.

Quotes

"Some Veterans will tell you that Service Dogs are more than man's best friend, they are companions who are an integral part of their day-to-day life. This project will help us study and learn how Service Dogs can help Veterans suffering from post-traumatic stress disorder."

The Honourable Julian Fantino, Minister of Veterans Affairs

"Since 2012, Wounded Warriors Canada has been the national leader in funding PTSD animal assisted therapy programs for Canada's ill and injured Canadian Armed Forces members and their families. The participant response from those who have received a Service Dog from the Courageous Companions Program that we fund has been overwhelmingly positive and, in fact, life changing. We applaud Minister Fantino's timely action and look forward to working with the Department of Veterans Affairs on this important pilot project."

Phil Ralph, National Program Director for Wounded Warriors Canada

"This pilot project is a concrete and positive step forward. As someone who has gained tremendously from my service dog, I'm proud to be involved in this effort to help Veterans with PTSD."

Captain (retired) Medric Cousineau, SC, CD, Founder of Paws Fur Thought

"The Mental Health Strategy for Canada, released by the Mental Health Commission of Canada in 2012, shared that shifting policies and practices toward recovery and well-being will require, among other things, finding innovative ways to support people living with mental health problems and illnesses to exercise choices in their journey of recovery. Certainly, the use of Psychiatric Service Dogs to assist Veterans with PTSD is an innovative, emerging recovery-oriented practice. We look forward to hearing more about the pilot project and the ensuing research."

Louise Bradley, President and CEO, Mental Health Commission of Canada

Memorial Paws Canada

"She is so beautiful. I am so happy. Do you think I can get more info?" I could hear the happiness in Darlene's voice but I could also hear the tears. Bittersweet emotions. "To think something so positive is going to happen."

"Darlene, I know. I am almost speechless." What do you say to a mother whose son has died for your country, a man who has paid the ultimate sacrifice for your continued freedoms? "I am sure I can reach out and get more info. It should not be a problem."

"She is so amazing." Darlene was referring to a young lady lab puppy and the photo I had sent her of "Recce" with her new handler.

"As I told you when you named the puppies, there is no guarantee what line of service work they will wind up in. Recce has shown an amazing skill for scenting and alerting and is going into advanced training as a DAD (Diabetic Alert Dog). She is the successor dog for this young lady. Successor dog is the term used for a handler's second or third and beyond service dog. Successor. Replacement dog would carry such a negative connotation. I know in my world there will never be a replacement for Thai. In the fullness of time, Thai will retire, become a house diva, and eventually cross the Rainbow Bridge. I will wind up with a successor dog to help me with my issues. But never a replacement. These dogs mean far too much to us for us to even entertain that phraseology.

"Darlene, I am sure I can make that happen." It would be my honour. After the call wound up, I was a bit of an emotional whirling dervish. How could you not be? I had just brought tears of joy to a mother who had lost her son to a war.

"Thai Girly, we had best go for a walk. I need to get my head back together." Thai looked up at me with appreciative eyes. The sole words she grasped out of that sentence were her name and walk, but that was all she needed to hear. She got up off her big comfy bed and stretched her "play bow extended stretch". Then she went and stood over by her leash. She knew what was happening next.

Whenever I need to think these days or to get unwound it happens by taking Thai for a long walk, down by the ocean and out to Hartlen Point. The solitude of nature and the ability to quiet the "chattering monkeys" in my head. The soft padding of her feet and the faint jingle of her dog tags create a soothing rhythm as we walk along.

"You know Thai Girly, in some ways that was way too easy." Thai looked up at me with her big brown eyes and cocks her head to the side trying to decipher what I was on about this time. I make jokes that one of the best parts about having Thai with me in public all the time is I can talk to her and people do not think I am as crazy as if I was talking to myself.

"You know Thai it would be too easy to do that for other families of the fallen. Maybe we could make something good come out of something bad." I was caught back up in a conversation that I had with one of our Memorial Cross Mothers who shared with me her daily pain.

"You never get over it. You just try and do the very best you can each day." Her words haunted me, not because they were untrue, but because they echoed a sentiment that lay deep down inside of me. Perhaps one of the struggles with PTSD is we do not like to admit that we have issues, issues that never go away from sights, sounds, smells and actions that will never be forgotten. The pain of losing your child would easily be in this category. So in many ways, she and I are kindred spirits, using the walks to the point to help deal with a pain that stays with you.

"Thai girl, what if we were to start naming puppies in the various programs just like Darlene did with Recce and Dragoon?" Last year on Canada Day, the CARES program had a two puppy litter born on Canada Day, and that was the spark that was to light the fire. The shared experience of Thai at Beechwood made it a natural for me to reach out to Darlene for names that she gladly provide. "Recce" since Darryl was in Recce platoon and "Gnomer" for the ceramic Gnome that accompanies Darlene, a gnome that had survived the blast that had claimed Darryl's life. A few weeks after the fact though, "Gnomer" had to be renamed. I had gotten a call from Sarah at CARES, Gnomer was getting confused. He thought his name was "MER" and everything was "NO." So Darlene renamed him "Dragoon" for the Royal Canadian Dragoons, Darryl's regimental affiliation, one which he shared with my father.

By the time Thai and I had returned from our latest trek around the Point, I had fleshed out the idea for Memorial Paws Canada. It could not be simpler. We would provide the families of our fallen the opportunity to name puppies in the program. That was it. The end. Short sweet and to the point.

My next call was going to be easy.

"Hey Darlene, got a question for you?"

"Hey anything for you." I knew she was agreeing before the ask because she knew I would not ask something that would be hurtful.

"Dar, how would you like to be our Honourary Silver Cross Mom for a program named Memorial Paws Canada? This initiative would be a puppy naming project, just like you did with Recce and Dragoon for our other families." I stopped talking and started listening.

"Of course I would. That would be so awesome."

With that simple conversation the wheels were set in motion to help honour our fallen by giving their families a positive. A simple gesture, but it would help with the one common thing that I had heard from the Silver Cross families on my walk. "Our biggest fear is that they will be forgotten."

We would try and ensure that the sacrifices of their sons and daughter, husbands and wives, fathers and mothers, would be remembered in the life of service as reflected in these future service dog puppies. A life of service remembered in a life of service. No greater devotion than a dog to its master.

What I did not know at the time that I put this idea together would be what would happen in the weeks that immediately followed. As I reached out to the various families I knew, or knew those who knew the families, a small magical miracle began to unfold. The families each had a different vision, a different thought and the names came forward. What is hard to capture is the excitement and the breath of fresh air of enthusiasm that blew forth. "Royal," "Sam," "Mission," and "Lux" came on the radar immediately. Each had significance and meaning. Royal was named after the Royal Canadian Regiment, Sam was short for "Samurai, "Mozart" named after a dog that was closely connected to the family, and Lux was the Latin word for light.

Our puppies needed names, and now they were getting names with a legacy, a meaning and a purpose that counts!"

A Mental Health Discussion
August, 2014

My meeting is set with the Mental Health Foundation of Nova Scotia. Even though I have no problem discussing my challenges with Mental Health Issues, this is tough. Not the subject matter, the place. The meeting is at the offices of the foundation that are in the shadows of the Nova Scotia Psychiatric Hospital, and for me, this is not a great memory. There is something about being locked in a room with no way to get out and knowing that you are being observed that sticks with you. Such is the Emergency Assessment Unit back in the day. I hope things have changed but the very thought of going inside the building still knots my stomach. This certainly was not a high point in my life which, because of my struggles with serious mental health issues, has had some very serious low points. In fact, some dangerously close to being "terminally irreversible" that I now prefer to put them so far back in the rearview mirror that they are but distant memories. But memories they are, no matter how deeply buried. There was a time, but thanks to Thai, and the support of my family, they are becoming more distant by the day, but still very much a reality at those points in time.

"Thai girlie, let's go to our meeting." Thai's big brown eyes and wagging tail convey hope, optimism and a "live in the moment" quality that helps to ground me and push aside the thoughts of the big brown brick building. Today I am here to meet with Starr Dobson, the President of the Nova Scotia Mental Health Foundation. I, we, Paws Fur Thought needs help and lots of it. We are getting reach outs from beyond the veterans community to help with Service Dogs for communities other than Veterans. I am hoping that I can rally more support.

"Good morning Starr." The bright colours of the offices are so far from clinical that it helps set a positive mood. There is enough dark and somber surrounding Mental Health issues that anything that can be done to set a positive tone needs to be exploited. The bright greens and blues do exactly that.

"Good morning Medric and Thai, you having a good morning?" Starr Dobson, the current president of the Foundation has spent years as a reporter and news anchor on one of the local television networks. She has an uncanny ability to read people and situations, probably a skill learned in her former profession. "Shall we go sit at the tables out front, grab a coffee?"

"And some sunshine… Thai loves sunbeams."

We settled into the corner table, and sure enough, Thai assumed a position guarding my back, even while soaking up the luxurious warmth of a Sunbeam.

Even though Starr had become well aware of mine and Thai's story as part of the Inspiring Lives Awards for the year, this was a chance to actually explain the intricacies of Thai and why more of her kind would be so essential moving forward.

"Starr, there are so many others. Red, White and Blue, A & A, Fire, Emergency Responders, Police, RCMP, Assault and Abuse survivors, are all communities that are susceptible to PTSD."

"I can see that." Starr's acknowledgment is sincere.

"Did you know that since the first of April we have had seventeen first responders go hard down?"

"You mean…" I think she was trying to figure out a nice way to say suicide.

"Exactly. Terminally Irreversible." I triggered and Thai was up on me in a flash. She knew and she had a job to do. Her paws were on my shoulder and I began to rub her belly and tell her what a good girl she was. But she was having none of it. Here, so close to a spot where I had been in a very dark moment, the trigger was a bad one. She was not letting up and I excused myself and knelt on the floor to hug Thai and really get in the moment with her. "You are such a good girl Thai!" My voice calm and reassuring. Once again she had headed off a full blown panic and anxiety attack. A few more belly and ear rubs, and Thai was actually sensing the change in my mood. As rapidly as she had reacted, she started to settle, and when I resumed my seat, she curled up on my boots, ensuring I was not moving without her being instantly aware.

"That was incredible. I have heard you describe it, but watching it was something very special." Thai's impact on Starr clearly registered and made a lasting impression.

"That's what I was talking about and that is why she is so important. So now that you have seen it, do you want to know how she does it?"

"Yes, please." Sincere, and heartfelt.

"Ok. So when I have an intrusive thought or other trigger, I have an amygdala hijack, Flight, Fight or Freeze. Cortisol gets driven down my HPA axis which in turn releases a pheromone in my skin. If a dog can discriminate a teaspoon of sugar in an Olympic sized swimming pool, they can react to that when in the same room, easily. She acts as an emotional early warning system for me."

"Incredible. Just amazing." I know it wouldn't have had nearly the same effect if she had not just witnessed it.

"But that is only half of the story. One of the ways to counteract the effects of Cortisol in your system is to flood it with Oxytocin. A real simple way to have that happen is to pat your dog. Interacting with your dog releases Oxytocin into your system. So my furry early warning system knows when I am experiencing problems, and she brings the solution with her. That is why she is an alternative therapy that is so powerful. She is with me 24-7-365, so just like my injury it is a marriage made in heaven."

Starr's knowing nod would pave the way to garnering the support we needed from the Nova Scotia Mental Health Association. Another victory and another convert. Well done, Thai… you really are something special

Beechwood
Early June, 2014

There is a snap and cracking pop from the flag that is standing straight out, perpendicular to the flag pole, on a clear windy day, "clear in a million" in aviator's terms. The hot sun was baking everything and everyone.

There was a throng of black leather and sunglasses, motorcycles and bicycles, all gathered at Beechwood National Cemetery in Ottawa for the National Capital Memorial Motorcycle ride. The Memorial service to honour our fallen and our ill and injured was about to begin. I was awash in sea of conflicting emotions. It was the first time that I had been back since the 19th of September when the Long Walk to Sanity had kicked off its final leg. I could see the tree and the rock that had been dedicated to the Soldiers of Suicide on the 15th of September. The rows of headstones laid out in precise fashion, each identical except for the inscriptions. Death, the great equalizer, had claimed many. Some were Combat Casualties like Darryl Caswell who had died June 11th 2007, victim of Afghanistan. Many others had answered the Reaper's call as the inevitable march of time watched the sands slip through life's hourglass. Still others were victims of an unseen assailant, claiming their own lives as a result of the serious mental health issues that arise after a war.

Thai's wet nose bumps my hand. I look down and she is bumping and rubbing me. Her alert. The skirl of the pipes providing the backdrop of the latest mental montage that had gone through my mind. I feel a profound sense of loss juxtaposed with both gratitude and a huge sense of accomplishment.

The fallen that were represented by their tombstones, ever present sentinels, marking the final resting places of those who had answered the call of their country's duty to serve. Some made the ultimate sacrifices and shall never grow old and I am reminded of the obligations, sacred covenant, that comes with putting individuals in harm's way to protect a country's freedoms and sovereignty. The families of the fallen will forever struggle with unanswered questions and mourning the loss, the chance to say a final goodbye, a chance to watch their children's children grow old and fill their life's destiny.

I am also overcome with gratitude, though mixed with guilt. I have survived. The internal war that I've fought with my PTSD and other serious mental health issues has been constant and ongoing since 1986. I have survived in a large part due to Thai's intervention in my life and I am determined to ensure that others get the kind of help I have received. She became the shining beacon of sanity in an ocean of darkness and despair. Her constant companionship and nonjudgmental understanding are welcome as she executes the skills she has to keep me back from the edge of the abyss. The darkness, all-encompassing, waits, a patient servant of the Reaper. Today I am so thankful that there are those who believed in me when I had long since stopped believing in me.

Candy, Kenya, Vardo, Omega, Korie, TJ, Sasha, Norm… the list goes on. The roll call of service dogs that Paws Fur Thought had helped fund and pair with other disabled veterans serves as a poignant reminder as to why the mission is so critically important. Recce, Dragoon, Sam, Mozart, Patty and Royal…… the names in the Memorial Paws program awaiting service dog puppies in training to help ensure that those families whose loved ones made the ultimate sacrifice would not be forgotten.

I look down at Thai, now curled up beside me, her head resting on my boot and I know the value of the gift I have been given. Thai has given me a new "Leash on Life" and in my world is priceless. The goal of helping others get their Service Dogs helps spur me through the days where my depression threatens to rear its ugly head.

This past week has been a huge emotional roller coaster and Thai and I have hung on as it has careened around the course of life with reckless abandon. On Tuesday past, Veterans Affairs Minister Julian Fantino announced the pilot project to study fifty service dog pairings to get the evidence base necessary to get formal recognition of service dogs as an adjunct therapy in the suite of PTSD/OSI tools. The announcement provided huge validation since the yardsticks have been moved considerably since my meeting with the Minister on the 17th of September in Manotick. A Department that was using Therapy Dog and Service Dog as interchangeable words had gone from research assessment to pilot project evidence based research project. Huge!

This announcement was followed up by a few hours on Wednesday with the Senior Military Mental healthcare team, trying to answer questions as they grapple with the implications of Service Dogs within the military. In my mind, the severity of injury that requires Service Dog intervention breaches the Universality of Service and will have career implications for the military member. It can't but not. How do you deploy to the field, to the ships, or operate in an operational air force unit with a Service Dog present. Lack of national standards are also very problematic for a rules based organization.

But the past week did not end there. Follow up visits with two of our handlers in Kingston, Ontario, and a visit to Muzzles and Snouts, Lisa-Marie Guernon's training facility in Prince Edward County preceded my trip to Bracebridge to meet Darlene Cushman, Darryl Caswell's Silver Cross Mother. My mind drifts to Darryl, and the scores of others, whose sacrifices have paid for my continued freedom. So it has been over the decades since Canada has become a Nation. Freedom is not free and somebody always pays the price. The headstones are stark reminders.

Darlene was hosting a Memorial Motorcycle ride in Darryl's Honour to raise funds for Homeless Veterans and to provide Service Dogs to our injured. Darlene, who had been the recipient of Thai's alerts in this exact spot a year earlier, understood the power and appreciated how Thai had worked. She too wanted nothing more than to help. While at the ride on Saturday, The Afghanistan Poppy Memorial was present due to the hard work of Warrant Officers Renay Groves and Gregg Huizinga and their team of seventeen dedicated volunteers. Bronze poppies, one for each of our fallen, adorn the monument, made from the wreckage of a battle damaged tank that was destroyed in the Afghanistan theatre of operations.

Stark, stunning and powerful.

A Guardian of our sacred obligation to never forget those who gave so much.

The work to continue pairing other sufferers with PTSD Service Dogs continues. The road can be lonely and challenging, but the sacrifices embodied in the Memorial, on the tombstones, and by the families make it easier to keep putting one foot in front of the other and marching on toward the goal of helping those who suffer. I feel their pain. My family has lived it. I have lived it, and thankfully, I have survived.

Weary and humbled there remains the nagging question in my mind. "How far did you go today? Further Than Yesterday and that is all that counts."

The Validation Complete
Mid-June, 2014

I stare at the computer screen. I am speechless. Breathless. Overwhelmed and ultimately validated. I blink and the words do not change. The floodgates open and the emotional tidal wave unleashes and I have a non-stop patchwork of memories. The heat of the days where the humidex clocked north of forty five, the miles when the pain in my feet was an excruciating burn and the miles of lonely empty highways where I legitimately questioned my sanity were all validated.

The Dominion Command Convention of the Royal Canadian Legion had been meeting in Edmonton and this bi-annual event is where Resolutions are tabled and voted on to guide Legion Policy and Procedures. I was staring at an email from the Nova Scotia Executive Director, Valerie Mitchell-Veniotte. I was incredulous and overwhelmed by the magnitude and the implications of what I was reading.

The convention delegates had just voted in a resolution that twenty five per cent of funds that Branches raise in their Poppy Trust Funds could be used to acquire Service Dogs for disabled Veterans.

The tears started to flow and shape tracks down my cheeks. Validation!

"Hey Joc. You are never going to believe this. I just heard from Valerie at the Dominion Convention…" I know that she had as much invested in this as I had as she had been with me every step of the way on this Long Walk To Sanity. The solution to quieting the voices in my head was to get help for others so that they could step away from the brink of the abyss.

"And?" Tentative, inquiring and unsure. Jocelyn knew the implications of what I was about to say, and depending on the verdict delivered, she knew that my mood for the coming days and weeks would be affected.

"The convention has agreed to a resolution that twenty five percent of Poppy Funds can be used to fund Service Dogs and that there is no preferred supplier."

"That is amazing. You must feel happy!" I was not sure where I was on the elation spectrum but I can tell you I was very happy and spinning in a sea of positives. My thoughts leaped to the Veterans we have helped to date.

A simple man with a simple idea. We get the largest Veterans organization in Canada to help fund Service Dogs for disabled Veterans while we try and influence government policy to adopt the use of Service Dogs as an adjunct therapy for those suffering from PTSD. Some people would cringe at the task. Given what happened on the North Atlantic, I could be very glib. "At least I don't think anyone is going to try and kill me while I try."

I felt I needed to call Uncle "Frank" Norman and let him know. Consigliore, advisor, mentor, and voice of sober second thought, Frank had been with me since I messed up the golden years of his retirement two years before. As he was want to say "I now have exposure to and am aware of things I wish I wasn't. But then again, sometimes we do not get to choose our battles." I think he was referring to how my circumstances had been foisted upon me.

"Good day." Uncle Frank usually seemed chipper, but today he wasn't.

"Hey Uncle Frank." We spent a few minutes catching up on events in which we both had passing interest or mutual investment.

"You know Uncle Frank, the next time someone tells you they are only one person, what difference can they make? You can tell them you know someone who would not take *no* for an answer and has pushed an agenda to the point where I can say we conquered." I was feeling really good about myself.

"What have you done this time?" Given what I had been up to for the past year he was never quite sure where I would be coming from.

"Well I was being no more than my usual pain in the ass self, and now another part of the puzzle has fallen into place." I relay the news that I had just received about the Legion, Poppy Funds, and Service Dogs.

"Well Done." Sincere, honest.

"You know Uncle Frank, those words they taught us? Truth, Duty, Valour. Nowhere in those words does it say Quit." The image of sitting on my ass having been destroyed by the lineman freight train at football practice was replaced by the look on my rooks face when she was thinking of quitting: "Quit and you will never know…"

Whiskey Tango Foxtrot Reprise
August, 2014

I am standing around with a group of Wounded Warriors, each of us battling our own injuries and demons. Some amputees, others burn survivors, and most if not all struggling with inner demons that occupy a place in their headspace. Entrenched and unable to remove the sights, sounds, smells and memories. Intrusive. Pervasive. Often times absolutely debilitating.

"Folks, when I got hurt in 1986, they did not even know how to spell PTSD let alone have an effective treatment plan." So in some ways things are better now, but there is a lot of real estate to cover and many are still subjected to treatment plans that are clearly ineffective. Sad but true.

"You want to hear a serious I shit you not story? You are never going to believe this crap. Timeframe? The early 90's, sometime after I left the military, I know I am struggling. Normal people do not think the thoughts I was and do the things I was doing. I knew I had a problem and that I needed serious help. So somehow I get geared up with this Spin Doc… and off I go. Maybe he could help me."

So far nothing in the story has given away where this story is heading and how detrimental it was to become to my recovery.

"So we are in my second appointment and right near the end of the session he asks me if he thinks my wife would join us for the next session. I tell him I will ask her, not sure what her response will be but I will call him and let him know. Off I trundle home and make the request. Sure. She is going to give it a shot. She knows I can't keep going the way I was."

Once again, kind of routine stuff. Verification from those living closest to you as to how things are really. Imagine someone with serious mental health issues unaware of the impact of their behaviours and actions. Imagine.

"So at the appointed time, my wife and I show up for the next session. We show and go through a bunch of questions, mostly directed at Jocelyn this time. About forty-five minutes into the session, buddy says he has got it figured out. Now Joc and I are both excited. Given my strange behaviours we were both hanging on to every word. Finally...... maybe the answer."

So buddy stares me square in the eye and says: "You are Tigger and your wife is Piglet!"

Whiskey Tango Foxtrot. WTF?

"Tango Three Mike you are one mile back. Confirm height, speeds and switches. Standby to drop, now now now. On the third now if I have done my job right we are weapons free and hopefully an entire submarine and its crew are going *Voyage to the Bottom of the Sea!*"

"I grab Joc by the hand and we head for the door. Neither of us had to say a word. We both knew. I mean I am struggling badly but this guy is nuttier than squirrel shit."

The group standing there has two different reactions. Some standing with eyes and mouth wide open, incredulous, and the others laughing.

"So guys and gals, as we struggle forward in 2014, the good news is that it is not the early nineties and you do not have someone trying to figure out which one of the Winnie the Pooh characters you are!"

Head shakes and some very derogatory comments directed at the "whack job" who was supposed to be helping me ensue.

Whiskey Tango Foxtrot....

Epilogue
01 June 2015

"Today, the Department of Veterans Affairs and the Government of Canada is pleased to announce the efficacy study into the use of Service Dogs for Veterans battling PTSD is about to begin."

Erin O'Toole, the current Minister of Veterans Affairs, was poised and confident behind the dais and the microphones. The television cameras were out in force. Erin had become the Minister in January of 2015. He was also a former Sea King TACCO and a Bay Street Lawyer. I drifted.

The diversity of images were as mixed as the maelstrom of emotions, and I was struggling. Thai had her "A" game going. She knew I was a complex mix of panic, anxiety and disassociation. She was body checking me and tugging on her leash trying to get me away from the stress.

The announcement was the culmination of all the hard work that had gone into the Long Walk to Sanity. The efficacy study was about to become very real. From having to listen to traditional medical practitioners mouth the platitudes of "There are no studies proving the efficacy of Service Dogs in PTSD treatment" to which I would rebut "There are no studies proving the inefficacy either and I understand that the plural of anecdote is not data, but anecdote one ups supposition!" Very real. The study has been formulated and now the government was releasing the funding.

"You do not have to walk anymore. You have made your point."

"But I am going to finish my walk, and I will if I have to."

The last exchange between myself and then Minister of Veterans Affairs, Julian Fantino at our Meeting in Manotick on the 17th of September 2013. We have gone from skepticism to research assessment to efficacy study and the development of National Standards for Service Dogs for PTSD. This has been quite a journey. Those words indelibly etched into my mind.

From long hot days out on the road where the loneliness and anxiety were crushing, to watching the Minister solidify the concrete and make real what we had set out to do.

Paws Fur Thought had set out to pair Veterans with their Service Dogs so that they could get their lives back and step back from the edges of the dark abyss of their own personal hell. I had wanted to get the efficacy study to be done. My plan to use the Veterans we had paired was not quite the plan that was unfolding, but at least the study was being done. The development of Standards so that VAC would have best practices to draw on was part of the collateral work that was being done. But so much more has happened. The Paws organization is expanding and the mission is being executed by a team who believes in the miraculous power of these highly trained Service Dogs to have such a powerfully positive impact on the lives of their veteran handlers and their families.

Thai's paws were heavy upon me. I looked down into her deep brown eyes. She knew better than all those around me the intensity of the internal conflicts that raged within me. The images of the North Atlantic. The hell that was a North Atlantic gale remains. But now there are images of dogs and smiling handlers. Paws Success Stories.

I quietly stepped away from the crowd and to where Thai and I could spend some quiet time. I dropped onto one knee, reached under her vest, and give her a gentle rub. "Thai you are such a good girl". Amazingly uncanny how she can read me and act as an emotional barometer.

"Let's go for a walk girl. I think we got some things to do." Quiet time. Fishing. Reading books. Listening to baseball. Watching some football. Driving, slowly, with no real destination or plan. Maybe write another book. Truth, Duty and Valour. Loyalty, Courage and Integrity. I had survived and made it home, finally, decades after I had deployed to sea.

"How far are we going to go Thai? **Further Than Yesterday, that's all that counts!"**

The End

Photos

Figure 1 The Seahawk, as captured by the Aurora, much earlier in the day before the Gale really raged

Figure 2 My Girls, Jennifer, Jocelyn and Lindsey

Figure 3 RMC Grad 1983

Figure 4 Drayton (DJ) Cousineau in Egypt in 1958/59 working on a recce vehicle that hit a land mine.

Figure 5 The Flight Crew: Back row Capt Hans Kleeman, Capt Ken Whitehead Front Lt USN Brad Renner, Capt Bill Ropp, Sgt Al Smith, Self, Missing: PO Bill "Doc" Hagey

Figure 6 CH124A Seaking (Editor's Note: This Bird was modified with Forward Looking Infrared Radar, Flir, and years after the rescue)

Figure 7 MIss Thai

Figure 8 Fun time and "Not all work and No Play". Mental Health Break for Thai.

Figure 9 Decision Day at Hartlen Point. Note the Inukshuk to the Right

Figure 10 Luke MacDonald, the Master of the Boot Plan

Figure 11 Chris "Red" Hatton and I shooting arrows and discussing my "New Normal"

Figure 12 Day One of The Long Walk to Sanity. The first 100 yards

Figure 13 Day One Motivational Poster.

Figure 14 Arriving at CFB Shearwater, Day One of the Long Walk to Sanity

Figure 15 The back of the Pawsmobile. "If we Send'em, We must Mend'em!"

Figure 16 The Pawsmobile with its Mission Statement

Figure 17 Brenda and Noble at the Fisherman's Memorial at the Cove in Eastern Passage

Figure 18 Paul "Trapper" Cane and LCol Vaughn Cosman, my walk coordinator

Figure 19 At the Heroes Highway Ride in Trenton

Figure 20 George and Vardo along with Dan and Kenya, Paws Fur Thoughts first two pairings, even before the walk finished

Figure 21 LCol Retd Bryan Bailey, Class of 83 RMC and MGen Retd "Uncle Frank" Norman, consigliore and guiding light at RMC's Wall of Honour

Figure 2222 LCol Vaughn Cosman, Nav School Classmate and OPI for the Long Walk to Sanity with the Minister in Manotick. The day it all changed!

Figure 23 Darlene Cushman, Thai and I at Beechwood

Figure 24 Moorbern Kennels puppies that are being donated to Paws and the Memorial Paws Canada project. The medals belong to the father of Cynthia Moorhead-Bernier, The Rev. John Francis Moorhead, Able Seaman, Gunner, WWII, Captain, Army Chaplain, Korea

Figure 25 LGen David Millar, Chief of Military Personnel and I discuss service dogs and their role with injured members.

Figure 26 Starr Dobson, CEO of Mental Health Foundation of NS and Thai at the Inspiring Lives Awards

Figure 27 Minister of Veterans Affairs, Erin O'Toole watching Thai Alert.

Figure 28 The Prescription for Sanity: Keep Calm and Walk the Dog, Repeat as Necessary.

Glossary:

AESOP: Airborne Electronic Sensor Operator. An NCO positon within the crew of a Seaking

AWOL: Absent without Leave. A Chargeable offence under the Code of Service Discipline

CAF: Canadian Armed Forces

CARES: Canine Assistance and Rehabilitation Educations Services. The Service Dog School that trained Thai and is located in Concordia, Kansas.

CAV: Canadian Army Veterans (Motorcycle Units). A Veteran Motorcycle Club co-founded by Paul "Trapper" Cane in 2003

CBD: Crash, Burn, Die. A dark aviator's euphemism for what happens after a crash.

CD: Canadian Forces Decoration awarded to CF Members for 12 years of good conduct and service

CF: Canadian Forces

CIMVHR: Canadian Institute for Military and Veteran Health Research. A collaborative of 30 universities overseen by Queens University and the Royal Military College of Canada.(RMC)

CMP: Chief of Military Personnel- equivalent to the Head of Human Resources for large corporations

CWC: Cadet Wing Commander at RMC

CWPRO: Cadet Wing Public Relations Officer

CWTO: Cadet Wing Training Officer – noted as chief disciplinarian and in charge of drill and parades

DS: Directing Staff – the staff, primarily Senior NCO's at various schools within the CF

ETA: Estimated Time of Arrival

LCWB: Last Class with Balls – the acronym that represented the last all male class of RMC "Redcoats"

MOC: Military Occupation Code. An identifier that defined trade or classification. An Air Navigator was a 31A while an infanteer was a 031.

MP: Member of Parliament. (US equivalent- Congressman)

NDHQ: National Defence Headquarters

NS: Nova Scotia

NM: Nautical Mile or Knots. 1NM equals 1.852 Km's or 1.15 Statute miles

OSI: Operational Stress Injury

POW: Prisoner of War

PT: Physical Training

PTSD: Post Traumatic Stress Disorder – Now commonly referred to as an OSI

RCEME: Royal Canadian Electrical & Mechanical Engineers

RCMP: Royal Canadian Mounted Police

SAR: Search and Rescue

SC: Star of Courage: At the time of writing there has been awarded only 447 times and to only 60 military members. It is the second highest Civilian award for bravery following the Cross of Valour (CV), and ahead of the Medal of Bravery (MB).

SOS: Soldiers of Suicide Also International Distress call and in days gone by, Struck of Strength.

TACCO: Tactical coordinator. A Specialized Air Navigator Sub trade that specialized in Anti-Submarine Warfare in the back of a Seaking Helicopter. The TACCO would take sensor input from the

AESOP to help compile the Tactical picture. The TACCO and the AESOP were both trained and shared utility flying duties such as hoisting, slinging and Helicopter in Flight Refueling.

TDV: Truth, Duty, Valour. The motto of the Royal Military Colleges of Canada

TRX: A type of fitness strap that allows for hundreds of exercises using the members own body weight as resistance.

USN: United States Navy

VAC: Veterans Affairs Canada, formerly, DVA: Department of Veterans Affairs

VC: Victoria Cross. The British Empires highest award for Gallantry in the Face of the enemy. Respected amongst the Commonwealth Forces as having no equal.

VRAB: Veterans Review and Appeal Board. A 3 person tribunal that rules on medical information in determining veteran's disability awards, benefits and pensions

Links:

Paws Fur Thought: www.pawsfurthought.com

Memorial Paws Canada: www.memorialpawscanada.ca

Book & Authour Website

To contact Cous for speaking engagements:

http://www.furtherthanyesterday.com/speakers-page.html

Topics Includes

1. Service Dogs
2. PTSD- Mental Health
3. Motivational – Be the Game Changer!

Blog: www.furtherthanyesterday.ca

Donations to the Paws Fur Thought program can be made through the following link:

http://www.pawsfurthought.com/donate.html

The Final Word

Folks many people have asked me how I found the time, strength and energy to write "Further Than Yesterday" since it is such an intensely personal journey that covers some very rough ground.

I would be completely remiss if I did not give a huge shout out to my Editor, who chooses to remain anonymous. I have known him on a personal level for many decades.

He is a very accomplished writer in his own right and has had a couple of very successful careers throughout his life. He also shares my love of Football and Baseball. But I have learned two very valuable lessons from him when it comes to writing and in the process earning the right to use the term authour.

`1. You cannot edit a blank page.** So you must write. Good, bad, or indifferent get your thoughts onto the page. From there the arduous process of drafts, revisions and technical stuff can commence. Until then, your wish to write a book is but a dream or a fantasy.

2. At some point you must write "The End". It is unbelievable the subconscious and psychological impact of two words, six letters. It is the catalyst and the start point of a turning those pages you have created into the story you wish to tell.

I have learned much in this part of the journey, and I am forever indebted to my friend, fellow authour and editor. He also taught me about defining the motivation for writing to the audience. In this case we are both committed to helping others obtain their service dogs to help them. I cannot repay the debt, but I can acknowledge it. **Invictus.**

Sneak Peek

A sneak peek into **"Further than Today"**, the next installment in the "Further Than" trilogy.

The Reapers Scythe.

No one gets out of the game of life alive. The dark images of death present a both a strange fascination and moribund reality. Death, permanent, irreversible and it is what awaits us all. Today though, I am drawn to stare at it from a different vantage point, and one, thankfully, I do not share with everyone. It would not be the natural order of things. In fact it would be reflective of a state of the world that is absolutely unnatural. We are born, we grow up, marry, have kids, watch them grow up, hopefully, have grandchildren and when the sands of time have slipped through our hourglass, we move on to whatever your belief system says comes next. But there are those who do not have the luxury of that sequence.

We, the unfortunates, get to bury our children, a thought so out of sync with nature that it does not even have its own word. Widow, Widower, and Orphan are all terms in our language. Most languages have words for these terms and concepts. What is missing is the word for the parent who has to bury their child. That funeral is one of the most painful, if not arguably the most painful thing one ever has to do. I know from firsthand experience.

The hole in my heart and soul is indescribable. The hollow emptiness that seems so pointless. There is no way to replace it, no way to make the echoes in your soul subside. I fear they will be with me forever. Those who have lost their sons and daughters to wars, accidents or illness have an unspoken bond, one that is genuinely forged in the fires of hell. How could it not be? You can share an entire dialogue in a word, a nod, or a hug that needs no further dialogue. The hurt is unlike no other. The senselessness, the pointlessness and the pain that never actually subsides can push you to very dark places.

But there is Hope. There are rays of sunshine and others who have been where I am. From them I learn to live with the pain and develop coping strategies. This is not the first time in my life that this has been necessary. The Grim Reaper has knocked on my door before. From trying to decapitate me in the North Atlantic to near fatal brushes with suicide attempts, the Reaper has swung his scythe. I was lucky. I was able to duck and thanks to Thai, my service dog, I am no longer anywhere near the brink of the abyss that has no return in the spectrum of Self-harm. Thai saved me, and together, we have helped others get their service dogs, and watched them move back from the edge of their Abyss.

In time, we have watched their struggles turn into their successes and accomplishments, victorious and worthy of the term Survivor.

These are their stories.